The B.A.B.Y.

(Best Advice for Baby & You)

Book

....

*The Essential Parents' Guide to Postpartum
Care for the First Few Days ... and Beyond*

Karen L. Brewer, BSN, RNC-MNN

PUBLISHED BY BOOKBABY
PENNSAUKEN, NJ

BookBaby
BookBaby Publishers
7905 N Crescent Blvd
Pennsauken, NJ 08110

Print ISBN: 978-1-54392-285-1
eBook ISBN: 978-154392-286-8

Contents

Introduction

. . . .

The anticipation and waiting are over!! You are in the home stretch and are either ready to deliver or have just delivered your brand-new bundle(s) of joy. You have been reading books, scouring the internet, and/or getting advice and info from your family and friends. For the first-time parents, you have feelings of excitement and anxiety for the new baby. Will the baby be born okay? Will I be a good mother/father? Am I ready for this? Then... after the baby comes, you become anxious over every little thing. Is the baby too hot or too cold? Getting enough to eat? Am I doing everything right? Am I doing anything right?

Relief, joy, worry overwhelm you. The first few days after delivery become a blur and you cannot remember anything. You panic!!! Your nurses have educated and instructed you on how to care for yourself and your baby, and maybe went over it only once or twice. Well, unfortunately you may only remember less than half (<50%) of everything that your nurse went over during your stay... maybe more like 25%. As the saying goes, "in one ear and out the other." That's not a lot of retention, but just remember how wild, crazy, and overwhelming the past few days have been for you! By the time you go home you'll be wondering, "What just happened?? It was all a blur." Thus, begins the worry...

Three things I tell my patients: *Do not* hesitate to ask questions, *do not* worry about asking them more than once, and *do not* apologize for asking them!! This includes all moms and dads, not just the newbies. Sometimes you just forget things from one child to the next, especially the "little details", and that's okay to ask questions again. Your nurse should not make you feel guilty for any of these things, and if they try to—*don't let them!*

Because you're getting inundated with so much information in such a brief period, and are trying to retain all this information on what is probably an immense lack of sleep—you cannot possibly comprehend it all. And *that's okay.* No question is a stupid question... no matter how many times you might ask it!! We as nurses want you to be well educated and comfortable with everything before you leave to go home, no matter if it's your postpartum care or your baby's care.

Teaching my patients and significant others how to care for themselves (and I do mean the guys, too) and how to care for the baby is so important. It is probably the most important task I perform as a postpartum nurse. Yes, I carefully assess and check all my patients, make sure they're pain-free (or as close to that as possible), and deal with any problems and/or challenges that come up during their stay—but I spend much of my time teaching the family about mom and baby care... or reminding and/or re-educating the experienced parents. Sometimes the smallest details get forgotten, so that is why I have taken the time to provide a more comprehensive reference guide to help with questions or concerns you might have before or after you are discharged from the hospital.

~Education is the shared commitment between dedicated teachers, motivated students and enthusiastic parents with high expectations.

— Bob Beauprez

Preface

．．．．．．．．．．．．

With over 20 years of in-hospital mother-baby experience, I have loved and continue to love teaching my patients how to take care of themselves and their new babies. But one of the things I noticed during my career is that parents have a lot of questions, and some of those have nothing to do with the routine care but are about… "little things." At least, what *I* think are "little things" can be very concerning for parents, even veteran parents that have not encountered something specific with themselves or previous babies. It's those concerns and questions that gave me the idea for this book. I started researching online to see if I could find something out there that has been written for parents to help address these concerns and questions, and I found that there simply is *nothing out there.*

There are self-help books for breastfeeding, postpartum depression, pregnancy, baby care and the like, but nothing specifically related to mom and baby care during their hospital stay and for things that might pop up shortly after returning home. At least— with the exception of buying several other books, or for piece-meal information which might have helped resolve their questions, it still will cost some additional money. And who wants to spend a lot of money for multiple books when there are other things that would be more important to spend your money on? I mean, *there is* now the new baby you must be financially responsible for and we all know that is *EXPENSIVE!* Let's spend our money wisely, shall we?

Even though patients are educated in the hospital, or at least *I hope* they are, sometimes the "little things" are forgotten; things that should be taught to every patient but *never* are. Nonetheless nursing care can be varied. Some nurses don't give thorough explanations of things, but only give very brief summaries of specific issues and move on. Some don't like to do the teaching and try to only give direct patient care, thus cheating parents of a well-rounded educational experience. And, not all nurses can give patients their undivided attention all the time, due to time constraints or having other more time-consuming patient issues. (Unfortunately, emergencies and problems to do come up that *must* take precedence.) So, the light bulb came on; that "aha" moment when I realized that patients might benefit from a book that would help address those questions or concerns with their selves and with their babies.

Now—not all the information is evidenced-based, because there may *have not* been a study done on a particular situation or matter, although a lot of information does come from evidenced-based practice. Some of it comes from reference books, journals, and web sites that are used to educate medical professionals throughout their careers. And—some of it comes from good old-fashioned nursing judgment and practice. Wherever the information comes from, you can be assured that it has been researched, documented, and referenced for accuracy… and tested in the hospital setting.

I would like to thank first, and foremost, my nursing educator guru and nurse manager, Kim Dishman. You helped nudge me along to do more with my nursing career just in the first few years I have known you, and I thank you for that. Without your encouragement and enthusiasm for my ideas, I don't think I would have had the guts to do this. Who would have thought I had it in me?? To my partners-in-crime: Gloria Theno, Amy Horton, Sheila Green, Elizabeth Murphy, Cindy Robinette, Terri Jenkins, Amber Tenay, and some others: whom I have laughed, cried, bounced around ideas, and had each other's back with. We have been together so long that I truly value your opinions… and trust you *explicitly*. To my newer nurse "buddies": Sara Gena, Kerry Davenport, Linda Grossglauser, and Michelle Andrews thank you for your support. And a special shout out to Bree Fallon, our OB nursing educator, for if not the continued support, honest opinions, and meticulous review of my transcript, I might have done a serious injustice to this book. You all rock!!!

And last… but not least, to my family.

To TJ and Jessica— Thank you for helping to support my nursing career all the way back to the beginning. I know I spent a lot of time missing games and activities while you were growing up, but I did it to make life much better for you and *I hope* it was.

To Jenna, who came along after the career change— You got the biggest benefit of my life-changing career move, for if I hadn't done it you may not have graced us with your presence. It was an immense struggle with two kiddos, but my career change soon allowed us to have three. So, I'm very glad you came along when you did!

To Bobby, my husband and best friend— Although you may have thought this idea was silly, and that your wife couldn't possibly be an author I say… ha, ha, ha… in your face!! LOL! No *really*, thanks for supporting me through all the many months it has taken writing this book and all the time spent to putting it, and my website, together. I know I have put off many things to write this, so I really appreciate the patience. I will get the rest of the house completed now— the housecleaning, the painting, the flooring, the decorating, etc. I promise!!

Karen

Mother's Care

·················

C are of the mother after birth is crucial to her well-being which assists her to not only heal after the delivery, but allows her to take care of the baby (or babies) and family as well. From the time of the delivery, mother's focus is usually about the baby and what life will be like in the days, months, and years ahead. How will the new baby fit in? How will I be able to cope? Many thoughts race through a parent's mind on how much impact will this new little being have on their family. It's essential to focus on the baby and what their daily needs entail, but mothers need to also be aware how much of their focus must be on themselves as well. When teaching various aspects of post-delivery care, one of the main topics that I emphasized on a regular basis is: *"You must take care of yourself... to be capable of taking care of your baby."* With this thought in mind, let's move on to taking care of mom. We will focus on both vaginal and cesarean deliveries with regards to recovery and care.

Immediate Post-Delivery

Immediately after delivery, you will begin the recovery phase of your postpartum care. Your blood pressure, pulse, respirations, and temperature will be monitored repeatedly, and you will be given various medications along with intravenous (IV) fluids to aid in your recovery. You will also be monitored for response to your body's ability to start moving normally (post-epidural, spinal or general anesthetic) which will allow you to be able to start caring for yourself. You may be given additional medications such as antibiotics if you have been diagnosed with an infection, or uterotonics (Methergine®, Hemabate®, Cytotec®, additional Pitocin®), which aid in uterine muscle contraction, if you are having a postpartum hemorrhage. There are other medications as well that may be given to you depending on your individual plan of care, but for the sake of this guide we will just focus on the routine care.

Fundal Massage

This is the part which all patients really hate when it is being administered. Your nurse supports the uterus from the bottom, right above the pelvic bone, and finds the top of your uterus at about your belly button, and then pushes down from the top then *SQUEEZES AND RUBS IT REALLY HARD!!!* If you're lucky enough to have had an epidural or spinal that has not worn completely off, then this is maybe only slightly uncomfortable. However, if you aren't so lucky… *WOW!* You may feel like you want to punch out your nurse for hurting you so badly! I assure you that your nurse is not a sadist. She is making sure that after your delivery, your uterus is contracting effectively to close off the blood vessels where the placenta was attached, and that any blood clots that might have been forming after the baby delivered are completely removed.

Clots in the uterus that aren't removed increase the potential for later developing a postpartum hemorrhage. It's also essential that any placental fragments are removed as well. Generally, your doctor will inspect the placenta after removal to make sure of this, but even the very smallest fragment might be missed. Remaining tissue can cause a postpartum infection— and we absolutely *do not* want to go there! Just be reassured, this intense fundal massage is generally during your recovery phase only, which is usually the first two hours.

After recovery is complete, your nurse will just be checking to make sure that your uterus is staying firm and in the right location, and should not massage anywhere near as hard (unless you have one who really is a sadist, then I feel for you.) If it is not firm, be aware that the heavy fundal massage *will be* commencing again until such time that it is firm. So, while you may think that your wonderful delivery nurse has now become Evil Incarnate, you will be thankful she is doing what is necessary to ensure you have a good recovery. Brace yourself, it really is a *"necessary evil!"*

IV Fluids

You will begin receiving IV fluids either right before you deliver during a scheduled cesarean section or when you come into the hospital for an induction or are in labor. Either way, this is to help get you and keep you hydrated during the labor/delivery process, and to rehydrate you after delivery is complete, as you lose fluids throughout either process. Lactated ringers and D5LR are the most commonly used IV solutions.

Depending on if you have a vaginal or cesarean section delivery is dependent on how long you will continue to receive these fluids after your delivery and recovery complete. For vaginal deliveries, IV fluids will usually be removed after recovery is completed and you have been up to void without any difficulties. For cesarean sections, IV fluids generally will be continued past the recovery period until approximately 12 hours or so, depending on the institution, and you are taking water orally without any nausea and vomiting, enough to help keep you hydrated without further use of additional IV fluids.

You may have the IV fluids *restarted* if you have any signs, symptoms, or complications, such as: dizziness/passing out during you 1st trip to the bathroom; fever; nausea and vomiting; increased blood loss, clots, or hemorrhaging; decreased blood pressure, etc., Once the crisis has resolved and you have recovered from whatever situation required additional fluids, then you will be removed from the fluids again.

Rehydration

After you have delivered, it is very important that you get rehydrated with plenty of fluids. If you have had or will have a vaginal delivery, your nurse will likely finish giving you IV fluids until she determines that you have been thoroughly rehydrated. She will also strongly suggest you drink plenty of water to keep you hydrated, which helps to aid in recovery. This does not mean drinking soda, tea, coffee, etc. to get the job done, although these may be had in moderation. Water is the preferred way to go to get rehydrated.

If you have had/or will be having a cesarean section, you will be slowly introduced to ice chips, and if you are tolerating that, then will move on to taking sips of water. Once you are tolerating that as well, you will be advanced to drinking water. You will, however, remain on IV fluids until you are putting out a significant amount of urine through the Foley catheter you have in place. Only then will you be removed from IV hydration and continue with drinking lots of water.

Getting Out of Bed/Back into Bed

Your nurse will check on you at various times during your recovery to check your Aldrete score: 1) how awake you are, 2) how well you can breathe, 3) what your blood pressure looks like, 4) how good is your oxygen saturation in your blood, and 5) how much function you have in your arms and legs after your delivery. If you have not had an epidural, spinal, or general anesthesia, then you will recover relatively quickly. This is used to help determine if you have any after-effects of your anesthesia, or will be able to get out of bed without any difficulty. However, you have had blood loss and some medications that may affect you when you stand up and move around, so she will also be checking repeatedly how you feel as you move.

Whatever you do— DO NOT get out of bed for the first time without your nurse present! Nothing is worse than a patient who thinks "I feel just fine. I can do this on my own." You can go from feeling just fine to "I'm going to pass out" in a heartbeat. So— make sure she's there!!! For cesarean deliveries, it may be several hours before you will be allowed to get up, but the same concept applies to you as well. I'll let you in on a little secret— we really don't like having to fill out an incident report if you have fallen— so, please, please, please—don't make us!!?? I am batting 1,000 with this very detailed suggestion, and not one of my patients have ever hit the floor on my watch— in all my 20+ years!! That's a record I intend to keep, as long as I am capable of still working on the hospital floor.

When you are ready to get up, position your bed so that the head is raised up. Bend your knees and place your feet flat on the bed. The closer you can comfortably manage to pull them up toward your bottom— all the better. Then place your hands flat on the bed next to your hips. Use your hands and feet to gently lift your bottom up off the bed and move over towards the edge of the bed. You may have to do this a couple of times to get to the edge, and that's okay. Once you have done this, rotate your hips to the side, place your elbow against the raised headboard and your other hand by your elbow or grasp the handrail, swing your legs over the edge of the bed and push yourself to a sitting position. Now— do not immediately get up! Sit there for a minute or two to make sure you have your bearings and that you are not lightheaded, dizzy, ears ringing, vision blurring, etc.

Once you feel stable, plant your feet on the floor shoulder length apart, look straight ahead and not down to the floor, push off the bed, and then stand up. Now again, wait at least 15-30 seconds to make sure you are still stable before heading to the bathroom or walking around the room for the first time. If at any time during this you start to feel lightheaded, dizzy, ears ringing, vision blurring— let your nurse know immediately! You can go from, "I am starting to feel…" to hitting the floor rather quickly. This way she can get you back to the bed quickly and safely. She may request assistance from other staff to help get you back to bed without incidence, so don't be alarmed when she does.

The concept of how to properly get out of bed is based on my observation of mechanics utilized by different nurses. I have found that in my many years of nursing that both vaginal and cesarean delivery patients can decrease the amount of potential pain they might cause themselves by following my method. *For vaginal delivery patients*: this eliminates "scooting" on your bottom area, which may be sore, swollen, and possibly all stitched up. Any way to decrease the amount of pain and discomfort in this area is always a plus. *For cesarean section patients*: this helps by utilizing your arms and legs to assist maneuvering into a new position without placing additional strain on the incision site. If you "scoot" on your bottom, you will be pulling your incision site from the lower segment. Since your vaginal skin is attached all the way up to your incision site, when you "scoot" forward that pulls your skin below your incision downward, causing pulling on the incision and unnecessary additional pain. And also, any time you can keep from using your abdominal muscles (which I might add are not functioning for the time being) to move around and out of bed— this is "a good thing."

Vaginal Deliveries

After your baby is delivered and you are fawning all over the new bundle of joy on your chest, your doctor is busy making repairs to your vaginal area and cleaning you up. You will be checked for lacerations, tears, any bleeding areas, and the appropriate repairs will be made. If you're lucky there aren't any repairs to be made— you get to skip the step of the repairs and just jump into the clean-up phase.

Once everything is completed on the doctor's end, your nurse will follow behind and clean your perineum, remove all the drapes surrounding you, possibly put an ice pack to your perineum— if you might be swelling soon, then taking your legs down from the stirrups and replacing the parts of the labor bed previously removed.

Once you have completed your recovery, you will be getting up to the bathroom for the first time after your delivery. Your nurse will assist you getting up for the first time, and then go over how to take care of your perineum once you have sat down on the toilet. The following is what I go over with my patients on how to care of yourself post-delivery.

Perineal Care

Care for your perineal area, which includes your vagina and rectal area, is very important to help eliminate the possibility of infection and to promote healing. Since the word "vagina" may be a medical term that makes the average person uncomfortable saying, various nicknames have been given to this general region, and your nurse may use any number of names. I've heard "*hoo-hoo*" or "*hoo-hah*" used many times throughout my career, so in hopes of lending a little humor to our teaching, I will utilize "*hoo-hah*" or "*nether region*" a few times during this lesson.

Vaginal swelling: After a vaginal delivery, you may have mild to severe swelling to the outer and inner folds of your *hoo-hah*. These folds are called the labia.

Due to pelvic pressure placed on your *hoo-hah* before delivery and all the pressure from pushing the baby out during delivery, both the inner and outer folds of the labia can become swollen. This can become very uncomfortable to sit on your bottom. So, whenever you can, lie down on either side and place a pillow between your legs. This can take a great deal of pressure off the area. Ice packs placed at the site soon after delivery will help with reducing the swelling and numb the affected area, so ask for it if it is not offered to you. When you *must* sit up, such as during eating or breastfeeding, you may want to lean slightly to one side or the other, and wedge a small, thin pillow or soft blanket under the raised "butt" cheek. Unfortunately, there is nothing you can do for the pressure if you must laugh, cough, or sneeze. Brace yourself the best you can, and hope that it doesn't hurt too much.

Hemorrhoids: These are another thing that can put additional pressure on your bottom. They develop with some patients during pregnancy due to the pelvic pressure put on the rectal veins, which causes some blood to collect in them. Straining to have a bowel movement, due to constipation, will also aggravate and possibly cause them to "*pop out.*" They may be mild to severe, and may become quite uncomfortable. Then the added pressure of pushing out baby can make them "*pop out*" of the rectum as well. Generally, they will recede back up into the rectum after delivery and the swelling subsides. The same issues apply to hemorrhoids as with vaginal swelling, regarding the pressure placed on them while sitting. The above-mentioned recommendations can help with these as well. Even if you do not feel like you have hemorrhoids, your nurse may find evidence of them.

If the hemorrhoids do not recede back into the rectum, you continue to have issues with hemorrhoids after discharge, and/or they continue to be a problem for you, follow up with your OB doctor and let them know. They may treat the issue or refer you on to a specialist who can treat them.

Hematomas: This can be caused by a rupture or trauma to the blood vessels without any tears or lacerations on the outer tissue during delivery. Blood then leaks or flows into the tissues causing the hematoma. Most of the time your body will reabsorb this collection of blood without any problem. In the event the blood continues escaping, and a hematoma forms and enlarges over time, this can become extremely painful. Generally, pain medications do not seem to relieve much pain, if at all. If it has been determined by your nurse, through continuous complaint of pain and getting absolutely no relief from medications, she will look at your nether region to check specifically for a hematoma to determine if this is the case. If it is, then the physician will need to evacuate the blood and repair the cause of the hematoma. This may cause some more soreness, but the pain relief should be remarkably better.

Episiotomies/vaginal lacerations/stitches: These are some of the issues that make *most* mothers tremble and quake during their recovery time. The very thought of having to go #2 puts the *"fear of God"* in them! The nether region is already sore, tender, or down right painful, and to have a bowel movement *any* time soon is mortifying! Our skin and *hoo-hah* can stretch, but some cannot stretch enough to avoid developing surface lacerations or tears in their nether region. Your doctor may perform/has performed an episiotomy to help provide additional room for the baby to come out, and will then repair that and any other lacerations deemed necessary. An ice pack afterward can help numb the area and reduce any swelling for you. (*See Topical Pads and Medications below.*)

Here is another little tip for those with vaginal or possible rectal repairs (Yes, some people will need repairs to the rectum too, if you have had what is called a 4ᵗʰ degree--- a complete tear through the rectal wall.) Sitting down on the toilet, chair or bed may cause those stitches to feel like they are going to pull completely out, due to the stretching of the skin when we sit down. A little technique that I thought up years ago, is to do— a Kegel. (You know, that exercise you've been taught, or read about during your pregnancy—) So, before you sit down, tighten up your vaginal and rectal muscles and *hold it,* then sit down and relax again. By doing this, what you are achieving is pulling the skin in a little bit more, so when you sit down, you don't feel like it's going to pull apart down there. Many mothers over the years tell me this really does help quite a bit.

Cleansing bottle/Hygenique® sprayer: Hospitals have assorted items to aid you in cleaning your nether region after having gone to the bathroom. Some may have a wall sprayer (Hygenique®) that works just like a removeable shower head to clean yourself. Others may have a clear, plastic cleansing bottle to add water and cleanse off with. No matter which method you use, be sure and use it after you do your business!!

Delivery compromises you by putting you at risk for infection. Your nether region is a portal for infection, so no matter whether you had a vaginal or cesarean delivery, be sure you *do not* skip this step. While you are still sitting down, completely clean yourself off with water. Once you are clean, then dry off with toilet paper. (Gently *pat* dry if you had a vaginal delivery— ouch!)

If you are having issues of burning from your lacerations or stitches while you are urinating, cleanse off with some of the water *while you go.* This will help to dilute the urine and lessen the burning sensation. (This is another little suggestion I thought of several years ago.)

Topical pads and medications: There are several possibilities of pads or topical medications you may be given during your recovery. Dibucaine is a topical cream or gel that can be placed directly on your *hoo-hah.* This medication is used for relief from itching and pain by numbing the area for you. Another one might be Dermaplast®, which is in the form of a spray. This has a numbing medication (benzocaine) as well, but it also contains aloe and lanolin to help aid in healing. Preparation H®, which is made of hydrocortisone, helps with burning, itching, and swelling. You may also be given witch hazel (Tucks®) cleansing pads to place directly on your nether region. These have a cooling and soothing effect on your stitches and/or lacerations. Any or all of them are great alternatives for those who do not take or want to take oral pain medicine.

You may decide you only want the witch hazel pads which is fine. If you choose to add the creams and/or spray to the pads, you can. After you have finished your business, cleansed with water and dried off, take two of the witch hazel pads and overlap them making a longer pad for more complete coverage. Place approximately 1-inch length of Preparation H (hydrocortisone) cream in the middle and smear it out. (Folding the pads in half, rubbing together, then separating will accomplish this.) Place the dibucaine cream *or* Dermaplast spray on top of the hydrocortisone. Stand up with your legs spread apart and tuck the pad gently up against your *hoo-hah* and rectum. Then bring your legs together, allowing your body to hold the pads in place, and pull up the *very sexy* granny panties the hospital provides for you. Leave the pads and medication in place until the next time you will be using the restroom and cleansing the area, then replace with new ones.

Perineal pads/panties: Your hospital will provide you with perineal (feminine) pads and disposable underwear or panties to use during your stay. Every time you use the restroom or take a shower, be very sure to change your perineal pad and any topical pads you may have left in place. This will help in avoiding infection. Your disposable underwear or panties are meant for short-time usage and when they get visibly soiled, be sure to toss them and get a new pair of them as well.

Moving Around in Bed/Moving up in Bed

Since your vaginal and bottom area is really sore, you need to take care not to cause yourself any unnecessary pain in that region. Scooting and sliding on your nether region will cause you pain, so here are a few pointers on how to avoid that.

When changing positions in bed, such as turning over to your side, draw your knees up and plant your feet on the bed. Next, lift your bottom off the bed and rotate your hips a little to the side you are turning over to. You may have to repeat this several times to get into the new position you want to be in, but this will allow you to turn over into a side lying position without causing any additional pain. When you want to turn back over to your back or over to the other side, just repeat this step as many times as you need to get into the new position.

Now, if you are starting to slowly migrate toward the foot of the bed, you can use some of this same technique to accomplish this. First, put the head of the bed all the way down, and then grab a hold of the upper bed rails toward the top. Next, draw your knees up far enough to allow for easily pushing off the bed with your feet without your feet slipping back down. Once you're in position, you want to lift up your bottom from the bed at the same time you pull with your upper arms and push with your feet. This technique helps eliminate any undue pain on your vaginal area, and moves you back up in a better position in bed.

Urgent/Emergent Issues During Labor and/or Delivery

This can be a scary, intense, and anxiety-filled time for parents during what they assumed would be a standard, uncomplicated vaginal delivery. Issues and events can occur during the course of labor which can be unpredictable and must be handled quickly to avoid a serious or life-threatening event for mother, baby, or both. Here are some events which can quickly change the course of the delivery from a vaginal delivery to a cesarean section.

Cord Prolapse

This is a very dangerous event which can happen during the course of labor—if the water breaks when the baby is not fully engaged against the head of the cervix. If the baby is "floating" in amniotic fluid and the water breaks, the cord can slip past the baby's head and pass through the vagina and out. If the baby's head then starts to engage in the pelvis, the cord can then be compressed between the head and the vaginal wall and cut off its own blood/oxygen supply, which can be detrimental to the well-being of the baby.

If this were to occur, you would find a nurse placing her fingers up into the vagina, and will be riding in the bed with you— while making a rapid trek with other delivery personnel to the OR for a cesarean delivery. Her fingers will remain up in the vagina to keep the baby's head up and away from the cord until the cesarean section is performed and the baby is removed.

Breech Presentation

Having a foot or buttocks touched by a nurse during a cervical exam is unusual, as most times a breech presentation has been previously determined and monitored regularly during your OB appointments. But babies can do acrobatic acts very quickly and turn into a breech presentation without anyone having knowledge that it has happened before you present to the hospital.

If a baby is breech, an OB doctor can attempt to turn the baby around during what is called an external cephalic version. They usually attempt this close to your due date.

This is usually performed in the hospital setting, in the event there is a need for an emergency cesarean. The version, if done between 37-39 weeks, the success rate is approximately 65%. Only about 6-7% of those babies revert back to breech presentation before delivery. If performed successfully, the doctor can then attempt induction at this time or wait closer to the due date. If the baby cannot be successfully verted or has distress during the procedure, then a cesarean section is in order.

There are certain criteria that must be met in order for the procedure to be performed. Your OB doctor will determine if you meet the criteria before a version is attempted.

Placenta Previa

In 1 out of every 200 pregnancies, this event might occur. Placenta Previa is where the placenta is partially or completely covering the cervical opening to the vagina. The placenta is a very highly vascularized (lots of blood vessels) part of the womb, which provides for nourishment and oxygen for your baby. If this is determined early in the pregnancy, it is monitored by the physician frequently by ultrasound to determine if the placenta has migrated away from the cervical opening. As the baby grows and the womb stretches, the placenta will usually begin to migrate away from the opening, eliminating the concerns for a cesarean section. In the event this does not happen, then it will be decided that a cesarean section is in order for the safety of both mother and baby.

If this has not been monitored previously by an obstetrician and a woman goes into labor, this could prove fatal to both mother and baby. Usually, vaginal bleeding during the pregnancy is a first indicator to a woman there is something wrong. She will usually present herself to a hospital to be checked and monitored. If the bleeding is severe enough and the previa is diagnosed by ultrasound, the doctor may perform an emergency cesarean section, if deemed necessary at that time. If the bleeding does start to slow down or stop, the doctor may opt to carefully monitor the mother in the hospital and delay delivery, in the event the baby is too early, and it might cause issues for him or her.

The longer a woman can remain safely pregnant is best for the baby's outcome, but if this becomes a life-threatening event, and emergency cesarean will be performed without hesitation.

Shoulder Dystocia

Large babies, disproportionate or small pelvis, post-dates babies, mother's short stature, or a history of a previous shoulder dystocia can place the mother and baby at risk for having a shoulder dystocia. A shoulder dystocia is when the baby's head has been delivered, but the shoulders cannot be easily delivered after. The shoulders are usually caught on the pubic bone or symphysis, and less commonly caught on the sacral promontory.

This is one of the most anxiety-provoking procedures during a vaginal delivery for doctors and nurses. If a shoulder dystocia has occurred, there are several procedures that can be administered to help deliver the baby successfully, but some not without possible issues.

The *McRoberts maneuver* is the first to be used. This is where the nurse or other personnel pull the mother's legs back into her chest and rotate them outward, which flattens out the sacral promontory and opens up the public symphysis— giving the pelvis more room to deliver the shoulders.

If the McRoberts maneuver is not successful, next would be the use of *suprapubic pressure*, where a nurse places their hands in a "cardiac resuscitation position" over the back of the fetal shoulder, pushing downward and away to attempt to rotate the baby's shoulder inward towards its chest. This can help to reduce the shoulder and allow it to present itself successfully.

There is another maneuver which can be performed, such as the doctor internally rotating the forearm over the chest and out of the vagina, which helps to give more room for delivery of the other shoulder. But using this procedure comes with the risk of breaking the clavicle or forearm of the baby to facilitate delivery, and/or causing nerve damage on the affected side.

Because of the concern for fetal distress, injury, or death caused by getting "caught" in the pelvis and cutting off oxygen to the baby, doctors will usually suggest that a cesarean delivery be performed before you go into labor.

Fetal Distress (Fetal Intolerance to Labor)

You may be going through your labor rather smoothly, until at some time during the labor your baby starts to show signs of distress. This is when the baby's heart rate starts a downward trend during the contractions, but is having difficulty recovering from them. If this pattern continues during each contraction or the baby starts showing signs of not recovering at all from the contractions, the obstetrician may order a cesarean section to deliver the baby quickly. All induction medications, if used, are turned off, and medications, such as Terbutaline, is given to you to stop all contractions and you will be prepped for surgery.

Cesarean Section Deliveries

This is a special section devoted to just cesarean section deliveries, which will affect the mother during their hospital stay or beyond. Cesarean section patients have more to deal with and have additional demands to help them with their recovery. If you have had, are planning to have, or unexpectedly had a cesarean section then you need to read all about it in this section.

Here your dreams of a vaginal delivery and normal recovery have been dashed, only to be changed— either due to predetermined medical reasons or urgent/emergent issues during labor— at the drop of the hat. You may feel inadequate as a woman because you could not deliver the "normal" way like women are intended to do. Well, let me tell you right now— that's completely *not true*!! You have carried this baby in your body for hopefully nine months, and certain situations dictate that you and your baby would be better off with a cesarean delivery— and sometimes it may be sooner rather than later.

We all know that nothing is black and white in our world, so why would the method of delivery be any different??? I can honestly say I have "ridden both sides of that fence." My first two babies were born vaginally, but my youngest thought she needed to be different— she didn't tolerate labor. I would have a contraction and her heart rate would get lower and lower, and then would come back up as my contractions subsided. It was hard to determine just what was going on at the time— did she have a tightened, pinched or knotted cord? was it due to positioning? We didn't know, so the safest way to eliminate the problem was to deliver her by cesarean section. I certainly did not like the idea of having a cesarean section, especially since I was completely dilated to 10 on the OR table, but she wouldn't even tolerate a light vaginal push… so…… cesarean section it was!

The decision was easy for me— my baby's safety came first. Since we had no clue what the cause of the decreasing heart rate was, I just gave the okay to change course— and to the OR we went. However, that decision can be hard when you're anticipating having your baby normally as opposed to "*abnormally*". You may be quickly thrust into this decision due to an emergent situation, or slowly acclimated to the idea during your prenatal visits due to breech presentation, too large of baby, issues with your anatomy, etc. No matter how it happens, it was not in your game plan.

But really— what is most important to you?? Mine was to have a healthy baby without any post-delivery issues. To me, it was not worth the risk to put my child in danger or risk long-term effects to my baby's mental capacity due to lack of oxygen. (Which prolonged decelerations in baby's heart rate is one of the baby's responses to lack of oxygen.) I didn't feel guilty for my decision— a positive outcome for both of us were my priority. You shouldn't feel guilty or inadequate because you had a cesarean section. Just remember the goal— healthy mom/healthy baby.

Certain factors may predispose you to a cesarean section for the safe delivery of your baby or babies, and possibly your safety as well. Here are a few of those factors:

- Multiple babies
- Maternal infection which make a vaginal delivery risky
- Unexpected labor events (discussed in the section before)
- Large baby
- Mother's medical condition which may make vaginal delivery risky

What to Expect During your Recovery

After you have finished with your 2-hour recovery you will be turned back over to your postpartum care nurse or your labor nurse, if she also does postpartum, for continued care. She will assist you with breastfeeding your baby, if you are planning this, since you will be unable to sit upright for a little while. She will also continue to keep IV fluids running and medicate you through your IV line for pain, itching, nausea and/or vomiting, or if needed, antibiotics.

If you had an epidural or spinal for surgery, you may be given Duramorph® (*morphine sulfate*) in your spinal catheter prior to being taken to the PACU (post-anesthesia care unit) after your surgery. This medication gives you long-term pain relief for 12-24 hours, depending on the anesthesiologist's choice. If you have general anesthesia during your surgery, you will be set up on a PCA (patient-controlled analgesia) pump during your recovery period, and given a pain medication for your use until you can take oral pain medications.

Since you have had a cesarean section, your recovery time is a little longer than with a vaginal delivery. The initial recovery time is the same two hours, but you will be on IV fluids longer, not getting out of bed for several more hours, and needing extra help with your care and your baby's care. So, we'll go over what you can expect after your recovery is completed.

IV Lines

You will have had an IV line started prior to your labor-turned-cesarean section or prior to your scheduled cesarean section. This IV line will help to administer IV fluids prior to and after your delivery, along with providing access to administer IV medications before, during, and/or after your delivery.

Generally, we will keep IV lines open and running after the delivery-- or lock off the site once we stop your IV fluids. We will leave it in for a little longer, at least until we receive results back from the labs we ordered for the morning after your surgery. If your labs come back during or after your surgery showing infection, very low hemoglobin, issues with your platelets, etc., then we already have your IV site still in place and we don't have to stick you again!! Also, if you are Rh negative and your baby's labs come back showing Rh positive, then we can leave the IV site open until you receive Rhophylac®, which can be administered in this site, so you don't have to get a shot in the gluteus maximus (bottom) again.

If there isn't any reason to keep the line open after all the post-delivery results are received, then we will remove it. I don't know about you, but I don't want to have to stick people any more than what is necessary, and I try to avoid having to restart it if it is pulled too soon and we need it back.

IV fluids

When you have a cesarean section, you will have an IV running for approximately 12-24 hours, or more, depending on how well you are getting/staying hydrated. For several hours after delivery, this will also be the site in which to administer IV medications, so we want to keep this open and available during that timeframe. If you have other issues, you may be required to have the IV site/fluids running for a longer period. So, there will be several things we take into consideration when we stop IV fluids.

First, we look at your hydration status, and we figure that by looking at your urine output. We have been pumping fluids into you since before delivery, but we need to get those fluids back out, too. When you get to the point of rehydration, you will start giving back a decent amount of urine. Second, starting as quickly as possible, we offer you ice chips when you can take them without nausea/vomiting. Then we slowly move you toward taking sips of water, and then on to drinking water. When you are drinking plenty of water, giving back plenty of urine, not running a fever— then we can get rid of the IV fluids. So, we will flush the IV line with saline solution after detaching the IV tubing.

IV meds

During your recovery period, you may be given several different medications such as for pain, shivering, nausea and vomiting, or itching. With the opioid pain relievers, you will be monitored closely by nursing staff and the anesthesiologist providing your care for any side effects, allergic or anaphylactic reactions you may experience during administration of the drug(s). Any or all of the drugs given will help to relief from your symptoms while you are in recovery

Demerol® (meperidine hydrochloride): This medication is given to you for some breakthrough pain and also from shivering. You will be watched closely in PACU for respiratory depression (slowing down or stop breathing), and for heavy sedation (making you *so* sleepy you may "pass out" from the use of this drug.) Respiratory depression and sedation are a very big concern since you have other pain medications on board at the same time.

You may have some breakthrough pain after you have returned to the recovery area after your surgery, so this might be given to you for the pain. You also may have a case of the uncontrollable shivers, which is a common phenomenon after surgery. Demerol is a medication which can help to get these shivers under control for you.

Stadol® (butorphanol): Another pain medication which may be given to you for some breakthrough pain after surgery. As with Demerol, you will be monitored for respiratory depression and sedation during your recovery. This drug is primarily used just for breakthrough pain relief.

Sublimaze® (fentanyl citrate): Fentanyl citrate is given for IV pain management either by IV injection or through a patient controlled analgesia (PCA) pump. Depending on the type of anesthesia used for your surgery, you may receive small dosages for breakthrough pain after an epidural or spinal anesthetic, or used in a PCA to be controlled by you when you feel the need for additional pain medication after the surgery.

This is another narcotic pain medication that you need to be closely monitored for respiratory depression and sedation during your recovery.

Morphine sulfate: Used for pain relief, morphine can be used in the form of IV medication given in a PCA pump after general surgery where you can pump the medication as needed during your recovery. Or, if you had Duramorph *(morphine sulfate)* added to your epidural or spinal after your cesarean, very small doses can be given for additional pain relief.

As with an opioid (narcotic) medication given for pain relief, monitoring for respiratory depression or sedation is necessary, along with other side effects such as allergic or anaphylactic reactions.

Toradol® (ketorolac): In most cases, Toradol will be ordered for administration to you after your surgery. This medication is like taking IV ibuprofen (see the section below under *Cesarean Pain Management*). Toradol works well in combination with any IV or epidural/spinal narcotic pain reliever at managing post-operative pain.

Zofran® (ondansetron): After surgery, you may have some nausea and/or vomiting, which is common. The use of preoperative and anesthesia medications along with the surgery itself may cause you to have nausea and/or vomiting afterwards. Zofran is one medication used to correct this issue.

Phenergan® (promethazine): This is another medication to combat nausea and/or vomiting, if you have it, after your surgery. Usually, Phenergan is used in the first line of defense in medicating for nausea and/or vomiting, then Zofran is used if the Phenergan is not effective, or still having mild symptoms.

Benadryl® (diphenhydramine): One of the most common, but irritating side effects from the use of Duramorph (morphine sulfate), which is used for long-duration pain relief post-cesarean of 12-24 hours, is itching. This is *not* an allergy, but it is still, none the less, an aggravating side effect.

Generally, you may start itching first on your nose or around the nose and mouth. Then the itching may migrate downward and start affected some other areas of your body, or may have a full-blown case everywhere on your body. Everyone is different as to if and how much itching you might encounter.

PCA pump

For those patients having general anesthesia or are allergic to some spinal narcotics used for cesarean sections, you may be started on a PCA pump in recovery to delivery pain medications during your recovery period. Fentanyl citrate, Demerol, and morphine sulfate discussed earlier, along with Dilaudid® (*hydromorphone*) are all medications used for PCA medication.

The PCA (patient controlled analgesia) pump allows you to give yourself a certain amount of the pain medication ordered to you if, and when, you feel the need for it. This can be good for you by allowing you to control when you get the medication and not having to call for the medications, then waiting until a nurse retrieves the medication and administers it to you. Even though you have control with giving yourself the medication when you want, you cannot give yourself too much medication because the pump only allows you so much control. The machine is programmed by the doctor or nurse with lockouts at certain lockout amounts or intervals so as to limit the amounts of medication given within say 6 or 8 minutes time. When you are taking water and/or food without nausea or vomiting, you can then have the PCA removed and start taking oral pain medications.

The downside to having a PCA pump is that when you fall asleep for extended periods, you may wake up and have too much pain as to be controlled by the use of the pump. If you are having an issue with pain control and you cannot take water or food without having nausea or vomiting, you must stay on this medication until you can get past that. You may be ordered, if the pain cannot be controlled, additional pain medications for IV injection, or a change in your lockout amount or interval on the PCA machine.

Ice chips/sips of water

During recovery, you nurse will start you off with some ice chips to wet your mouth, as it will be very dry after surgery. Over a 30-60-minute period, you may continue to suck on ice chips off and on to make sure you are tolerating those before moving to sips of water. Once you are good to go, she will switch you to taking sips of water— and I mean *sips*. If you try and guzzle down the water too fast, it usually comes back up shortly thereafter. I don't think you want to be throwing up after just having major surgery, but if you insist— go right ahead. Many have thought this wouldn't happen to them, and they did it anyway, only to find out I was right.

Why your body wants to regurgitate up nice, cold water is not something you would think it would do, but it does. You have an empty stomach which doesn't react well to iced cold water, so it decides to get rid of it. Not something you want after surgery to your abdomen, which would cause you to have pain, and I know you don't want additional pain. So, take it slow and easy to get your body used to it, then you will be able to advance to the next good thing— clear liquids!

Sitting up in bed

When you come out of the operating room and are moved to the PACU (post-anesthesia care unit) for your initial recovery, you are lying flat on the gurney or regular hospital bed. You will continue to rest and recover in this position for about an hour. If you are still on a gurney, then shortly you will be moved onto a regular hospital bed. Once in this bed, you will be slowly moved up to a sitting position.

Now the best way I found is to move the head of the bed up only three or four inches, say for 20-30 mins at a stretch. This way you slowly acclimate to the change in your position. If you move up to quickly after the surgery, you may become lightheaded, dizzy, and then become nauseous and/or vomit. This can be caused by a couple of factors.

First, the surgery itself causes the body to become weak and feel fatigued, like you had a really hard work-out and total exhaustion kicks in. This is a very normal occurrence after surgery, which is also part of the natural healing process, and would be very unusual if you didn't feel this way. Then anesthesia medications can affect your blood pressure by causing it to drop (hypotension) and also cause body fatigue. There is also the breathing factor involved. When you have surgery and have pain after, you tend to breathe shallow, which decreases the oxygen in your blood, which, in turn, decreases how much oxygen is getting to all of your cells. These, and some other potential causes (infection, fatigue prior to surgery, dehydration, etc.) are to blame for this.

So, to eliminate the potential of this happening, moving the head of the bed up a little at a time, then resting, then moving it again, then resting and so on will make the transition to sitting up so much easier.

Incentive spirometers

If you had general anesthesia during your surgery, when you have completed your recovery in the PACU and have returned to your room, you should be set up with an incentive spirometer and given a demonstration on its use by a respiratory therapist.

This device is used to help you remove the remaining anesthesia from your lungs and to prevent the development of pneumonia. It will help to open up your lungs fully and help you cough out the remaining anesthesia. You will be using this device every hour while you are awake and when you awaken after sleeping, and continue until you are up and walking around.

The downside of using this device is that when you open up the lungs it will force you to cough repeatedly. This, of course, will not feel very good on your incision, so supporting your abdomen well will help prevent some or all of any additional pain. (See the section below under *Some Incision Do's and Don'ts* for bracing your incision.)

Dangling and getting out of bed

When you are ready to sit on the side of the bed and then get up, position your bed so that the head is raised up. Bend your knees and place your feet flat on the bed. The closer you can comfortably manage to pull them up toward your bottom— all the better. Then place your hands flat on the bed next to your hips. Use your hands and feet to gently lift your bottom up off the bed and start to turn a little *towards* the edge of the bed while moving *over towards* the edge of the bed. You may have to do this a couple of times to get closer to the edge, and that's okay.

By the time you get to the edge of the bed, your legs should be starting to hang over the edge. Once you have done this, put your weight more on the side closest to the headboard and slowly rotate on your hip, place your elbow against the raised headboard and your other hand by your elbow or grasp the handrail, then swing your legs over the edge of the bed and push yourself to a sitting position.

Once you are in a sitting position on the side of the bed, sit there for a few minutes to get acclimated to sitting in that position. Let your feet dangle off the side of the bed and move the legs around while you are dangling. Wait to see if you get lightheaded, dizzy, ears ringing, vision blurring, or starting to have some nausea. This way, if you start having any of these symptoms, you can lie back down in bed. Sometimes you will have some of these symptoms because you haven't moved this much since the surgery, and need to try it out first before you start to stand up.

When all is well, and you are having none of the symptoms, you then move a little forward and place your feet shoulder width apart on the floor, look straight ahead and not down towards the floor, and use your hands on the bed to help push yourself up into a standing position. Remember to use all arms and legs during this maneuver so you are not putting any undue stress on the incision site. If you have forgotten why, go back to the section of *Getting Out of Bed/Back into Bed* above. There— now you have gotten yourself out of bed.

Foley Catheters

Due to the fact you will be immobile from surgery, and for several hours afterward be unable to get up and empty your bladder, you will be sporting one of these until we at least get you up and moving. Some people complain about them because they are uncomfortable, and they can be, but in general we try and remove them as quickly as possible anyway, so the sooner we get you up and moving the sooner we can remove them.

During the time frame you have your catheter, we will be able to monitor closely how good you are giving back all those fluids we've been pumping into you. It's not unheard of to lose quite a lot of fluid during the surgical process, so we need to replenish it and start getting urine back. We also look at and smell your urine, because the urine can tell us several things. (It's still too dark, so not getting hydrated; it's cloudy... could it be an infection of some kind; does it have an unpleasant abnormal odor...? Again, possible infection.

Now, there is something else to watch for while you still have the catheter on board. If at any time you start feeling like "I need to go pee", like your bladder is filling up, then let your nurse know. Sometimes after surgeries, the catheter tip in your bladder gets displaced, causing it to "butt up" against the side wall of your bladder and not allowing the urine to drain out. (At the same time, the balloon which holds the catheter in your bladder blocks off the other drain hole.) If it can't drain; your bladder will fill up. This can contribute to lower abdominal pain at the incision site due to the pressure from the filling bladder pushing on it— from the inside. Be sure and let your nurse know so she can fix that for you.

When the catheter can be removed, I give my patients the option of having the catheter for the night or getting it out sooner. If they really want the catheter out as quick as possible, then they must be capable of walking to the bathroom and tolerate being out of bed without difficulty, along with having good output and no fever. Some want that "darn thing out", so let's do what we need to make it happen. Others don't mind having it, and like the idea of not having to get up every 1-2 hours to void— like they have for the past few months. So, we leave it in until morning— then it *must come out.*

Once the catheter is removed, and you are taught *hoo-hah* care, you will have about 4-6 hours to pee on your own. If you cannot urinate on your own, we must empty out the bladder for you, by reinserting a one-time catheter briefly to do just that. Most of the time this is unnecessary, as patients are capable of urinating on their own, but sometimes it doesn't work— and here are some reasons why.

One, trauma to the ureters, urethra, and bladder. That little ol' tube that pulls the urine out of the bladder and pushes is out of the body gets traumatized when the catheter is placed. The bladder is manipulated during the surgery, pushed/shoved out of the way to get the baby out. It is now "frozen" and unable to do what it was intended to do— empty your bladder. When that happens, it needs to take time to "wake up" and start working as it did before, but sometimes it takes longer than we want, hence the need to empty the bladder.

Second, if the bladder gets overdistended (very full), then we are possibly back to the problem of potentially displacing the uterus, therefore, increasing the chances for postpartum bleeding/clotting and/or hemorrhaging, like discussed earlier. (See section on *Voiding*)

And if you are still unable to void after being emptied out, then a short-term foley catheter will be replaced and you will be further evaluated. However, as stated before, this is very "few and far between." It just doesn't happen very often.

Perineal care

Your perineal care will be pretty much the same as it would be for a vaginal delivery. After urinating, use your plastic cleansing bottle or Hygenique sprayer (attached to the bathroom wall) to cleanse thoroughly to clean away any dried or fresh blood from your hoo hah. If you have not used a

Hygenique sprayer, make sure your nurse shows you how to set up and use it. As stated in the vaginal care section above, delivery compromises you by putting you at risk for infection. Your nether region is a portal for infection, so no matter whether you had a vaginal or cesarean delivery, be sure you *do not* skip this step. While you are still sitting down, completely cleanse yourself off with water. Once you are clean, then dry off with toilet paper normally. Continue to do this each and every time you use the toilet for as long as you are bleeding.

Ambulating in the halls

This is *necessary* when it comes to recovering from a cesarean section. When you get up and start walking around on you own, you will need to start walking around the unit as well. This is very important for your recovery, so be sure you *do not* avoid this during your stay. And if you are up walking around, back and forth in the room *doesn't count!* I cannot count how many times I asked my patients if they walked in the halls and how much, and I get the answer "I walked around the room." And my reply to this would be, "I didn't ask you about walking around the room, I asked if you have been walking in the halls." Most of the time their answer was none. To this I would reply, "Then I will tell you why it is important to walk in the halls and not just in the room..." and so I will communicate to you the reasons as well as the benefits as I do with my patients.

The first benefit of early ambulation is reduction or elimination of blood clots forming in your legs. Deep vein thrombosis, or DVTs, is a very significant post-surgical complication to avoid. These clots can travel to your heart, lungs, or brain. After any surgery, a patient is at risk for developing blood clots in their legs, therefore, ambulation is the key in prevention of this potentially deadly complication. By ambulating in the halls, that long-distance walking helps with venous circulation in the legs. Anytime the circulation is decreased, blood can pool in the lower extremities and increase the chance for the blood to clot. During the early recovery period, until you are allowed to ambulate, you will be wearing pneumatic sequential compression cuffs. These cuffs aid in keeping the blood circulating in your legs until you can get up and walk around. Once you have the green light to walk, it's important to keep that circulation going.

Another benefit is improved patient outcomes and recovery. Studies show that early and frequent ambulation helps patients recover quicker and require shorter hospital stays. By ambulating, you are accelerating your recovery by moving around more frequently, which, in turn, enables you to care for yourself and your baby, thus making your transition from hospital to home easier for you.

Last is— ambulation helps to get the motility (movement) going again in the bowels. When you have abdominal surgery, the trauma to your intestines from being moved around causes them to "go to sleep". They shut down, and therefore, stop all movement of anything in your bowel, including pushing through the gas. When this happens, the gas can build up and start causing you sharp, abdominal pains— and pain medications *will not* have any effect on this. By getting up and ambulating in the halls, at least three times a day for about 10-15 minutes each, you will get the motility in your bowel going and start passing some of that gas.

Now, you may build up with more gas than you get rid of, and this can happen, even if you are passing some gas. If you are, and you're walking in the halls like you should, be sure and let you nurse know if it is getting uncomfortable for you. She can give you something to aid in passing more gas.

When I have patients, who are passing very little or no gas and are becoming uncomfortable, I start them off with a more holistic method than jumping right into medication. My concoction— a cup of warm prune juice *followed* by a cup of hot tea or coffee, *caffeinated.* Now, you may think…*eeeww!! Prune juice!!* I can honestly say warm prune juice *does not* taste bad. I've even had a few nay-sayers turn up their noses at that only to find out it wasn't as bad as they thought. And in all my years, only about a handful refused to even try it— and they were *very* "picky" eaters.

Now, the reasoning behind the warm prune juice and hot tea/coffee is simple. Prune juice is a natural laxative (now you know why the old folks eat them prunes and drink that juice!) Tea or coffee *with caffeine...* natural stimulant. And— both of them being warm to hot help to stimulate as well. Woo-hoo— there is a method to my madness!! In all the many years I have given this two-fisted concoction, I can honestly say it worked well for them— *AND* they didn't have to resort to using a Ducolax suppository to get the job done. I can't even tell you the last time I had to give a patient one.

Your nurse should be asking you if you are passing gas, and you need to be honest. Be sure and tell her if it's just a little or a whole lot. You may be passing what you think is a lot of gas, but sometimes you may be building up with more gas than you are getting rid of. And don't be embarrassed to do so in front of her, or anyone else for that matter. If you do not want to pass gas in front of anyone, ask them to leave the room briefly. It's important that you do not hold on to the gas and not let it release. You are recovering from major surgery and have issues that need to be resolved, and bowel function is one of them. *So, let 'r rip, tater chip!!*

Rocking chair

If is available at your hospital, this is another useful tool to use when working on getting the gas to move through your system. The back and forth rocking helps to keep you in motion so the gas bubbles can move around. You can use the rocking chair when you are just sitting around the room, or if you are unable to ambulate due to assorted reasons or complications.

Chewing gum

It's been found through research that chewing gum after surgery can decrease the time when you start passing gas, therefore, improving the return of bowel function. This causes the digestive juices to start flowing, which in turn aids in returning bowel function. If you are unable to start eating soon after your surgery, due to nausea/vomiting or other complications, this may be a temporary alternative to feeding your irritable stomach.

Incisional Care/Issues

When you have a cesarean section, the surgery takes approximately 30-40 minutes from start to finish. Several layers are cut through to get to the uterus and remove the baby, so several layers are sewn back up. The outer layer of skin is either sewn together, stapled together, or a combination of sewing/ gluing together. Your doctor may also put over the site several strips of tape called steristrips. Generally, the suture used today is an absorbable suture, so removal is not required. Staples on the outer skin will be removed either just before you go home or a few days after surgery in the doctor's office, then steristrips will be placed along the incision site. These strips will generally begin to "fall off" on their own within 5-7 days. If longer, your doctor will have you remove them yourself. Depending on your physician's preference, it can be any one of these methods.

First we're going to go over care of your incision. Once your pressure bandage is removed, approximately 6-12 hours after surgery, the incision site is inspected to see if there is any active bleeding, oozing, redness, swelling, bruising, or gaps in the incision. It is also important to leave the dressing off to allow for air circulation to the wound, allowing it to heal. Your nurse may place a sanitary pad across the site, without taping it down, and this is okay. Air can still get to the site for healing, but it can also help with *two* things: monitoring for any oozing, or color of drainage and how much, *and* putting a bit of padding across the site to protect it from bumping up against things like the sink or counter.

Oozing or bleeding from site: If you have drainage showing on your pad, let your nurse know so she can see if it is normal amounts of drainage or if it warrants further assessing and/or care. Do not be too alarmed if you do have some. Sometimes a pocket of fluid close to the surface of the incision will push its way through. This can be normal, but if you are unsure, then check with your nurse. Make sure you change your pad each time you shower or clean your incision, so you are not placing a soiled pad back over the site. We don't want any infections.

Cleaning your incision: When you shower for the first time after your surgery, do not be afraid to clean your incision— in fact, we want you to. This keeps bacteria from setting up residence and infecting your wound. After you have showered your body and/or hair, take a bit of soap and water in your hands and lightly rub across the incision completely and then rinse. Once your shower is finished, towel dry yourself as normal but lightly pat dry your incision. If when you finish drying, feel along your incision site. If it is still damp, take a hair dryer on a cool, low setting and completely dry the site.

Now depending on the time of year (summer vs winter) and if your belly tissue hangs down enough to cover up your incision, you may need to use extra care. When it's hot and you sweat, that extra flap of belly tissue—called a pannus— can allow for moisture to collect in your incision area. That trapped moisture and warm body allows for bacteria to grow and flourish, which we all know is not good for your incision. So, you will need to clean the incision site more frequently, and when you are just sitting around your house, periodically take your hands and gently lift up your pannus to allow air to circulate around your incision and help keep it dry. At any point in time you see the incision is getting reddened, having unusual drainage, has an unpleasant odor, is warm or hot to the touch (warmer than usual) then let your doctor know as soon as possible. If you cannot see the site yourself, even in the mirror, have a family member check it for you.

Numbness at site: For most patients, the area on and around the incision site will be numb for some time. This is normal, as some of the nerves have been severed due to the surgery. Generally, it will take several months or even years for the sensation to get back to normal. As the nerves regenerate, feeling will begin to come back.

To help with inflammation, you may use an ice pack periodically during your recovery period. If your nurse does not offer this to you, just ask. (See the information below under *burning on or around the site* on how long and how often to use an ice pack.)

Burning on or around site: For some patients, there is no numbness, but the feeling is as if your skin has been sunburnt and you do not want to have anything touching it. I know this does happen, and some nurses may not have any idea why you are having this kind of irritation, but I can tell you it is real— because I experienced it for myself. Again, it depends on how the nerves are severed as to which sensation you will have, but numbness is the most typical feeling.

If you *do* have the burning, irritating sensation on or around your incision site, there are a couple of things you may do to help with it. First off, is placing the sanitary pad across the site. It will help keep your clothes from rubbing up against it, and again help protect the site if you bump up against it. If this does not work for you because it is still irritating, placing an ice pack periodically across the site might give you some relief. Do this for about 20 minutes at a time, maybe 4-6 times or more per day. Whatever helps give you relief. But *do not* continually have an ice pack on there. You can cause skin burns, frostbite, and damage deeper under the skin down to your tissues and cells.

During your recovery in the hospital, your nurse may offer this to you. If she doesn't, it doesn't hurt to ask for one. Ice to the incision can help with not only inflammation, it can help with pain as well. After several days, or when you go home, placing warm packs to the site periodically will also help with getting the circulation going, which helps promote healing. Whichever method you use, or if you use both, be sure and wrap the ice pack or warm pack with a towel or washcloth to prevent burns, frostbite, tissue damage, etc.

Bruising around site: You may notice when you inspect your incision within the first few days after surgery that you have some bruising on or around the site. Any time there is surgical manipulation of the skin there is a potential for bruising. So, do not be surprised to see this. However, you may see a lot more bruising than you may expect, and maybe swelling, especially on the lower segment of the incision site. *Do not* be alarmed if you do. There is a perfectly normal explanation for this as well.

When your doctor is cutting through the layers of skin, tissue, fat, etc. they get down to the bladder. To eliminate possibly nicking or cutting into the bladder, they move the bladder out of the way by placing a bladder blade over the top of the bladder, and the surgical nurse or tech pulls it down toward your hoo-hah. Because of the slick surfaces from blood and fluid, sometimes the bladder blade will slip out of place and rake over the tissues, causing added trauma to the area. This additional trauma will cause bruising and swelling to those tissues.

Pain more on one side: There may also be some additional pain, more so on one side or the other of your incision site. This is due to the side the doctor preforms your surgery on. If your doctor is right handed, they will stand on your right side during the procedure. If a southpaw, then the left side. The doctor will pull and tug harder on the side closest to him/her, and all the sutures of each layer will be tied off on their side. Both of these issues will contribute to the additional pain to that side of your incision. And— you may have twinges of pain on that same side long after you heal. This is due to the adhesions (internal scar tissue) which has formed more on the affected side.

Pain from additional surgical procedures: There are a couple other reasons you may have additional pain from your cesarean section surgery. When having your tubes tied during your cesarean, the doctor is in your abdomen for a longer time and is manipulating all of your internal organs more. This causes additional trauma in and around your abdomen and muscles which would lead to more pain.

Another reason might be if you had previous cesarean sections or abdominal surgeries in the past, you may have an overabundance of adhesions (internal scar tissue) which would be necessary to "break up" or release from other organs and tissues in the surrounding area. This also would contribute to the additional pain from your surgery.

Some Incision Do's and Don'ts

Since you have just had major surgery, there are a few things you need to be cautious of during your recovery time. It's easy to forget, especially if you have never had surgery, that you cannot move around as easily as you have before. Getting in and out of bed, or even turning over when you sleep takes a little forethought before you engage in your task. This also goes for bending, reaching, stretching or twisting. Any or all of these ways of moving can cause pain, and in some cases extreme pain. So, we will go over proper mechanics of movement during your recovery.

Some of the "don'ts": Reaching, stretching, twisting while you are sitting or standing can also cause incisional pain as well. We generally take for granted that we can still move this way even after surgery— but in reality, you may cause yourself additional pain and nobody wants to have additional pain. So, *think* before you move. "Will my movement cause me pain?" "How can I best move to avoid additional pain?" Just be mindful of what you do and how you do it, and your recovery will go smoother.

Lifting your legs off the bed when you are lying down or bending at the waist when trying to sit up can also cause pain. When you do this, you are engaging your tummy muscles in and around your incision site. Some of those muscles have been severed during the surgery, so lifting your legs and engaging those muscles to work will start to cause you undue pain over time, so refrain from doing this as well. You may think you are helping your nurse out by lifting your legs for her, say, when she is putting on/taking off your pneumatic pressure cuffs— *but* let her do the leg lifting for you.

Bracing your incision: Three other issues that may come up during your recovery period: laughing, coughing, and sneezing. *Oh, NO!!* The last thing you want to think about is having any one or all these problems cause additional pain. Patients have been told over the years to place a pillow over your incision and brace it with your hands to alleviate abdominal movement, thus avoiding more pain. I find this method not as beneficial as one I have adopted many years ago.

A colleague of mine suggested this method, and I find that it is better than the old one. If you must laugh, cough, or sneeze, curl around your abdomen, crossing your forearms over your belly and try grasping your sides with your fingers and hold. By doing this, you will place more counter-pressure against your abdomen by using your shoulders and forearms, than just using your hands. This will give you more control by giving what I call a "brick wall effect." Your abdomen will not move nearly as much, if at all, and may cause you little or no pain.

Moving your body up in bed: Sometimes when you are sitting up in bed or changing positions while you are sleeping, your body starts to migrate down toward the foot of the bed. The more this happens, the more you start to slump in bed when you are sitting up which puts more pressure against your incision. When this happens, there is a simple way to move yourself back up in bed without putting any undo pain or pressure on your incision site.

First, put the head of the bed all the way down, then grab a hold of the upper bed rails toward the top. Next, draw your knees up far enough to allow for easily pushing off the bed with your feet, without your feet slipping back down. Once you're in position, you want to lift up your bottom from the bed at the same time you pull with your upper arms and push with your feet. This technique helps eliminate any undue stress and pain at your incision site, and moves you back up in a better position in bed. But *make sure* you move the head all the way back down before you do anything else, otherwise, you will be going against gravity and may cause yourself more soreness or pain if you do not.

Turning over in bed: Changing positions in bed, from back to side _or_ side to side, is done a lot like when you get in and out of bed. (See section _Getting Out of Bed_, under _Immediate Post-Delivery_ to refresh your memory.) You _do not_ want to twist at the waist to roll over. What you want to do is draw your knees up and plant your feet on the bed as close to your bottom as you can get. Lift your hips up and rotate your hips a little, then set your "butt" back down. After rotating your hips, scoot your shoulders back the opposite way just a little. Repeat the process in little increments until you have gotten into the position you want to lay in next. This will put very little strain on your incision and lessen the chance of causing pain to your abdomen.

Pain Management

Be prepared to read several pages throughout this section, as it is a very important one to make your recovery the best it can be— for you and your baby. This topic is where there *are* several instructions I can emphasize with patients and their pain management, which will be the same issues for both types of deliveries. However, I will separate some of the information into vaginal deliveries and cesarean deliveries, for the pain management will generally be very different for each.

Your nurse will be asking you, "How would you rate your pain?" or "How would you rate your pain, on a scale of 0-10, with 10 being the highest?" Some patients seem to have a great deal of difficulty with this pain scale, in that they may be laughing and joking, or talking to others and seem just fine… but will rate their pain like-- a 7 or 8. A patient's pain is subjective. We cannot feel their pain, so we must rely on their pain rating to determine how well the pain is being managed. But when the pain does not reflect how the patient is acting, then as nurses, we must be diligent to explain the pain scale, further allowing us to obtain a more accurate score.

One of the fabulous nurses I work with has a cute little analogy she uses when explaining the pain scale to patients. "If your pain is a zero, then you are having no pain. If your pain is a 5, then you might feel like crying, but if your pain is a 10, then you *will* feel like *"OH… MY… GOD… JUST KILL ME NOW!!! Because I now have my arm cut off without any anesthesia!!"*

Before giving a pain score to your nurse, be sure and move around a little in bed just for a few seconds to gage the current pain better. If you haven't been moving around, usually your pain is not as high as it is when you do. This helps to give a more accurate pain score for your pain. If you have recently been up and about the room or halls, make sure you use *that* pain rating if you are now resting or sitting again. Having an accurate pain rating will give you a better idea of how intense it is and if you require pain medication to manage it. If you are having a mild to moderate amount of pain, you may only need a small amount of pain meds to help you get relief. If it's moderate to severe, then a higher dosage and possible higher concentration of meds may be in order.

There are times that you may want to be proactive with your pain management, and that is very *okay*. You will have uterine cramping as your uterus is working to get smaller and smaller after delivery. Those cramps may be mild enough from a first delivery; that you may just feel a small amount of cramping but do not require any medications for it, and that's fine. If it intensifies, you can request some at that time. But if you have had several babies, usually but not always 3 or more, your cramping will continue to increase in intensity. I usually have moms, by the time 3 or more babies have come along, feel like they are "*going through labor all over again.*" Yes, it has been described as that, so prepare yourself for it to happen! If it doesn't, you can count yourself lucky— but be prepared on the next go-around. (File it away in that brain of yours for future reference.)

Breastfeeding will also cause your uterus to contract as well. It's your body's natural way of triggering the oxytocin in your brain to cause contractions in the uterine muscle, which assists with the decrease of heavy bleeding and clots, and helps your uterus to get back in the pelvis to its pre-pregnant state. So, it is a good thing, even though it "doesn't feel too *whoopy.*" Just be reassured this will only be intense and will lessen in its severity over a very short time.

When the cramping is just starting, it usually starts off mild and then quickly and steadily increases in intensity. I do instruct my moms that taking some ibuprofen ahead of time might help to decrease the severity, or help them get "on top of the pain" before it increases. Some will want to have the ibuprofen given to them when they can have it, so they can hopefully stay on top of it. A warm blanket or heating pad can also help decrease the cramping, but that and the ibuprofen are about all that can be given for it. (This is one of the issues that affect both vaginal and cesarean deliveries equally.)

There will also be general muscle aches and muscle soreness after either type of delivery. For vaginal deliveries, you may have muscle aches/soreness from all the pushing and pulling during delivery. You put your arms, shoulders, face, back, and legs to an extensive workout during the pushing phase, so why wouldn't you be sore all over?! You will be experiencing on or about the 2nd day after delivery that you "feel like you have been hit by a Mack truck!" Or, you might feel you had the most extensive workout in the gym, only you had it in the delivery room. For cesarean sections, you will be pulled and tugged around, and muscles are messed with in your abdomen during the surgery, so there is where some of your soreness comes from.

You may also have pain in your back and that may be caused by two things or both. First, if you have an epidural or spinal prior to delivery, you might have soreness at the injection site from the medication used to numb the area. This medication can cause bruising to the tissues, therefore, soreness around the site. You will also have soreness from the insertion of the epidural needle itself, causing more soreness at the site. Then second, you may have pain in the muscles of your back, particularly the lower half. This can be caused by the simple fact you no longer have the baby's weight in front, so you're realigning your posture to compensate for the change in weight distribution. During your pregnancy, this would have been a gradual change in posture, whereas, now it is a sudden change. That sudden change puts a great deal of strain on those muscles, therefore causing a backache. Makes sense? Good—moving on!

For those who are going to be *or* are breastfeeding, be reassured that any of the pain medications given to you during your recovery process is *okay* for breastfeeding. We *certainly* would not be offering any of these medications to you to take if they were not. They have been studied and determined to be safe with breastfeeding by the American Academy of Pediatrics (AAP) and National Institute for Health (NIH), and properly categorized as far as how much, if any, effect they have on babies.

The drugs you may be taking range from, Non-Steroidal Anti-Inflammatories (NSAIDs) such as acetaminophen, ibuprofen, naproxen, ketorolac, etc., to antibiotics and have been found to have no effect on breastmilk production or effect on breastfed babies. Narcotics (oxycodone, hydrocodone, hydromorphone, morphine, fentanyl) used for cesarean sections and vaginal deliveries, respectively, were found to have little or no effect on their babies within the first few days after delivery. This is possibly due to the little or no quantity of narcotic passed through the colostrum. Once the milk came in, babies *may* have become more sleepy and harder to arouse with the higher amounts now present in the breastmilk, but the strength of the prescription was also of a higher dosage. (20 mcg per dose versus 10 mcg per dose.) These were also found with babies whose mothers were taking narcotic medications for longer than 10 days, which is the usual length of medication prescribed for discharge prescriptions.

While unsure of other institutions dosage of prescription narcotics for post-partum cesarean sections, our institution utilizes the lower dosage of narcotic for effective pain relief, which is 10 mcg (5 mcg of oxycodone per tablet.) So, you can rest assured that taking pain medications, even narcotics, are safe enough to take for short-term therapy during your recovery period without causing too much drowsiness or having babies difficult to arouse for feedings. And don't forego your comfort and good pain relief for the fear of it causing ill effects on your breastfed baby. Remember, you must take care of yourself, too.

Now, for the differentiation of pain relievers between vaginal and cesarean sections. First, we'll look at the vaginal pain medications and what they are indicated for, then move on to those given for cesarean sections.

Vaginal Pain Relief

Generally, patients giving birth the old-fashioned way will have pain in 1-4 primary areas. First will be, of course, vaginal pain. Due to trauma of the nether region (swelling, lacerations, tears, episiotomies, and stitches), any one or a combination of several can cause pain to be mild to severe. For this kind of pain, meds can range from plain Tylenol® *(acetaminophen)*, a pain reliever without any narcotics, all the way up to Percocet® *(oxycodone w/ acetaminophen.)* The other areas: back, muscles, and uterus would be taken care of with ibuprofen, which we discussed above.

Mild pain: (1-3) For the most part, plain Tylenol *(acetaminophen)* can be used for mild pain relief or be used by patients who absolutely do not want any meds with narcotics in them. These are available in what we call PRN form— *as needed only.*

Moderate to severe pain: (3-6) These medications listed, such as Norco® or Vicodin® *(hydrocodone w/acetaminophen),* Ultram® *(tramadol)* and Tylenol® #3 *(codeine w/acetaminophen)* may be used for moderate to severe pain. Norco is the medication most used for vaginal area pain on a routine basis in our hospitals and is only available to the patient *as needed,* unless your physician specifically orders it routinely for you.

Depending on how much pain you are in, you *do* have the option to take this routinely— can be generally taken every 4 hours— for a very brief period of time (like during your hospital stay), and resort to taking it only as needed as the pain begins to subside. Either way will depend on how you are feeling and how much pain medication is needed. Our health system and doctors do not have these medications as scheduled meds, only on an as needed basis, unless indicated.

Severe pain: (7-10) These medications would be ordered for those who have very intensive and deep vaginal repairs done. If a patient has what is called a 3rd or 4th degree repair, doctors will generally order Norco to start and move up to Percocet® *(oxycodone w/acetaminophen)* if needed for pain relief, as this type of surgical repair goes into or through the rectal muscle wall. This is an extensive repair and patients will *most assuredly* feel the intensity of it. We have been known to call these kinds of repairs "vaginal c-sections." You are in so much pain you do not even want to sit down on anything— toilet, bed or chair!! *OUCH, OUCH… OUCH, OUCH, OUCH!! Not at all comfortable!!!*

So, to sum it up, ibuprofen would be used for muscle aches and uterine cramping. Acetaminophen for mild pain, Norco or Vicodin for moderate vaginal pain, and Percocet for severe pain. You should have prescriptions given to you when you are discharged from the hospital for any or all of the medications you were receiving during your hospital stay.

Cesarean Section Pain Relief

This is a different ball of wax when it comes to pain relief. You have just had major surgery with your lower abdomen cut open, baby removed, and then everything is put back into place and/or reattached, so your pain will naturally be more intense. Surgery of the lower abdomen is a *major surgery,* so you need to be aware that it is essential for you to get good pain relief. Below we will go over the different types of pain relief, when you start taking oral medications after a longer recovery, how to wean yourself off the narcotic pain meds effectively, and why the need for use of narcotic pain meds.

Mild pain (1-3): Very few post-cesarean patients will be in this category. These will be the women who have a very high threshold for pain and do not require much in the way of medications. I have seen some just take ibuprofen and do just fine, but, again, these are a rare few. If I find that they need a little more incisional pain relief and don't want to take any narcotics, then I will suggest at least some acetaminophen to help with it. Both ibuprofen and acetaminophen work very well together for overall mild pain relief.

Moderate to severe pain (4-6): From past experience caring for post-cesareans, the majority of women fall into this category. Use of a narcotic pain reliever together with ibuprofen, and taking and weaning off the meds as described below under *How to Take Oral Medications,* works well at controlling pain for these women.

Severe Pain (7-10): Not very many women fall into this category, but there are some that do. These women have a very low threshold for pain, and getting the patient's pain under control is very challenging. Additional narcotic pain meds may be ordered, on top of the narcotic they already have, to get better pain management for them.

When a patient falls under this category, there may be extenuating circumstances that may be contributing to their pain. The patient may not be walking in the halls to help relieve gas building up in the abdomen, thus they are very distended and having gas cramping pain. They also may be moving around incorrectly, such as not getting in or out of bed correctly; reaching, stretching, twisting; laughing, coughing, sneezing a lot; or having an overdistended bladder which pushes up against the incision from the inside. Another reason could be the "knees" of the bed are up so high that their thighs are pushing up against the incision site. Or, the patient has gone way too long without having any pain meds before the pain got out of control.

There may also be patients who have an unrealistic idea of *not having any pain from the surgery,* so any pain they do have they may consider as severe. They may also not have an accurate grasp on the pain scale, so they give a higher number than it really may be. The nurse should be mindful to fully describe the pain scale again to these patients if they may be scoring the pain too high for what they may be feeling.

The last reason may be very concerning, in that it may be due to the surgery itself. It's possible there may be some blood oozing from one of the many areas inside the abdomen where the doctor might have a missed "bleeder" which wasn't tied off or cauterized. This can cause abdominal pain as the "free floating" blood collects in the abdomen. If this is determined, additional surgery would be needed to correct this problem.

Whatever the reason, it would be more prudent for us, as nurses, to evaluate other possible reasons before getting an order for additional narcotic pain meds.

IV Pain Relief

First you will start out with either an epidural or spinal and may be given Duramorph (*morphine sulfate*) in the OR before you leave. This is long-acting morphine, usually lasting about 12-24 hours for continued narcotic pain relief. During that timeframe, if you have any break-through pain, your nurse will be able to give any one of several IV pain meds to get you over the hump. Usually they are low dosages of fentanyl, Demerol *(meperidine)*, or additional morphine to aid the Duramorph, but may be others. Toradol *(ketorolac)* is a non-steroidal anti-inflammatory drug *(NSAID)*, like having "IV ibuprofen." This works well in conjunction with your narcotic to give you good overall pain control. If you are allergic to morphine or any of the narcotics given, the anesthesiologist will find another medication he/she can use.

PCA pain relief

If you have a general anesthetic in surgery, afterward, you will be set up with a PCA pump (patient-controlled analgesia) and a medication you can have, such as Morphine, Demerol, Dilaudid, or Fentanyl. This is where you administer the pain medication to yourself, but the dosage amount will be controlled so you cannot give yourself too much. One of the problems with PCAs is if you fall asleep and your pain starts to climb, you may get behind on the pain relief, and this makes it a little harder to keep the pain under control. But with a PCA, you can switch over to an oral narcotic a lot sooner, as soon as you are tolerating oral hydration and/or other clear liquids.

If you are allergic to many of the IV or oral narcotics, then the doctor will give you what you can have, although you may not get very good pain relief during your recovery. (I feel bad for any patient who cannot take the appropriate pain medication(s) in order to get good pain relief. Some people are allergic to some— or *a lot*— of pain medications, which makes it hard to find alternative ones that can help get and keep your pain under control. Alternative non-medication therapies might have to be utilized in their particular case.)

Oral Pain Medications

When you can take oral medications, then Percocet *(oxycodone w/acetaminophen)* is generally the drug of choice for an abdominal surgery of this kind, at least with our physicians. This medication is usually given in conjunction with Motrin *(ibuprofen)*. These two medications together work very well for overall pain relief from the cesarean section. Percocet is given for the actual surgical pain, whereas, ibuprofen is given for generalized pain such as muscle aches, soreness, and cramping. Some facilities may order Ultram *(tramadol)* which is a narcotic-like medication for moderate to severe pain relief.

Depending on your institution, you may be given Vicodin *(hydrocodone w/ acetaminophen)*, or Norco *(hydrocodone w/acetaminophen)*, for your incisional pain management. These narcotics give a little less pain relief than the Percocet, but may be your hospital's course of treatment for cesarean pain. Most hospitals I have researched usually give Percocet for post-cesareans.

How to Take Oral Medications

When I tell my cesarean patients how I recommend they manage their pain, I suggest that for at least the next 2-3 days— the length of their hospital stay— they take the pain medicine when they can have it. That means around the clock, 1-2 tablets every 4 hours for their oxycodone or hydrocodone and usually every 8 hours for 800 mg of ibuprofen, starting off with 2 tablets of your narcotic. (The timeframe rarely changes on the ibuprofen for our patients, but your doctor may order it for every 4-6 hours with the appropriate dosages accordingly.) I do wake patients up to give pain medication unless they request I alter the time a little to be when the baby feeds. This way the patient has continuous pain relief and it stays under control.

If a patient is sleeping through their dosage time, or sits around in bed for a long time and does not take pain meds, then when they attempt to move around or get out of bed their pain immediately goes from a comfortable 2-3 up to 5-8. When pain jumps up like that, it affects you in several ways.

One— you now don't want to move around and do the things you need to do (walk to the bathroom, attend your baby, walk the halls, etc.). Moving around and being active are important for recovery. Two— now your pain is no longer under control, and you will be playing "catch up" with it. This may take several dosages of meds to get it back under control. Then, the pain itself may cause you to get nauseated, and heaven forbid, vomit. Not a good thing to cause yourself when you've had surgery. Now you're vomiting, and the pain is getting even worse for you. Not good! Another problem you might encounter is not being comfortable enough to sleep. If you can't sleep, you can't heal, then every problem you are having can get worse and worse. See how one little thing can have a snowball effect?? This is the reason I strongly recommend *careful consideration* on the subject of pain management when recovering from a cesarean.

Women with History of Opioid Use

For those with a history of opioid use/misuse during or prior to the pregnancy, there will be a screening by the physician before the administration of any opioid substance in the postpartum period. Non-opioid drug therapy may be used, along with alternative pain therapies, such as uses of heat or ice, meditation, etc. to control patients pain and manage it.

If found to be concerning for physicians on behalf of the infant born to an opioid-addicted mother, or had prior opioid abuse in her history, opioids may be prescribed to the mother to reduce the chance of the infant developing Neonatal Abstinence Syndrome (immediate drug withdrawal from opioids after delivery). Additional medical support may be needed for these infants to help recover from exposure to opioids during their mother's pregnancy.

Weaning off Oral Narcotic Pain Meds

Now, when it comes to weaning off your narcotic, this is what I suggest to the majority of my patients, and to you. First, continue to take the ibuprofen throughout the whole pain management process. This will be the last pain medication you will be using at the end. Now for the narcotic: Take 2 tablets around the clock the first few days. You can best determine when the time is right based on your pain. When you get to the point when you are moving around, and the time comes due for your pain medicine, but you do not feel you need any pain meds at all— or very little— then cut the dosage in half. Now start taking one tablet every 4 hours instead of 2. If your pain at the end of these 4 hours starts jumping back up and you find out you might have cut down the dosage too quickly, then you jump back up to 2 tablets and start the process all over again. If not, and your pain is still under control after 4 hours, then continue to take the new dosage of your narcotic for a while.

The next step is the last step in the tapering process. Now when you again get to the 4-hour mark and you do not feel like you need to take any pain meds at all, this is when you start stretching out the time in which you take the next dose. Take your next dose only when you *just* start to feel some pain, but it's still low on the pain scale, and continue that process over the next few days. This is how you will successfully wean off these narcotics— and feel better in your healing process!

Lastly, you can do the same with the ibuprofen now that you are off the narcotics. Same process, but maybe even a shorter amount of time!! See, education is the key to this issue, and anything else you might encounter along the way.

Now, with some patients who only want one Percocet and do fairly well with just the one and don't want to take a second Percocet if they are having just a little more pain, I have even combined that one Percocet with taking another one acetaminophen tablet to go with it. This way they still get at least *half* the narcotic dosage and *all* of what they would have been getting in acetaminophen. They, of course, still take the ibuprofen along with the different dosages for good overall pain relief. Then they use the same principle of weaning off these meds like discussed above.

Not all patients rate pain in the same way— and that's normal. Some patients have a higher threshold of pain than the average person and they do not require meds in the same way— and I respect that. Therefore, I don't force pain meds on any of my patients. I just educate them in what would be the best for their recovery. If I notice that they are refusing pain meds and are not handling their pain well, I will continue to encourage them to a least take a dose or two, so they can get comfortable or get some much-needed sleep. For those patients who absolutely do not want to take the narcotics during your recovery, and can tolerate not having it, which some people *do* have a high tolerance for pain— you may take plain acetaminophen (Tylenol) along with the Ibuprofen (Motrin) if you would rather. If your physician did not order the plain acetaminophen for you to take, just as your nurse to see if it can be ordered for you. At least you will benefit from the acetaminophen, which would have been combined with the narcotics if you would have taken those, and still have that along with the ibuprofen in your recovery.

Physician's Ordering Style of Oral Meds

Now, with cesarean sections, pain management is a little bit different. Some physicians order the patients pain meds to be given around the clock, and then order it for as needed at a later time. Other physicians may only order your pain medications PRN— there's that acronym *AGAIN*, meaning *as needed*. Either way, you will have some narcotic orders for your surgical pain management.

Generally, like in our hospitals, the narcotics used for incisional pain is scheduled where you *can* take it PRN every 4 hours, but since it is not ordered to be given routinely, *do not* assume your nurse will bring it to you automatically when it can be given. Some nurses may ask you to call them when you want more pain medicine, and some may ask if you would like them to bring it to you when you can have it: *each and every time.* Then some nurses, like me, will offer to bring the medication, when it can be given, on a routine basis to keep you as pain free as possible. I highly recommend the latter way being best for the majority of patients, and I will tell you why...

Reasons for Recommended Oral Pain Meds

After having surgery, you will be getting up and moving around rather quickly—usually within the first 6-12 hours. You will be sitting up to breast-feed or bottle feed baby, taking care of baby's needs, getting up to go to the bathroom, walking in the halls, showering, etc. To allow you to accomplish these tasks and stay comfortable, you will more than likely need to take pain meds regularly for both incisional pain and muscle soreness/cramping. Be sure and move around in bed before you give your nurse your pain rating, so you get the proper dose of meds you need currently. (Just like it was discussed in the beginning paragraphs of the *Pain Management* section.)

Every one of these tasks are important for your well-being and recovery, so take care and be in control of your pain management. If you are as comfortable as we can make you, your recovery will be quicker and more controlled—and give you a more pleasurable experience. Just remember, after surgery no one is completely pain free, so don't expect that you will be. I tell my patients, if we can keep your pain around a 2-3 then you are getting good pain relief.

It cannot be said enough that pain management is a very important part of any patient's recovery. We, as healthcare workers, consider this "The Fifth Vital Sign." I know there are problems of opioid abuse out there and it's directed at the healthcare industry for issuing vast amounts of prescriptions to patients. I believe, but it has not been or can be studied, that patient education is key to providing a remedy for this growing problem. If patients are handed a prescription for pain medication, they should also be educated in how it should be taken for their current pain and how to best taper or "wean off" of it as pain is decreasing. I'm sure that most everyone out there who has been prescribed narcotic medications by physicians were not properly given instructions or education. I know several, in my family alone, that have not. This can be simply remedied by doing so. I am a firm believer in pain management for patients, but education is the key to making it work for the best and for the shortest duration of time needed.

When you are getting ready to go home, you should have prescriptions given to you before you are discharged from the hospital for any or all of the pain medications you were receiving during your hospital stay. Usually this is about 10-14 days' worth of pain meds, but more than likely you may not finish the whole prescription if you wean off of the meds as we discussed earlier. Plus, don't forget to get your Colace to go with the pain meds. This is an over-the-counter medication which you will not receive a prescription for, and your doctor may not remember to tell you to keep taking it, so be sure and get this too. You will still need this while you are taking the narcotic pain meds, and maybe even a while after you finish them.

Pain Management Conclusion

I know this was a long, and drawn out section with regards to pain management, but I decided it was a very important one to be very specific when teaching. It's one of the most critical areas which gets glossed over during patient care, whether the patient is in the hospital or not. You cannot have patient satisfaction if one of your issues, like pain, is not kept under control— and pain is a significant factor. I look at pain management like I approach my patient care— I treat all my patients the way I would like to be treated if I were the patient. With that said, I will leave you with the last line of a favorite poem of mine, "Invictus."

...I am the Master of my fate, I am the Captain of my soul.

-William Ernest Hensley

You are the master of your healthcare, so be diligent and stay in control of it! Fight for what you feel is best for you and the rest will fall in place. I believe all patients should stay in charge of your care during their lifetime— I hope you will as well!!

Voiding (Urinating)

You may hear your nurse use the term "voiding" instead of urinating when they ask when you have gone to the bathroom. It's the term used by doctors, nurses, or other medical professionals, and sometimes we forget you may not have ever heard it. (I know I've had a few people look at me rather strangely when using that term.) Even so, your nurse will be asking you *if* you have urinated, *how* much, and, as well as, *how* often? These three things are very important in your recovery after delivery.

The first question you will be asked is *have* you urinated? If the answer is "*no*", then we will want you to do so within 4-6 hours after a vaginal delivery or within 6 hours after your catheter removal (whether vaginal or cesarean.) Your nurse may suggest you increase your water intake; making the urge or need to go come quicker. She may suggest while you are attempting to void is to have the water running in the bathroom to make you think about urinating. She may also have you get in the shower, if you are stable enough to, and let the water run over you. She may even tell you to just let loose in the shower if you can, that it's okay to do so. Sometimes these tricks are effective enough to get the ball rolling. If you still cannot go, we will check to see if your bladder is full or over-distended and if it is, we must remove the urine. That means using what is called a straight catheter to empty it out but then we will remove it again. Patients ask, "why can't I pee? And I tell them, due to the initial trauma to the urethra, the tube that releases the urine from the bladder, it may not bounce back quickly enough to empty out your bladder. Then your bladder will fill up and over-distend, causing your urine to back up into your kidneys. *NOT* a good thing! Can anyone say... "pain and infection??"

Next question is *how* much did you urinate? Was it just a little; emptied some but still feel you could go more; or do you feel as if you completely emptied your bladder out? If it was a little or just some, then we will continue to monitor you a little closer to make sure your bladder gets back to full function within the designated timeframe. Sometimes you may start and stop frequently when first going as well. This is a *normal* thing. You may have to sit on the toilet for a little while to finish. If it is completely emptying, then that's a good thing. That's what we are looking for when we ask you if you have urinated: *complete bladder and urinary tract function.*

Lastly, we will want to know *how often* you have gone. If you haven't been told by your nurse, you need to make sure and go at least every 2-3 hours to keep your bladder emptied out, and more so if you are drinking a lot of water or other liquids. (Preferably water!) If your bladder has a chance to over-fill, it will cause your uterus to become displaced to the right or left, and if it's *really* overdistended it will elevate your uterus up higher than it should be (which should be at your belly button or below.) What happens then is the uterus, being out of place, cannot contract like it needs to in order to close off the blood vessels where the placenta was attached. Therefore, the uterus becomes soft or *boggy*, making you prone to blood clots, postpartum hemorrhage, or both. Not a good thing when you had a significant amount of blood loss already.

One of my biggest pet peeves when taking care of patients is that any or all visitors think that it is *okay* to use the patient's bathroom while they are visiting. HEL-LO-O-O PEOPLE!! This is a HOSPITAL, not a public place to share bathrooms! I strongly suggest to my patients not to allow their visitors to use their bathrooms. You, as a patient, are *compromised* and are prone to contract infections. You may have stitches, lacerations, and/or tears from a vaginal delivery, or just vaginal bleeding from a cesarean section, which either one makes you vulnerable to infection from bacteria or other diseases. And— you *never know* what someone might bring into your bathroom which might infect you.

Now, with that said, if you feel comfortable that your husband/significant other and/or your children are not infected with anything they might pass on to you, then I will leave that decision *up to you.* But... be aware, even *they* might bring something in to you if they have used any public facilities in the recent past. (Especially at any outdoor events, such as Johnny-on-the-Spots. Yuck, yuck, and triple YUCK!!! Those are just Naaa--STY!!) So, use your good judgment before you let anyone pass through your bathroom door, okay? There are facilities available in the hospital close-by, which are especially designated for visitors.

Bleeding, Clots, Hemorrhaging

This is a very common issue which can happen to any patient during the delivery or in the next few hours, days or weeks ahead. As a patient, you must report to your nurse anything that is unusual or "out of the norm" with your bleeding. If you aren't sure if it is a problem, ask anyway. It's always a better idea to "err on the side of caution" than to assume that the bleeding is okay or ignore it. This can put you at greater risk and your life in danger if it is not checked and addressed in a timely manner.

It is very normal to begin bleeding again after giving birth. I know, you've had nine months of not having that blasted period and now it really must start up again?! I don't know of any woman who wants to start that back up, even if it must start-- *and* it will, *and* it is supposed to happen even if we don't want it to. At first, the bleeding will usually be a little heavier than your normal period. For those of you who have normally heavy periods, they may be more like those or maybe a little heavier. Over the next few days they will decrease in amount and start to darken, just like it does as you start to taper off.

When the bleeding becomes concerning, is when you are filling your pad very quickly. If you are bleeding heavily, usually it will fill up the center of the pad within an hour and become a lot heavier in weight. When this happens, let your nurse know so she can check it and determine if additional actions need to be taken, or maybe to watch and wait to see if it will resolve on its own. If she checks you and it's due to a soft or boggy uterus, expect to have a wonderful, heavy-duty massage again!! IT'S CRUNCH TIME!! You know, just like the ones right after delivery that were not very fun? Well, most of the time this does the trick and no other interventions are necessary, so it really is a good thing. But— if you have returned home from the hospital and this happens, *call your doctor.*

Bleeding can be caused by any number of things. One of the most common is an over-distended bladder. When your bladder over-distends, or fills up way too much, it can displace, or push, your uterus over to one side or the other, which then prevents it from contracting. When the uterus cannot contract, it cannot close off those blood vessels where the placenta was attached. This then causes additional bleeding from the uterus being relaxed and not contracted which in turn, causes uterine bleeding to resume, pool in the uterus, and form blood clots. The best prevention of this problem is to get up and empty your bladder every 2-3 hours, or *more frequently* if you are drinking a lot of water.

Another issue with heavy bleeding is that it may be brought on by too much activity shortly after delivery, and that counts for when you go home and the next few weeks to come. Your body needs to heal, whether from a vaginal or cesarean birth, so over the next few weeks you need to be taking it easy and not *over-doing* it. One of your body's natural ways of telling you that you are: *is increased bleeding and clots.* When you take 6-8 weeks off from work during your maternity leave, it's for a very good reason— to heal!

Blood clots form when the blood pools in one area or another in the uterus, cervix, or vagina and start to thicken up to the consistency of a piece of raw liver. It is *normal* to pass a few clots after delivery. They usually are very small little pieces you may find on your pad or notice when you dry off after voiding, like what you may have during your monthly periods. They may be a little larger or stringy. You may also pass one or two golf ball-sized clots and then no others, and that can be normal too. Anytime you are not sure if it *is* normal, be sure and ask your nurse.

Another reason for a moderate to large amount of blood loss can be caused by vaginal or cervical tears or lacerations that were not found after delivery, or even uterine tears or lacerations which cannot be seen further back in the body. Sometimes these "bleeders" may slowly trickle, but fill up your peripads rather quickly, or they flow freely and rather quickly causing rapid blood loss.

You may need to be given medications to stop the bleeding, which is better sooner rather than later. If the issue is related to a blood vessel or vessels that are leaking and causing the hemorrhaging, then the doctor will need to make the repairs. And if the cause is something that cannot be quickly determined and corrected, then your doctor may need to take you back into the operating room and perform surgery to find the source of the bleeding, and correct it.

In most cases, this can be fixed rather quickly with a few stitches here or there, however, there are some rare instances which the bleeding *cannot* be stopped, and it becomes life threatening to the patient. In this unfortunate event, the doctor may perform a hysterectomy just to save your life.

So, do not take your bleeding lightly— or might I say, *heavily*. Because if it is heavy or producing lots of little clots that would equal a big one, or passing large ones, it can have very serious consequences. If you are not sure, ask your nurse. She will either check it and give you reassurance that it's "o*kay*", check it and watch it more closely if it's more clotting than normal, or contact the doctor and report what is happening so that further care can be administered quickly. Or again— call your doctor if you are already back home.

Other Medications/Supplements

You may be given other medications or supplements during your hospital stay which are used to either aid in your recovery or help give you a needed boost. We'll go over all the types of medications used for both.

Colace or Peri-Colace

Colace® *(docusate sodium)* is a stool softener that helps to make the stool, well— *softer,* so when you go for the first time after delivery, this reduces the chance of having a harder stool to pass. It helps your body to draw more water into the bowel, thus making the stool softer. Peri-Colace® contains an added laxative to the stool softener to help increase the effect of stool passage. Several things affect your ability to go to the bathroom easily after delivery:

- medications (especially narcotics)
- decreased intestinal motility (moving the food down the GI tract)
- dehydration
- not eating proper foods (dietary "roughage", such as fruits and vegetables)
- vaginal and/or rectal repairs
- hemorrhoids
- cesarean sections.

You do not want to strain or cause increased pain in your nether region or your incision, so you generally will be offered this medication to make it easier to go for the first time or so. It can be taken twice a day to help you along for that first stool that you may be dreading, and it's highly recommended that you take this along with your narcotic pain medications since constipation is one of the side effects. If you are taking narcotics, be sure and pick up some Colace along with your prescriptions when you discharge from the hospital. Take them the entire time you are taking the narcotics. Even if you are not taking narcotics, is okay to take this medicine just to make it less difficult to have that first stool, so take it if is offered or ask for it if it is not. Also, increase your dietary fiber intake and continue your increased water intake. You will feel much better if you do.

Miralax/Milk of Magnesia/Ducolax

These types of medications Miralax® (*polyethylene glycol*), Milk of Magnesia® (*magnesium hydroxide*), and Ducolax® (*bisacodyl*) will help you if you are having a tough time with producing a bowel movement after you deliver. Sometimes, during your recovery period and beyond, you may have extreme difficulty having one or more bowel movements, and you need something stronger to get everything moving through. These medications are laxatives, and they work on the small intestine to help push the waste through more quickly and easily, and draw in even more water, but they do have side effects during that "hastening" period, mostly the Dulcolax.. You may be bloated, gassy, crampy, and need to "run" to the bathroom more quickly with these medications because they work faster on your digestive system.

These should only be used if you are already prone to having constipation, if you take narcotics, and are not eating and drinking properly after delivery, *and* you become *very* uncomfortable due to the build-up of gas and/or stool. If you use the Colace (whether you are taking narcotics or not) and eat the high fiber foods and drink plenty of water, you can avoid using these medications unless necessary.

Miralax and Milk of Magnesia are both oral medications, but the Ducolax is offered in suppository form which will make for quicker results. However, most of my patients, when asking for gas or bowel relief, usually shy away from taking Ducolax, since this medication goes up the *wazoo*. Warm prune juice followed by hot tea or coffee can have a fairly quick result in good intestinal relief from gas, but not necessarily a quick effect on a bowel movement. I tend to offer this alternative to my cesarean section patients because they generally are having more issues with gas bloating, cramping, and sharp pain verses bowel movement issues earlier on. (*See the section relating to *Cesarean Section Recovery*)

Today is not like it was many years ago, when your mothers were told that having a bowel movement before they were discharged was a *"must."* Physicians now know that our bodies will function properly within a few days, and having a bowel movement will come within a brief period of time without becoming a concern. But if you do have difficulty either before or after you have been discharged, these are some of the medications that can be highly effective for you.

Tums/Gas-X/Phasyme/Mylicon/Mylanta

These types of drugs, Tums® (calcium carbonate) and the others (simethicone) are used for reducing gas and bloating, which is causing heartburn, or gas discomfort and indigestion in your stomach and/or gut. These come in a chewable tablet for quicker digestion and relief.

With some women, indigestion, gas, and bloating is a big problem during pregnancy due to the baby pushing all your intestinal organs up and out of their usual places. But sometimes after your delivery, you may still have some issues that have not gone away, so taking these medications may help you with that.

Prenatal vitamins

During your pregnancy, your obstetrician or general practitioner would have ordered prenatal vitamins to give you additional vitamins and minerals you may be lacking, or that your body will use up more quickly during the pregnancy. Doctors will also recommend using prenatal vitamins even after delivery, and especially if you are breastfeeding, as they will aid you in recovery and with the vitamins and minerals you need to replenish.

My personal OB/GYN, and colleague of mine, told me that she recommends prenatal vitamins to be used as a supplement even if not breastfeeding or pregnant. She informed me that they are a good overall supplement to use for years to come. So, if you have taken the prenatal vitamins during the pregnancy, I would recommend that you take them after delivery— and beyond. If you do continue to use them, even if you are not pregnant now or don't plan to become pregnant again, be sure to let your husband or significant other know why you are taking them— so you don't freak them out if they see the bottle!! I know my husband did when I started taking them again years later after we quit having any more babies.

Iron tablets (ferrous sulfate)

If you are anemic, which is when your body does not have enough iron in your blood to carry oxygen from your red blood cells (hemoglobin) into all the other parts of the body, your doctor may prescribe iron tablets or gel tabs to be taken. You may become anemic during the pregnancy, which can hinder your body in providing much needed oxygen not only for yourself, but for your baby as well. Severe anemia, left untreated can cause anemia in your baby, maternal death, and stillbirth or fetal death. So, this is very, very important that you *do not* take anemia and its treatment lightly.

If you become anemic after you have delivered, were anemic during the pregnancy, have an ongoing anemia even when not pregnant, or become anemic due to a larger-than-normal blood volume loss during delivery, your doctor may prescribe iron tablets to be taken during this time. There may be other blood-related issues you may deal with which are not very common, but if you do, your doctor should provide you with information and appropriate care.

If you have a significant drop in your hemoglobin after your delivery which the iron supplements will not be sufficient to boost your iron levels, your doctor may order a blood transfusion of a couple units of red blood cells. This will help you bounce back much quicker from the severe drop in your hemoglobin. Then they may also order iron supplements to continue boosting the red blood cell production.

During my career, in fact just within the last 2-3 years, I had a Micronesian patient who did not seek prenatal care. Whether it was due to not knowing how to go about getting prenatal care or not wanting prenatal care due to religious or cultural beliefs, when she came into the hospital to deliver it was found that there was no fetal heartbeat, and she was severely anemic when her bloodwork was drawn. She was close to full-term and came into the hospital in full labor. To me, this was a very sad and needless fetal death that could have been prevented by simply having prenatal care (even if it was just a few clinic visits) to determine the anemia and taken iron tablets, or had iron infusions which might have prevented this from happening. Very, very sad situation to have happen.

Vaccinations

We receive numerous vaccines when we are infants all the way up through middle school. Recently, there have been additional vaccines offered to older high school and college students for things like cervical cancer prevention or meningococcal meningitis. But some vaccines must be given again, as boosters, when the time frame has elapsed, and the previous vaccines are no longer effective. The Centers for Disease Control recommend updating these vaccines as soon as it is deemed safe.

Hepatitis B

This is a series of shots given over several months to protect you from contracting Hepatitis B, and, in turn, passing it on to others— including your unborn baby. If you have not received this vaccine and would like to, talk to your doctor when the best time to receive the vaccine. It is not offered in the hospital during your stay.

MMR (measles, mumps, rubella)

During your prenatal visits in the obstetrician's office, your doctor will ask you when you last had your vaccines and will also test your blood to see if your measles, mumps, and rubella vaccine is still protecting you. If it is not, or only giving you partial protection, your doctor will recommend that you have a booster shot given in the hospital after delivery or any time later after the baby is born. This *cannot* be given to you during pregnancy, as this is a live virus and may be passed on through the placenta to your unborn baby, so it will be offered to you after birth.

Tdap (tetanus, diphtheria, pertussis)

This is a vaccine is only good for approximately 10 years, and it is recommended that everyone get booster doses after that time. If you do not know how current you are on this vaccine or it has been more than 10 years since your last booster, it is recommended that you receive a new booster shot. For women, you may receive this during your pregnancy between the 26th and 36th week, preferably closer to the 26th week, as it can safely pass on immunities to your unborn child. The longer your antibodies can increase in your body before birth, the more antibodies are passed on to your baby, protecting him or her until they will begin receiving their own vaccinations. Because of this, it is better to receive it before birth. If you do not, it will be offered to you during your hospital stay. It is highly recommended you receive it— *I strongly suggest you do if you need it.* If you have had other children, but cannot remember if you have been given this vaccine, the CDC also recommends that you go ahead and get it. An additional booster will not cause any problems, so if you don't know for sure go ahead and get it again.

Pertussus, or whooping cough, is one of the diseases prevented by this vaccine that is the most needed for your protection and your baby's. Whooping cough can be very serious, and potentially life-threatening to your newborn baby. If you have not been vaccinated in a long time or have never been vaccinated, you can pass this on to your baby if you are exposed to it. Getting the vaccine in the hospital is better than not receiving it at all, but *be aware* it takes about two weeks for the antibodies to start producing in enough quantities for you to be protected from the disease. During those two weeks, your baby will not be protected from others who might pass on the disease to him or her— and *only then* if you are breastfeeding your baby. You can still pass on these antibodies, but your baby will be exposed for those two weeks and can still contract it. If bottle feeding, then your baby will be exposed until such time they receive their DTaP shot at about 2 months of age.

I cannot imagine how devastating this can be for an infant to contract this horrendous disease. When my oldest daughter was in middle school, there was an outbreak of whooping cough within our school district and she did not contract it but did "carry it" home to me— and I contracted it. I didn't put two-and-two together until several years later that I had been exposed to it and contracted it. I had been immunized throughout my childhood, but was unaware that a booster was needed for continued protection. It was a miserable two months of coughing, so hard that I couldn't catch my breath or so hard it would cause me to choke and gag. Infants and small children are vulnerable and are frequently hospitalized due to its devastating effects. If you refuse some of the other shots because you have your reasons or just don't want them, please *don't* pass this one up!!!

Be sure that anyone who comes in direct contact with your children on a regular basis: babysitters, teachers, preschool or daycare workers, family members get vaccinated. Most day care centers and schools require their employees to be vaccinated before coming in direct contact with children, but there are others who are not— grandparents, aunts, uncles, cousins, etc., that might not have had a booster. If anyone comes in frequent contact with your children, insist they get the vaccine if they haven't.

Influenza vaccine

These are also offered to moms-to-be and patients who have not been vaccinated during the flu season, which is usually between October 1 and March 30. They are safe to be given during the pregnancy, and can be given at any time during the current flu season.

It is also highly recommended by the CDC that pregnant women receive this vaccine, to prevent them from contracting it. The influenza virus can be even more devastating to pregnant women due to her bodily changes during her pregnancy. Heart, lungs, and immune systems are altered, therefore putting them at risk during the flu season. Just like the Tdap shot, it can be given during the pregnancy if you are within the current flu season. It will allow your body to build up antibodies, which can be passed on to your baby prior to the delivery, thus protecting them during the season as well.

The misnomer with this vaccine is that a large amount of the populations "think" of the influenza vaccine as preventing the stomach "flu" or virus.

This is actually incorrect!!! What this vaccine is preventing is the influenza virus which can cause respiratory congestion (mucus filling up the lungs) to respiratory distress (where you have difficulty breathing or cannot breathe) to respiratory failure and/or heart failure— and/or death. The stomach "flu" is generally not going to cause respiratory distress or heart failure, it's just a short-term bug which over the next few days will be resolved thru vomiting/diarrhea, fever, muscle aches, and/or chills. Once your body purges and rests, then it will heal.

Pneumococcal vaccine

This is generally offered to individuals who would be at a higher risk for contracting pneumonia. Patients who currently smoke or have within the last year, have recurrent bronchitis or other respiratory issues, have or had asthma and are currently using inhalers or other respiratory meds to combat the issue, or have been diagnosed with emphysema or COPD, should be offered this vaccine.

With these types of respiratory issues, this puts these patients at higher risk for contracting the pneumococcal virus. So, it is offered— like the influenza shot— to these patients during the pregnancy or after the delivery.

Lab Work

During your prenatal visits with the doctor, you will have had lab work done in your physician's office usually during first prenatal visit. These labs will then be repeated upon admission to the hospital because your previous results will have changed since the beginning, or since the last time your blood was tested. This will give your doctor vital information which helps them to decide what treatment will be administered to you.

Lab work will also be drawn again the morning after delivery, or sooner if there were complications during or just after delivery. Your doctor will want to see what changes have occurred, which will allow them to give the appropriate follow-up care you need.

CBC (complete blood count)

This gives us a baseline to see how your white blood cell count is (shows if infection present), hemoglobin & hematocrit (shows oxygen carrying capacity of red blood cells), platelets (shows how well your clotting ability is when you bleed, which you will), glucose (for blood sugar levels), blood type & screen (to check your blood type and screen for antibodies), and various other labs which might need to be done based on your individual pregnancy.

ABO & Rh factor incompatibilities

When checking your blood type & screen, the lab is testing your blood type so your physicians caring for you can get the appropriate blood needed, should you have an emergent situation requiring a transfusion. A, B, AB, & O are the four blood types, but most are not compatible with each other. Each type of blood has antibodies against the other types, except for O negative. O negative blood has no antibodies with its type nor does it have antibodies from the (–) Rh factor, so this blood can be used with *any* blood type, including Rh (+) or (–) patients. (This is the reason O neg blood is considered the *universal donor*.) The screening is done to determine if you have the (+) or (–) Rh factor in your blood as well. The Rh factor are antibodies that can attack the opposite Rh factor, so if you are Rh negative (–) and your baby is Rh positive (+), this can affect any future babies you may have if it is not taken care of. (If you *know* you are Rh (+), you may skip the next two paragraphs.)

Generally, when mom is pregnant, and she has the (-) Rh factor, she will get a shot around the 28th week called Rhogam and then another after the baby is born, if the baby's blood type has a (+) Rh factor. By getting the Rhogam shot, the mother's (-) Rh factor will not attack the next baby's red blood cells if it happens to be (+) Rh. It can be a little confusing if your physician has not already explained this to you, but it's one of those easy fixes with Rhogam. It can have serous (immune hydrops fetalis) or even deadly consequences for the next baby, if not corrected with Rhogam.

Immune hydrops fetalis is a life-threatening anemia in newborns at delivery which ABO blood group and Rh incompatibilities can occur, a (-) Rh mom is not desensitized soon after a (+) Rh baby is born, or a miscarriage has occurred. This issue causes a large number of red blood cells in the infant to be *destroyed*, which may cause severe anemia, bruising of the skin, respiratory issues, total body swelling, jaundice, or heart failure. Treatment would potentially be blood transfusions, needle aspiration of fluid from abdomen and/or around lungs, respiratory assistance with breathing, and medications to help kidneys remove excess fluid or control heart failure. Being prepared for this eventuality may be necessary if the mother is (-) Rh and she has:

- no prenatal care and is not sure if she has ever had a miscarriage at any time;

- not sure if she has ever had a miscarriage and informed her physician or obstetrician;

- had a miscarriage, but never received Rhogam after the fact and is pregnant again.

Group B beta strep (+ or -)

This is another lab test that you are checked for during your prenatal visits, usually at about 36 weeks, but is important for the doctors to know before a vaginal delivery. Group B Beta Strep can be part of any women's normal vaginal tract flora. If the mother is what we call GBS (+), then she has the flora in her vaginal tract that can cause her unborn child to become infected when born. If antibiotics are given during labor at least 4 hours prior to delivery, it then has the ability of crossing over the placental barrier, and providing protection to the infant from the GBS (+) colonization of bacteria. This prophylactic treatment of antibiotics greatly *decreases* the chance for the bacteria to infect the infant and cause a variety of issues, which can lead to intensive care for the newborn in a Level II or Level III nursery— should they become infected. If you deliver prior to or quickly upon admission and are not able to receive this treatment, your baby will be monitored for signs and symptoms of infection and treated accordingly. Treatment, however, is not necessary if you will be delivering by cesarean section, because the baby will not be passing through the vaginal tract which is where the Group B Beta Strep is located.

Hepatitis B, syphilis, gonorrhea, HIV (or AIDS)

These are other diseases which can be potentially harmful to your unborn baby or be harmful during a vaginal delivery. Generally, your physician will test for this as well during the beginning of prenatal care, however, you must give permission for the testing of HIV. If these were never tested prior to delivery (in the event you *did not* receive prenatal care) or the hospital does not have access to your records because you are delivering at a different hospital than planned, they will be done upon admission.

To Mothers Using Illicit Drugs or Having Limited/No Prenatal Care

I wanted to add this section within this book as well, to cover this particular group of mothers who plan it is to deliver in a hospital setting when the time comes. This section *is not* put here to criticize these mothers who have been using illicit drugs during the pregnancy or decided for personal reasons not to receive regular, if any, prenatal care, but to discuss the importance of full disclosure of information requested by your nurses or doctors upon your arrival.

Your doctors and nurses are professionals, and with their professions they have a duty to give the best care to every patient who comes into the hospital for treatment, regardless of the patient's personal choices or situations. To give the best care they can give, they *need* to know *your complete history*. This includes telling them things that you feel might make them judgmental toward you. I cannot predict whether your nurse or doctor may not have something to say to you with regards to what information you give them (regrettably, there are those who may give you a "dressing down" because of it) but they *need* all the information they can get to make sure you and your baby do get the best care they can give. Just so you know, they will not withhold treatment from you on anything they deem necessary for a good outcome for you or your baby because of this.

This is *so* important to be totally honest with your nurse during your initial assessment and screening. He or she will get information from you regarding your medical, family, and current history. This will help ensure that if you have anything in your history that might play a role in your delivery and for your baby afterwards, that you get the appropriate care needed.

If you have used illicit drugs (marijuana, cocaine, crack, meth, prescription pain killers, etc.) during the pregnancy, *especially* the last few days before arriving at the hospital, be sure a tell your nurse or doctor of this— and be *honest and specific*. If you received a little prenatal care elsewhere, they will attempt to get records of what had been done during those visits which will be important to them. If you have had no prenatal care at all, or they cannot get your records in a timely manner, your doctors will order what is necessary to check you and your baby thoroughly.

For patients falling in all these groups, the first thing collected will be your blood for testing. This will give a current look at your body system functions and to give them a guideline to what specific actions will be necessary for your care. If you have used illicit drugs in your past or have had no prenatal care, they will request a drug screen to test if there are any drugs still in your system which might be contraindicated (not advised) with other painkillers or medications you might receive in the hospital. Your baby will be tested *as well* after delivery: *urine* to detect drugs passed on within the past few days, and *meconium* to detect what you would have taken at an earlier time during the pregnancy. This is also helpful for baby's treatment. If you have limited or no prenatal care, additional testing would be required to check for any disease processes [sexually transmitted diseases (STDs) or other contagious viruses easily transmittable] which might impact your care and require additional precautions.

With some STDs, there would be a need for a cesarean section because a vaginal birth might be dangerous for your baby. Vaginal herpes, chlamydia, gonorrhea, and syphilis are the main STDs in which cesarean births would be needed for a good outcome, and reduce or eliminate risks to your baby.

Testing for HIV and AIDs (another group of STDs) or any acquired virus through other means (shared needles or other equipment; contact with another's bodily fluids through broken skin, wounds, open sores, etc.), which the doctors and nurses caring for you and baby want to be aware of. Consent from you must be given to the hospital staff for this testing, however, it is preferred you get tested if you do not know you have it or not— and it's also ethical to provide this consent for protection of the hospital staff as well.

Although vaginal delivery does occur with these viruses successfully, testing will be necessary in providing information for a primary care physician and/or pediatrician for follow-up care. The testing is also necessary for the protection of the hospital staff caring for you and your baby. Additional precautions need to be taken for patient isolation, and universal precautions for appropriate hand hygiene and use of non-porous medical articles of gloves, gowns, and masks.

Ultrasonography (getting an ultrasound) would also be ordered if time allows before delivery. This gives information to the obstetrician and nurses with regards to:

- the possible age of baby (in weeks);

- how big your baby is;

- which position the baby is lying in;

- if there is anything visibly wrong with the baby, cord or placenta;

- where the placenta is positioned;

- and how much amniotic fluid is present around your baby.

This also helps with determining if it would be safe to deliver vaginally— or if a cesarean section would be necessary.

You should also expect during your hospital stay a visit from social services, per the obstetrician's orders. This is necessary in helping to:

- determine your current living conditions and if it is a safe environment for your baby

- determine if any additional services might be necessary to help you and baby once you leave the hospital

- provide information for financial assistance programs

- get signed up for WIC benefits or Medicaid

- provide aid or information for homelessness, abuse, or baby needs

- offer drug rehabilitation programs

Our goal is to provide optimal care for you and your baby, and acquire useful information which will allow us to provide that care in a safe and secure manner. All information remains confidential and is only available to the nurses and doctors providing that care. Our *"ultimate goal"* is for the best outcome— for both you and your baby!

Q & A on Other Post-Delivery Concerns

This is the section we will cover numerous questions or concerns that might pop up during your hospital stay or even for a time after you return home.

Q   *Why am I running a low-grade temperature? Should I worry about infection?*

A   You may run a low-grade temperature for a couple of reasons. Either spinal or epidural anesthesia may cause you to run a low-grade temperature for a brief period of time during or after your delivery. This is nothing to worry about, unless you have other complications with having the anesthesia, which your nurse will be monitoring you for during your stay.

The other would be if your milk has come in. Some moms have what is called a "milk fever" which really isn't a fever at all. It occurs at the onset of lactation, or milk production and lasts only a few hours. If you were to have any type of infection going on, your temperature would be at least 100.4 degrees or higher and for a longer period of time. Again, your nurse will be monitoring your vital signs for any indication of infection during your stay. If you have been discharged from the hospital and are running a fever of at least 100.4, then you need to contact your doctor.

Q   *Do you have any pills to dry up my milk since I am not breastfeeding??*

A   Unfortunately, this is something which is very outdated. You probably have your mom or grandmother or older acquaintance giving you that piece of advice to ask about it. Simply put, this hasn't been done for many years. There are several ways to help suppress your milk production during the beginning of your lactation.

This process may take a week or two, but remember every woman is different and it depends on your body's amount of milk production. And just remember, even if you are formula feeding, any milk you have already pumped, or hand expressed, can be fed to the baby. Even a little bit is good for them.

- Wear a well-fitted support bra;

- Use cabbage leaves placed on breasts, then exchange the wilted leaf with a new one when needed;

- Pump or hand express breasts only enough to reduce discomfort but not enough to empty them. When there is milk still in the breasts, your body will start decreasing the amount of milk it will produce;

- Taking a warm shower will stimulate the let-down reflex and relieve some of the pressure;

- Use ice packs to help reduce the pain and tissue swelling.

- Take ibuprofen or acetaminophen (Motrin or Tylenol) for pain relief (** *Do Not* take additional Tylenol if you are taking narcotic pain relievers at the same time, as they already may contain acetaminophen)

Q   *I weighed myself on the scale in the hall, but I didn't lose but a few pounds. How come?*

A   You would think that just having had your baby that you would have lost more than a few pounds after delivery. I mean, there is the weight of the baby, so you should have at least lost that much, right? The answer is "*not necessarily so.*" The reasoning for this is there is the enlarged uterus, additional blood volume from pregnancy, swelling of the breasts in preparation for lactation, and the extra fluid pumped into you during your labor or cesarean section. This all accounts for very little weight loss after delivery, even though we would like it to be a lot more.

Q   *Why am I swollen? (or swelling more?)*

A   During the pregnancy, women will sometimes retain some of the fluid in legs, feet, hands, and face which the physician will monitor through-out your recovery for any underlying complications. Any of the fluid you might have retained during pregnancy and all the fluids given to you before, during, and after your delivery can cause you to swell— or to swell even more than you already have. With the added infusion of IV fluid during labor and/or delivery, this can "get worse before it gets better." You may wake up at any time and realize your fingers and toes feel like "sausages," or that you feel like "you are walking on soggy sponges."

After delivery, your body is reverting to its pre-pregnant status now that you are no longer pregnant. Due to all the hormonal and physical changes going on, you may very well swell *more* within the next couple days or *start* swelling even if you had none prior to delivery. This is what we call *Third Spacing*. Fluid is finding its way outside the body's cells and floating in the spaces around the cells. This is a normal issue which usually takes a few days or so to remedy. One way to help rem-edy this is to drink lots of water. It really sounds funny we would ask you to do this, when you already have lots of "water swelling" already, but your fluid in your hands, feet, legs, and face is really not in your cells— it's now *"third spacing"*, or going outside the cells into the tissue and floating around. By drinking water, what you are doing is causing an osmotic process which helps to "draw" the water back into the cells so your body can flush the excess fluid out. You will definitely know when this is happening, because you will start going to the bathroom frequently and urinating quite a lot each time.

The second, is to get up and walk around, *not* sitting for extended periods of time. By getting up and moving, you are helping to get the circulation going, especially in your lower extremities to help move the fluid out.

When you are sitting, or lying down, the third way is to elevate your feet to help shift the fluid in the lower extremities away from your feet. If the swelling or edema get extremely bad, it can put pressure on your blood vessels, which might cause your blood pressure to increase. This swelling can also cause constriction of the nerves, which may cause pain, tingling, or weakness in your arms, hands, legs or feet. Once the fluid begins to shift and your body starts the fluid removal process, you will notice relief from the pain or swelling.

Q   *Why am I crying or emotional? Hot? Sweaty?*

A   There are several of the strangest things you might notice after you have delivered your baby. Why am I burning up? Feeling like I've been in a sauna? Getting drenched in sweat? Crying at the "drop of a hat?" You've been in good control, or feel you have, since you delivered, but these things seem a bit strange to you. Why are they happening? Is anything wrong? The answer is a big resounding…. "*NO!*" All of this funky stuff happening, is all due to— "hormones." Hormonal and physiological changes.

Now that you are no longer pregnant, all the hormones that shifted around when you first became pregnant, and physiologic systems that changed to accommodate the pregnancy, are now *shifting back* to your pre-pregnant state. These hormonal and physiologic changes can last for a few days to a few weeks. So, if you are throwing off the blankets, trying to strip down to the bare minimum of clothes, asking for a portable fan— or feeling like everything is falling apart or you want to cry over what you think is the silliest thing, just remember— *it will get better* with time, when the hormones readjust to their normal state.

Postpartum Depression: I had to put this one in right behind the hormonal fluctuations, as this kind of falls along the same lines with crying or emotional issues discussed before, but usually this is just a little bit different— it can be more severe.

Postpartum depression is a condition which generally does not start affecting you right away. This comes with time, approximately 3-12 months after delivery, and may be minor or major in severity. This can affect 1 out of 7 women in the postpartum period, and in which a family history of mood disorders can predispose you to this condition. Other risk factors include:

- depression or anxiety during the pregnancy;
- stressful life events during pregnancy or postpartum period;
- infant NICU admission or preterm delivery;
- poor family or social support;
- history of depression, and;
- problems with breastfeeding."

Any one or more of these risk factors can make things difficult for you and your family.

Unfortunately, you, as the patient, may not notice this creeping upon you and taking hold, or notice the "signs to look for" when watching for PP depression. This is where your husband, significant other, family, and/or friends can help you. They will be able to see the signs; when you may not.

Some of these signs might be:

- loss of weight and/or appetite;
- depressed mood;
- crying;

- not wanting to take care of yourself or baby;

- feelings of helplessness or hopelessness;

- wanting to withdraw from everyone.

The others will more likely be able to see these changes coming about when you may not. If it is brought to your attention you may be having signs of PPD (Postpartum Depression), contact your OB doctor (if it is within your recovery before your follow-up visit), or your Primary Care Physician. They may be able to prescribe medications to take for short-term mental health therapy, and then wean you off once the crisis is resolved.

Q   *Why do I have trouble sleeping?*

A   That first night, or day (depending on when you deliver) you may be physically exhausted and may want to sleep, but are having trouble getting there. For a majority of women shortly after delivery, they find out sleep is somehow eluding them and don't know why. There is a simple explanation for this problem— Adrenaline Rush!

I tell patients this adrenaline rush is caused by the birth of their baby. Between the excitement of the birth, the inundation of visitors, numerous recalls of events during the delivery, and the fact you "cannot shut your brain down…" it's no wonder why you are having trouble sleeping. It also makes it difficult to get sleep when your baby is right in the room with you, and any little squeak or squawk brings you to immediate attention.

You hold your baby, cuddle and kiss, and are in total awe of this new life before you. You don't want to put your baby down or send your baby to the nursery for fear you might miss out on even one precious moment of your baby's new life. And thus, we move on to…

Q   *Why am I so exhausted?*

A   Think back to just before you came into the hospital and what all was going on. Have you been getting any sleep during the last week or so before coming into the hospital? How long were you in labor before you delivered? Were you anxious and not sleeping because you had a scheduled delivery date the next day? Any one or a combination could be playing a role in this sleep deprivation. Then after having the baby, and being *"adrenaline rushed"* you have now compounded this problem. Nothing like starting off *"behind the eight ball"* when it comes to sleep. Next there are the new demands of feeding the baby every 2-3 hours, changing diapers, soothing or comforting a crying baby— and it snowballs!!

Once you are able to sleep, try and get as much rest as you can between your baby's feedings Sleeping for a couple hours at a stretch over several hours will help you overcome this deprivation. You'd be surprised at how a couple hours of solid sleep between feedings will help to rejuvenate you, and two or three more of these "power sleeps" will help even more. But just remember, this will go on for months, with a few curveballs thrown in (colicky baby, sick baby, overstimulated and cranky baby, etc.) Do the best you can to rest *when* you can, because there is a light at the end of the tunnel— I promise!

Q   *Why am I lightheaded? Dizzy? Loopy?*

A   There may be several causes for you to be lightheaded or dizzy during your recovery period. The first and foremost would be blood loss. During the delivery process, generally blood loss for a vaginal delivery is less than 500 ml, and for a cesarean delivery is less than 1000 ml. With blood loss, this decreases the amount of blood flowing in your system, and the amount of red blood cells which help to provide oxygen to all your body systems. This can cause you to be lightheaded or dizzy easily. This is one of the reasons we discussed earlier about getting out of bed slowly— and with your nurse present at least the first time.

Another probable reason could be lack of sleep in combination with your pain medications. When your body is trying to heal, sleep is a key component to recovery. If you have not had sufficient amounts of sleep, and you put pain medication on top of that, it may make you feel loopy, dizzy, in a "fog". The pain medication is helping give you pain relief and in turn helping to relax you. If you are already exhausted, the pain medication can amplify the effect, causing you to feel "out of it." *Listen to your body!!* If you are depriving yourself of sleep, with your body trying to heal from the delivery, you are just compounding the problem for yourself.

Be sure you are getting in and out of bed slowly during the first day or so, and not moving too quickly— take your time! Also, when you get into the shower, *do not* take a hot one! Hot water will zap what little energy you may have and increase the chances of becoming dizzy. Hopefully, your hospital has a shower bench available for your use, so be sure and use it at least the first time.

Q   *Why does my tailbone really hurt when I sit?? I can't put hardly any pressure on it!*

A   The cause of tailbone pain (coccydyna) is due to the vaginal delivery of the baby. The delivery may be difficult due to a large baby or fast delivery, small or abnormally shaped pelvis, or abnormal position of the baby as he is delivered. The joints between the individual coccyx bones can break open causing pain or a coccyx bone can become fractured. As the baby is being born, it may force the coccyx back, damaging the joint. Unfortunately, there is not a cure for this. With time, approximately 4 weeks for a joint break and 8-12 weeks for an actual bone fracture, the tailbone will heal.

Here's a list of helpful things to aid in healing:

- Rest and stop any physical activity which causes you pain. This will help in the healing process.

- Apply ice to your tailbone for 20 mins every hour for 48 hours while awake— *DO NOT* apply ice directly to the skin.

- Avoid sitting a lot, and when you are sleeping, lay on your stomach to take pressure off the tailbone.

- When you are sitting, alternate between sitting on one cheek or the other.

- You can breastfeed side-lying to avoid sitting up during this time. If you must sit up, sit on a cushion or inflatable donut to take the pressure off your tailbone.

- Take prescribed pain meds for your pain. Your doctor should suggest certain meds for pain relief.

- Take a stool softener throughout this healing time to avoid constipation. Straining will put extra pressure on your tailbone causing additional pain.

- Drink plenty of water and eat fibrous foods (fruits, vegetables, legumes, nut, beans, etc.)

Follow up with your doctor on your progress. If it is not healing well or at all, they will help find other treatments to aid in your recovery.

Q   *Why is my lower back so sore?*

A   Two common issues can cause lower back pain after delivery. First off would be having an epidural or spinal during your delivery. During the procedure, the anesthesiologist will numb the area around the site of placement. This will cause tissue bruising in that location, which will lead to soreness. Then the anesthesiologist pushes the spinal needle into the epidural space of your spine, which takes a little added pressure to achieve. The combination of these will cause some of your back pain after delivery.

The second cause of your lower back pain would be from the redistribution of weight after the baby is delivered. During the pregnancy, your posture slowly changed to redistribute your growing weight. This gradual change did not cause back pains until the weight became heavier out front later in the pregnancy. Now that the baby has delivered, the weight distribution shifted suddenly so now this quick change has strained your lower back muscles.

Q   *Why do I feel sore all over??*

A   Well, this is a fairly easy question to answer— you've just been through labor and/or delivery!! For vaginal deliveries: you use a lot of muscles you don't normally use, and they have had a workout!! About Day 2 you'll feel like you have been hit by a *Mack truck*, with the sore muscles all over your body. For cesarean sections: most of your muscles and organs in your abdomen have been pushed and shoved around during the procedure, which will make you sore. Ibuprofen (Motrin) is recommended for pain relief for your soreness.

Q   *Why do I have difficulty going pee?*

A   During the delivery process, whether vaginal with an epidural, or cesarean section with and epidural or spinal, a foley catheter was inserted to empty your bladder when you could not get up to do so on your own. When a catheter is in place, the urethra (the tube which empties your bladder) and the bladder itself becomes inactive. Having the catheter inserted and left in for even a brief time can block the nerve signals to your bladder when you attempt to urinate after its removal. This is called a neurogenic bladder.

Trauma from a vaginal delivery (swelling, lacerations, episiotomy repairs, etc.) and abdominal surgery, general anesthesia, pain medications, and IV fluids from cesarean sections are causes for a neurogenic bladder.

This issue will most times resolve on its own without intervention. It may take some time for those signals to fire again, so the urethra can resume emptying the bladder, and you will be given a few hours for this to start functioning on its own. When it starts working again, it may be slow going— so be patient. You may start and stop several times before you feel you have emptied your bladder. But if it doesn't start working in a timely manner and your bladder starts to fill, it will be emptied by your nurse.

Q   *I feel the need to pee, so why is my catheter not working?*

A   One of the problems I have found with my cesarean section patients is having a foley catheter that does not empty like it should. The catheter has two oblong holes on each side of the tip, but one side can be covered up by the balloon which keeps it in the bladder. That leaves only one hole to allow for drainage. With continuous movement and the position changes you make in bed, the catheter can "butt up" against the side wall of the bladder. Now *both* slots are blocked so the bladder fills up and you feel the need to urinate. Let your nurse know when this happens so she can help drain the catheter and keep the bladder empty until its removal.

Q   *Why does it burn when I pee?*

A   Episiotomies and lacerations to your hoo-hah after a vaginal delivery can be painful when you urinate. The more concentrated your urine is, the more it will burn. While you are going to the bathroom, try using your peri-bottle or Hygenique® sprayer while you are going. The water will help to dilute the urine and lessen the burning sensation to your cuts and lacerations. Continue to do this until they start to heal, and it no longer burns.

If the burning sensation feels like it's coming from *inside* you, let your nurse know as you may be developing a urinary tract or bladder infection.

Q   *My stitches feel like they are pulling out when I sit down. What can I do??*

A   The suggestion I made earlier in the book seems to work well for my vaginal-delivered patients when they sit down. When you were pregnant, your doctor or nurse may have instructed you to perform Kegel exercises to help strengthen your pelvic muscles to prepare for delivery. As you get ready to sit down, do a Kegel, hold it, then sit down and relax. This will help draw in your muscles and vaginal skin so when you sit and relax, it won't pull as much. Do this anywhere you sit— bed, chair, toilet, car seat, etc. until you no longer feel the pulling and tugging.

Q   *I feel like I've got more pressure on my bottom (or) I feel like my knees are pressing against my incision. Why is that happening??*

A   One of the things I found with our newer Hill-Rom hospital beds is that when you move the head of your bed up and down, the knees of the bed start to slowly rise on their own. This is such a subtle change over time you don't even realize that it's happening. Because of this, patients have either had more unusual vaginal area pain or pressure than before, or cesarean section patients have their thighs pushing up against their incision, also causing additional unknown pain. Once the knees of the bed were moved back down, this produced instant relief from situations and reduced the rating given for their pain.

When you go to get out of bed, be sure to check that the knees of the bed are completely down before you attempt to crawl out. This way you will not be "crawling out of a hole" in your bed. I find it's bizarre that something so simple can cause pain in either patient, just by "having a ghost in the machine..." but it's an easy fix with a remarkable outcome.

If your hospital has newer beds and you find you are having this problem, then try this solution. You will be glad you did!

Q   *I cannot hold the baby? So, why are my hands tingling and/or numb?*

A   When you have additional swelling after the baby is born, usually if you already had swelling prior to delivery, the added swelling in your hands, arms, etc. are putting pressure on your nerves— making your hands feel like they are "going to sleep." This is known as *Carpel Tunnel Syndrome.* As the fluid start to leave your body and the swelling goes down in your hands and arms, the tingling and numbness will subside.

If you had the swelling and carpel tunnel syndrome prior to delivery, it can get worse before it gets better, just like post-delivery swelling all over your body. Again, drinking lots of water will help to draw the fluid back into your cells to be flushed out, and walking the halls will help with circulation of this fluid.

Q   *I'm having terrible shoulder pain... What is causing this?*

A   For patients who have had a cesarean section, they may find this to be a problem. There are two schools of thought with regards to referred shoulder pain after surgery. One thought is, this is caused by the trauma of the abdominal surgery, and due to the manipulation of the abdominal muscles. The other is, it's a sign of gas build-up in the intestines, causing carbon dioxide-induced irritation to the phrenic nerve which causes pain in the C4 area of your neck.

Usually this pain is located at the right shoulder verses the left. I have found the right shoulder seems to be more accurate, but I have had patients with both at the same time. As the patient ambulates or rocks in a chair and starts passing gas, the pain in the shoulder starts to work its way out.

Q   *Why am I shivering uncontrollably right after delivery??*

A   Again, there are several schools of thought with regards to postpartum shivering. Sudden thermal imbalance from separation of the placenta, postpartum hemorrhage, sudden decrease in body temperature following delivery, hormonal changes immediately after delivery, and anesthesia-related affects can contribute to this. Thermal support such as warm blankets will help, along with administration of meperidine (Demerol), if an epidural or spinal had been administered. This usually resolves within the first couple of hours after delivery, or during the recovery period.

Q   *I have an excruciating headache that will not go away unless I lie down... What is causing this?*

A   If you have received an epidural or spinal prior to delivery, sometimes this is a side effect after the catheter is removed. If your body does not "clot off" the puncture site on the spine, cerebral spinal fluid can leak out, which in turn can cause this headache. By lying down for an extended period of time and taking pain meds, along with caffeine intake, this might resolve on its own. If it is severe enough as to cause incapacitation, the option for a blood patch to be place over the puncture site might be in order. This blood patch will cover the site and stop the leakage of spinal fluid, which will then reduce the headache and resolve it. The anesthesiologist will complete this task.

If the headache is accompanied with epigastric pain, increased blood pressure, visual disturbances, shortness of breath or painful breathing, or altered mental status, they may be symptoms of preeclampsia/eclampsia in the post-delivery phase. Usually this is found with patients who showed signs or symptoms prior to delivery, but it can begin after delivery in some patients even without having prior preeclampsia. With either of these findings, let your nurse know immediately so that proper assessment and treatment can be started as soon as possible.

Post-Hospital Complications or Emergencies

There can be complications after delivery, such as hemorrhaging, which can quickly become a very concerning issue with your nurses or the doctor. Some of these post-delivery complications occur during your hospital stay, and can be addressed and managed quickly. But, over half of all postpartum complications can occur in the *days, weeks, and months* after delivery. Don't think that you are in the clear after you have delivered and recovered some in the hospital. You may just find some of these issues occurring to you after you have been discharged.

After you have returned home, you may find that your vaginal bleeding has picked up and become heavier than it had been. Sometimes this is due to increased activity on *your* part. (I know there are some of you out there who feels the need to keep busy all the time, but this time *is not* one of those times.) Let others do what needs doing and concentrate on just taking care of yourself and your baby.

When you go home, it is important that you take it easy for a few weeks before you increase your activity. This gives your body time to heal after the delivery, *even* after a vaginal delivery. Delivery is a very traumatic event for your body and it needs time to heal, so don't try and over-do it too soon. If you all of a sudden start doing more around the house such as laundry, dishes, cleaning the house, along with taking care of your baby, you might find your bleeding picking up and becoming more reddish in color again. Areas in your uterus that had clotted off may have "broken back open", which would increase the reddish bleeding. This is a good indication you are doing too much and need to *slow way down.*

There are other signs of complications you need to look for after going home. More and more hospitals today are giving a hand-out regarding complications to mothers before they discharge from the hospital. This hand-out is written by AWHONN (Association of Women's Health, Obstetric, and Neonatal Nurses) and provide information of signs and symptoms you need to be looking for, which some might become *medical emergencies!* (If you do not read anything else the hospital hands out to you at discharge, be sure and read *this* one.) If you didn't receive this hand-out upon discharge, here is the contents of the warning signs given in the acronym P.O.S.T. B.I.R.T.H.:

- Pain in the chest, *and/or*

- Obstructed breathing or shortness of breath, which either of these two can mean a clot to your lungs or are having a heart problem;

- Seizures, which can indicate the condition of eclampsia;

- Thoughts or feelings of hurting yourself or your baby may mean you are having postpartum depression

Any one of these are a life-threatening emergency and you need to seek help immediately by *calling 911.*

The following symptoms are indications you need to call your health care provider (generally this is your obstetrician as you are still under their care for at least 6 weeks post-delivery):

- Bleeding, soaking through a pad in an hour and/or blood clots the size of an egg or bigger, may mean you are having a post-partum hemorrhage;

- Incision that is not healing, or increased redness or pus at the site of an episiotomy or cesarean incision may indicate an infection;

- Redness, swelling, warmth, or pain in the calf that is painful to the touch may indicate a blood clot:

- Temperature of 100.4° F or higher, bad smelling blood or discharge may indicate infection;

- Headache (very painful), vision changes, pain in the upper right area of your belly can all indicate high blood pressure, or the condition of post-birth preeclampsia

Your obstetrician will determine if you can come into the office to have this checked out, or if you need to go to the emergency room for treatment.

Any time you have anything that just doesn't feel, look, or smell right— just *trust* your instincts. You should always seek medical advice or care if you are not sure. It is *always* better to err on the side of caution and just make that phone call. Doesn't matter if it is day or night. If it's at night, there should be an answering service to connect you to the obstetrician on call.

The "OTHER" Topics

This is the section which may become what I look at as potential problems and you may find yourself faced with during your hospital stay. They are not care-related issues, per se, but can have an impact on your recovery or affect you when you are going home. Or— they might be just a few little issues that might bother you or your spouse/significant other. Let's discuss some of these potential issues and see if being proactive can make a difference.

Visitors, Visitors, Visitors...

Everyone has been anticipating the baby's birth for some time now and the cannot wait to see the little bundle of joy, and that is great, wonderful, stupendous!!! And of course, we as parents want to show off our prodigy with the *entire world* (or at least with everyone we know...) However, sometimes visitors do not think to call before they show up to make sure you are ready for them, or even see if it is a convenient time for you to receive them. They just show up and expect you to welcome them with open arms... and you do! "Oh, what's one more visitor." Go ahead and let them in— but, trust me when I say— you may *regret* it later.

Think in advance long before you head to the hospital how this might all go. When you start going into labor or your water breaks, you may be in for several long hours before your baby arrives. (Heaven forbid this happening in the early or late evening after you have been up since early in the morning.) Or— if you are scheduled on a pre-appointed day to be induced or have a cesarean section, and your brain doesn't want to shut down the night before because of your anticipation of the coming event, you may get behind on much needed rest.

If you're going into this already tired and then have multiple hours added on to your schedule with your labor and/or delivery, then you are already starting to get behind. Next you will have broken sleep taking care of and feeding your newborn— *if you can sleep at all,* now that you are adrenalin rushed with all your excitement of having your baby. Add some more hours in for all the visitors to come in and see you and the new baby. They don't all come in at once. *NO-O-O-O*... they come in one... right after... the other, so it's continuous for hours on end. Kind of seeing where I am going with this??

When the exhaustion finally hits you, it hits you hard!! But you don't get any reprieve, because now the baby is not sleeping very long and keeping you awake: demanding to breastfeed, crying because she wants to constantly be held and doesn't want to lie in her crib; crying because he needs a diaper change, or his little penis hurts from the circumcision; crying for something to constantly suck on; crying because they have a tummy ache from the formula, or need to burp. The list can go on and on and on. Add to it the new guidelines for many hospitals for babies rooming-in with their mothers, and you *can't* send your baby to the nursery so you can get some sleep. Now you're pain meds aren't working very well because you are so exhausted and can't get any sleep. Again, the list can go on and on *ad nauseum*.

Do all those well-meaning visitors deal with what you are now dealing with when they go home??? Have some of those visitors who have children forgotten how restrictions on visitors in the past allowed them to get some sleep... *and* could send the baby to the nursery when they wanted... *and* feed sugar water bottles to after breastfeeding when babies were still hungry? With all the changes over the years from *then* to *now*, your parents or grandparents or older visitors may have forgotten or don't know (or, heaven forbid, don't care) that it's not the same for you as it was for them. Or your younger visitors think this is entertainment time— and you and the new baby *"are the entertainment!!"* Now they come in and stay, and stay, and stay... and STAY... *FOR HOURS!!!* They think it's party time... so let's party!

The last thing with regard your visitors is— *don't* allow them to visit you while they are sick!! This is considered a well unit in the hospital, so you don't want them coming in and exposing you and your newborn to colds, flu, chicken pox, etc. (And *we* certainly do not want to be exposed either.)

During the official flu season, visitors that have any signs or symptoms of having the flu will not be allowed in to visit. It is recommended that only essential persons to the mother's well-being visit. This is in accordance to the Centers for Disease Control (CDC) guidelines during the flu season, which runs from October thru the end of March, to prevent transmission to the mother or baby. Also, children who are approximately 13 years of age or younger will not be allowed in *at all,* unless they are siblings with no signs of illness. Since they come in constant contact with other children and can contract or pass on the flu easily, they will not be allowed to visit. Generally, this ban does not take full effect unless there is a documented local outbreak of the influenza virus.

So, with that said, think long and hard before your let every Tom, Dick, and Harriet come in to visit you in the hospital. Once those few potential sleep intervals between the baby's care and your care while you are in the hospital are gone— they are gone for good. Then in a few days you head home, and you will be *so* sleep-deprived you cannot tell if you are coming or going. Oh, you'll survive it… other people managed to do it… but is it worth it in the long run???

It's okay to limit your visitors, tell them not to come see you and the baby right away, in fact don't even tell anyone when you are heading to the hospital. This is your special time with your spouse, significant other, or support person. Take your time just to enjoy this event without sharing it with everyone in person. Share it on social media, emails, face-time, Skype, or what have you— but only when you are ready to. In fact, have your spouse/significant other/support person do this for you so you can rest.

You need this time for adjustment with your newborn and your new family, so take all the time you need. And— if any of your family and friends become offended that you have put them off for the time being, just remember… they all waited nine months to see the new baby *just like you,* and will it not hurt them to wait a few more days for you to rest and adjust to your new family. I always say, "If they get *mad*… they can get *glad* in the same pants they got *mad* in." It is your right to say, "no visitors— I need some sleep," or "we are having a rough time today— can you come back tomorrow?" Don't feel as if it is your responsibility to "entertain the masses", and cater to their wishes and whims. In reality, shouldn't it be the other way around? They should be thinking of you and your baby's and family's needs and catering to you all instead.

Inexcusably Pushy Visitors

It's only natural that people want to come to the hospital to see you and the new baby. They've been waiting a long time too, waiting "with bated breath," but sometimes people get a little overzealous in their quest to see this new baby. Grandparents can be the most exasperating when it comes to their grandchild.

I am all for visitors coming to see you and the baby, but when it comes to ignoring what is being asked of them or getting rude with the nursing staff, is where I draw the line. I couldn't tell you how many times I have run across a grandmother or aunt or best friend who insisted that they were to be in the delivery room with the soon-to-be-mom, when in reality the soon-to-be-mom has no intention of having other people in the room besides the dad. I have even called security on some people because a situation escalated, and the visitor became verbally abusive to staff. Unfortunately, we are a society of *"ME, ME, ME"*, and if I want something I can get it without having to follow the rules— *and* If I complain long and loud enough, I will get what I want no matter what!!

One of the many issues we face in the hospital is with family members or close friends *"pushing"* their way in to be with mothers and fathers-to-be during the birth of the baby, or to have access to the patients before recovery is complete because they can't seem to wait any longer. Unfortunately, in today's society we have a lot of people out there who don't know limits or boundaries, and are trying to push their way into the delivery room or taking over in the days after the delivery. They think they can bully others (such as nurses, doctors, or other hospital staff) into letting them do what they want, regardless of rules or regulations the specific hospital has in place. Those rules and regulations are in place to provide a safe environment for the delivery and to maintain the health of mother and baby.

Family and friends tend to forget they are in a hospital setting during the birth and recovery of a baby. They wouldn't, in a normal course of a hospital visit, push their way in to the post-surgical area after a loved one's surgery, would they? No— they would wait until the hospital staff would tell them it was okay to "come in now" once everything was completed. What makes delivering a baby any different? I'll tell you— a new baby is now involved and according to these types of people they think *"all bets are off"* and they don't have to abide by any hospital or doctor's rules.

If you want to have others in the delivery room with you (except during a cesarean section), there may be limit to how many can be in there. The decision would be up to the hospital's protocols, and also with the doctors, on the specific number who can bear witness to the event. If you do not know what will or won't be allowed— just ask your nurse and she will tell you. When you know what is okay and what is not, you will be able to make the decision on whom you want to be with you and your significant other— *or* if you want *none* to be present. Be sure and share those wishes and rules with everyone who might be there waiting for the delivery. This way they will already know what is to be expected of them.

And speaking of decisions— regardless of what others want, it is ultimately your decision if you *even want* them in the room with you! Trust me when I say, there are some that may try and by-pass all the rules *or your preference*— and just sneak into the room anyway. I have seen this happen repeatedly. Sometimes they get away with it because the staff's attention is focused elsewhere at the time, but there are times when they are prevented from making entry into your room and disorderly conduct begins. Hospital staff will have no reservations in contacting security if a scene is started on the unit.

Well, when it comes to visitors— and that means everyone except the persons wearing a matching band to the baby— they don't really matter to the nursing staff. Don't get me wrong— we are very cordial to the visitors, and laugh and joke with them when they are present, but, overall, they can be disruptive to you and your baby's recovery. The only people that matter to us is you, the baby, and the father/significant other. We are here to make sure both you and the baby are healthy, and things are going well for you all as a family until you are discharged. You and baby are our #1 priority, not the visitors, so whatever you decide to do during your stay is all that matters.

If you don't want any visitors while you are in the hospital, let your staff know. If you don't want certain people to come, tell those people in advance of your hospital stay so they know ahead of time.

This is supposed to be a *very happy and exciting time* for you and everyone involved, and we don't want to take away the enjoyment from anyone during the birth of your baby. Just be sure everyone who will be waiting for the birth to occur knows there *are* ground rules, just like in any other hospital setting, and we expect them to be followed without causing any undue stress on you, your support person, or the staff. So— let's all get excited and have a happy and healthy delivery and everyone can celebrate!!

Social Media

After the delivery and recovery are complete and you share your news with everyone who's been waiting at the hospital or with text messages if not present, you may have to relay your instructions on how or what social media platforms they can or can't use to pass the information on to others.

During the excitement, everyone else wants to share the news of your baby's birth, but do you want that to happen? Shouldn't you be the one to decide if you want that information posted on FaceBook, Twitter, Instagram, Skype, or what have you? Or if you want to post it out there yourselves?? Since this is your "special" newsworthy event, I believe that you should be the one to do the posting or deciding where or if you want it posted or not.

This might be another thing you need to discuss with your family, friends, and associates about your personal decisions regarding posting this without your permission. Be sure and share those choices with everyone, unless you are okay with any or everyone passing on the good news.

Hospital Gifts

If you still insist on having visitors in the hospital, and you have a lot of the *"gift giving"* kind, I would highly recommend you tell them *not* come bearing gifts— at least not while you are in the hospital. Family and friends are always well-meaning when they bring something for you or your baby— or the siblings, but they tend to forget one tiny little thing. Who must haul all of gifts, flowers, etc. home?? Do they?? No— *YOU* do!!!

I cannot count how many times parents were inundated with so many gifts and flowers which needed to be taken home, that when it came time to load their vehicle— there wasn't any room to get mom or baby or both in it!! Some parents realize this issue and either have dad start hauling things home when they go home to take care of other kids, pets, stay at home— or enlist the help of family or friends to take some things home for them while they are still in the hospital. Some parents have left the plants, flowers, leftover goodies for the nurses to enjoy, and that is certainly not the intention of the gift-giver. They don't buy them for *us* to enjoy— they bought them for you. So, ask your visitors if they insist on gifts to please bring them when they visit you at home, or send them to your residence if they are unable to come see you anytime soon. This way you have one less stressor upon discharge, and you can get home safely without impairing your driver's visibility.

Baby's Care

· · · · · · · · · · · · · · · ·

This is the section you will most likely be referring to often, given that your new baby is here. As parents, we tend to be more concerned with our children than ourselves, but we must not overlook our own care just to focus on the baby's. Remember, you must take care of yourself in order to take care of your baby.

A lot of events and situations during the infant's time in the hospital, and shortly after returning home, are very normal and routine. Some things might appear abnormal but are considered expected during the baby's first few days after delivery. Focus will begin with everyday assessments, activities, changes, and education, then move on to some more issues which creep up unexpectedly, but are still normal in this timeframe.

Every post-delivery situation is unique to the recovery of each baby, with exception to eating, sleeping, peeing, pooping, crying, etc., but sometimes little "curve balls" can be thrown into the mix. They may cause you some anxiety and concern when they happen, so we will address all the possible "routine" stuff and then come back and talk about the "other" stuff. Be reassured that even if something is "out of the ordinary" in your mind does not mean it's a "bad" thing— it just sometimes happens and usually resolves itself in its own time. This is one of the reasons for providing this information to you; to help educate you ahead of time or be a reference during this time to help put your mind at ease.

Beginning with Recovery

Congratulations!!! Your baby is born— and now begins the recovery process for him or her— *or* them. The mouth and nose are suctioned out by your doctor, the cord is clamped, then cut, and the baby is place on your chest within the first minute or two. Your nursery nurse will then take over from there to dry the baby off with a towel, removing wetness and vernix from the baby's skin and head, all while stimulating the baby to let out the first cry, then placing a cap on the baby's head. By rubbing the baby's skin, she is removing almost everything covering the baby's exposed skin which can quickly decrease the baby's temperature. During this time, the baby is getting body heat from you by laying on your chest, thus helping maintain a more stable body temperature. Rubbing the skin also helps to elicit the baby's first cries, which help to "open up" the airway and expand the lungs, and to provide oxygen and help the lungs absorb the amniotic fluid remaining there.

You'll see when your baby is crying good and loud that their bluish skin color begins to turn pinker and pinker the more they cry. It's a good thing to allow your baby this time to cry excessively for a while after birth. This gives the lungs ample time to absorb all the fluid inside, and continue providing much needed oxygen to all the body's cells. Once the cord has been cut, this is a very important step for your new baby. You are no longer providing that oxygen for them, so they must be able to provide it for themselves now...♫♪ *so let her cry!!* ♫♪

During the "crying time", your nursery nurse will quickly check the baby's vital signs and do visual assessment to determine their well-being. Soon after, if you are breastfeeding, the nurse will assist you and the baby with latching on to the breast for the first time. Your doctor will begin to repair any necessary episiotomies, tears, or laceration as well, or finish with your cesarean section surgery. Your delivery nurse will continue to monitor and assess you as well during this time and provide you with IV hydration and pitocin if you have had a vaginal delivery— or continue with all of this once you are taken to the recovery room after your surgery is completed.

[**Some hospitals are now changing their procedures to allow for cesarean section deliveries to experience much of this immediate delivery occurrence, where they were not allowed to before. (Our facility calls this the *"gentle c-section."*)]

The recovery period for the baby generally lasts two hours, so you will see the nursery nurse recheck vitals and reassess the baby at several intervals during this time. Generally, this occurs every 30 mins; for the first two hours. Depending on your hospital's policies and procedures, this time is also put aside for bonding time between the parents and baby. Other procedures, such as weights and measurements, medication administration, baby's first bath and such will be delayed to give you this time to bond as a family unit.

A lot of hospitals across the nation have gone to this method of recovery for the family to enhance the bonding experience. Whether this is your first time delivering or your 6th— enjoy this time alone, without visitors swooping down on you and invading. Nothing is worse than not having gotten mom out of stirrups and the room a mess from the delivery, only to have your room— and *your privacy* invaded by impatient family members. (Or— barge into your room as soon as you return from your surgery.) They have waited just as long as you all have to see your new baby, but this is your right as a family to have this time alone together— and will be the only *"first time"* you'll get, so take advantage and enjoy!! Better yet, tell all of them who plan to be there at the hospital, in advance, that this *will* be happening. (Even if the hospital doesn't follow this procedure.) Put your foot down and declare, *"No Negotiations… at all!",* regardless of which way you deliver. If they know this ahead of time, they will be expecting it and should have no hard feelings about it.

When you and your baby have completed the recovery period, and your visitors anxiously come in to greet the newest addition to your circle, you will be allowed to spend this time however you want. Just remember, you've just been through delivery and are more than likely exhausted from your experience, so don't let them overwhelm you for hours on end. You and baby— *and* daddy need rest, feeding time, bonding time, etc— and the adventure has only begun.

(See the section on *Other Topics* under *Visitors, Visitors Visitors.*)

Detailed Recovery for Baby

In this section, we'll discuss in a little more detail the baby's recovery period, and shortly thereafter, so you will know what to expect as each event unfolds—and the reasons *for* them to occur.

Suctioning out the baby

Right after the baby's head is born, your OB doctor will take a bulb syringe and remove any excess fluid still in the baby's nose and mouth. This will help to unblock their airway so that first breath can occur. If your baby had his first stool inside before he was born, and it is very thick, the doctor may use a suction catheter to remove this from the mouth. (Sometimes those darn babies will try and cry just with the head delivered— it happens!)

As of 2005, it has been recommended, that deep suctioning (in the back of the throat and down the airway) for the babies who passed their first stool prior to delivery should not be suctioned with suction catheters at this time. The doctor will just use the bulb syringe to complete the fluid removal in the mouth, but the baby will be monitored closer for any signs or symptoms of meconium aspiration. This can make the baby sick, but most time they tolerate this without any additional concerns. If baby is having difficulty recovering from this, appropriate neonatal support therapy will be initiated.

Vital signs

Right after the baby is born, the nursery nurse will check the baby's heart rate, respirations, and temperature. These vitals give the nurse a baseline as to how the baby is transitioning from the delivery, and a guideline as to how the baby continues to complete transitioning to the outside world— all on their very own. Any one or all can be outside the normal range, telling us the baby may be needing additional medical care above and beyond that of a well-transitioning baby. These vitals, whether a sick or well-baby, are closely monitored all throughout the time in the hospital until discharge, as they can change at any time during their stay.

- Temperature: If baby is not maintaining this well, whether too high or too low, it could indicate there might be infection present and, therefore, may need additional medical interventions to correct this. We want the temperature between 98.0 and 99.0.

  Skin-to-skin contact with mother can help keep those temperatures up, but if the baby is not warming up this way, then placement under a radiant warmer will help with this and is generally used for a brief period of time.

- Respirations: How fast or slow the baby is breathing and if they are making sounds when they are breathing can help determine if there is respiratory distress or possible infection, or both.

  Sometimes right after birth a baby may struggle with breathing because of airway blockage from substantial amounts of fluid in the nose and mouth that had not been completely removed at delivery. Additional suctioning with a bulb syringe may be needed, along with a little supplemental oxygen.

  If the baby does not spontaneously breathe on their own, CPAP (Continuous Positive Airway Pressure) may be administered with a mask and oxygen source to help push air into the lungs and start spontaneous breathing. Most times, this is a short-term solution that quickly improves the baby's airway within a few minutes, and no other assistance would be necessary.

- Heart rate: If this is too high along with fast respirations, this can indicate the beginning of respiratory distress or infection. If too low, the baby may be already in respiratory distress and the heart is having difficulty pumping due to lack of oxygen.

Generally, if the heart rate is too low, it is due to a respiratory issue where the baby is not breathing well on his own *or* at all. Respiratory assistance would be necessary to remedy this, along with possible medications to help in resuscitation. Your nurses and doctor will assist your baby to overcome this rather quickly, so unless your baby has other issues which might be contributing to this problem, they should do just fine. Additional monitoring would be needed for a time in the Level II nursery to make sure your baby recovers well and can return to normal newborn care.

Combinations of these can have indications of other potential issues such as low blood sugars, temperature instabilities, apnea (periodically stop breathing), etc., which is why they are monitored.

Apgar scores

This tool is used within the first few minutes of life, which also helps determine how well the baby is transitioning, but quicker. These are done at 1 and 5 minutes after birth and are scored based on these five observations rated 0-2 for a maximum score of 10:

- heart rate: 0=None, 1= <100 BPM, 2=>100 BPM

- respirations: 0= No cry, 1= Weak cry, 2= Vigorous cry

- muscle tone: 0= Limp 1= Some flexion, 2= Active

- reflex: 0= No response to airway stimulation, 1= Grimace to stimulation, 2= Grimace and cough or sneeze during stimulation

- color: 0= Entire body blue or pale, 1= Good color, but blue hands and/or feet, 2= Completely pink or good color

These can quickly indicate the need for assistance with their airway or breathing, but the majority of routine births usually score in the 8-9 range at 1 and

5 minutes, usually taken 1 off for color and 1 off for tone. Just know that when your baby has been given a low Apgar score(s) at some point during the first few minutes of life, does not mean the baby will have issues later in relation to this. This is just a quick indicator for us if baby will need assistance to help with breathing.

Baby's measurements

After a few hours when the recovery period is over, or you're anxious to know sooner *(who won the baby pool???)*, the baby will be weighed and then measured for length, head circumference, and chest circumference. These measurements are not just information about your baby for you to have, they are useful diagnostic tools in determining your baby's plan of care during the hospitalization.

Ballard scoring

This is an assessment tool used to help determine the gestational age of the baby with relation to the physical and neurological characteristics found at birth. Usually this is within a week or two of the number of weeks you were pregnant, or may be helpful in determining if your dates were inaccurate based on the assessment. This is also a helpful assessment for healthcare workers to determine the baby's age if the mother has no idea how many weeks she might have been pregnant, and to determine if the care given matches the baby's needs based on the gestational age assigned to the them.

If this is close to the gestational age based on your dates and you are 37 weeks or more, then usually normal routine baby care will be provided. If the dates are determined to be < 37 weeks or greater than 42 weeks, then the healthcare given will be based on this assessment and any other findings indicating additional individual care. This should be discussed with you by your nurse or physician if this becomes necessary to let you know what is going to be happening and why.

This scoring also helps to chart the results on a scale, along with weight and length, which helps to categorize the baby as Small for Gestational Age (SGA), Large for Gestational Age (LGA), or Average for Gestational Age (AGA). This helps to determine any additional procedures which would be required to be performed if the baby falls out of the AGA range.

Vitamin K

Vitamin K is given to all newborns within the first 24 hours of life. Babies are born *with limited* ability for their blood to clot, which increases the chance for bleeding issues. This is called vitamin K deficiency. Bleeding and can be very serious to the newborn. This shot helps to boost the clotting of the blood and prevent complications, and has been given routinely in hospitals since 1961.

Erythomycin eye ointment

This is a prophylactic antibiotic placed in the baby's eyes to prevent ophthalmic neonatorum, a disorder which can cause corneal scarring, ocular (eye) perforation or blindness if the baby is exposed to the bacteria from Gonorrhea or Chlamydia in the mother's vaginal tract during a vaginal birth and not treated. A newborn born by cesarean section would not be exposed to these types of sexually transmitted diseases, but the CDC *and* US Preventative Services Taskforce recommend that *all* infants receive this antibiotic at birth. This is due to baby's potential exposure to other infections such as Herpes simplex or Staphylococcus Aureus which may also cause eye damage.

After its application, baby's may have redness and swelling around the eyelids, occlusion or blockage of the lacrimal ducts (tear ducts), and some yellowish discharge for a brief time. If the discharge is of concern to the pediatrician, additional eye medication may be ordered.

Hepatitis B vaccine

This is a vaccine recommended to all persons for the prevention of contracting this virus, which attacks the liver, and is offered to the parents for the baby's first vaccination shot to be given in the hospital. The liver is a vital organ that filters out the toxins and broken-down red blood cells (bilirubin), processes nutrients for your body, regulates the composition of the blood, and it makes certain proteins: Vitamin A, cholesterol, and clotting substances.

Having the Hepatitis B virus can damage the liver's ability to function by causing lifelong infection, cirrhosis of the liver, liver cancer, liver failure, and death. With the Hepatitis B vaccine this virus can be prevented, so the vaccine is recommended to be given as a first dose in the hospital at the time of birth. The two remaining doses in the series will be given in the pediatrician's office before the 18th month of age. If you are unsure whether you want to have this first administered during your hospital stay, you can decline at that time, and have your baby receive the complete series in their office.

Blood sugars (blood glucose)

Prior to the delivery, or at some time after, it may be determined your baby needs to have her blood sugar checked. There are several factors which would indicate the need for testing the baby's glucose levels and possibly for several intervals. Babies born *before* 37 weeks or SGA (small for gestational age) will have a series of glucose checks starting 30 minutes after the first feeding and each time right before the baby feeds over the first 24 hours. Babies born LGA (large for gestational age) or to mothers who are either insulin-dependent diabetics or have gestational diabetes (during the pregnancy) will be screened 30 minutes after the first feeding and before feedings during first 12 hours of life.

When babies are born and fall under these two categories, they are at higher risk for their blood glucose levels to drop (Neonatal Hypoglycemia), therefore, monitoring is necessary to ensure the glucose level do not drop too low and require intervention to bring those numbers up to the required levels.

Recently, the use of a glucose gel within the first four hours after delivery have been very effective in rapidly raising baby's blood sugars to appropriate levels, and have decreased the need for IV glucose therapy and separation from mothers. This has helped keep the mother and baby together, which has helped with continued breastfeeding prior to and after discharge.

AGA babies, who fall out of these categories for monitoring, may also require blood glucose testing if they become symptomatic of Neonatal Hypoglycemia. They may become too cold, which the baby must expend more energy and use up more calories to try to self-regulate their temperatures, therefore, cause the glucose levels to drop. Other symptoms of Neonatal Hypoglycemia we watch for are poor feedings, floppiness or lethargy, jitteriness, apneic episodes (stop breathing for greater than 20 seconds), losing their pink skin tone, seizures, weak or high-pitched cry, eye rolling, and tachypnea (more than 60 breaths per minute.)

Baby's 1st bath

To bathe or not to bathe… that is the question. Do you want your baby cleaned and "baby fresh" smelling, or do you want the vernix (the greasy, whitish covering on the surface of the baby's skin) to remain for at least 24 hours or more to gain the benefits before the vernix is shed?

There are still the old school nurses who "bathe the baby within about the first couple hours after birth" and get all the "yucky gunk" off the skin and out of the hair. But there has been research out there for a few years that waiting to bathe the baby, or not bathing at all during the hospital stay, is very beneficial.

It's been found that there are antimicrobial properties in the vernix to protect from infection exposure during delivery, and natural skin emollients to keep the skin softened. It also becomes a skin barrier while the baby is in the uterus, protecting him from amniotic fluid maceration (shrinking), and helps maintain electrolyte and fluid balance by greatly decreasing the transdermal (skin) releasing of those electrolytes and fluids.

More hospitals and birthing centers are migrating toward this practice, based off the evidence provided from several studies. It's up to you as parents if you want to follow this new practice to not bathe. It won't hurt your baby if you decide you want your baby bathed, but it might be very beneficial for him not to be. Just remember, it's ultimately your choice.

If, or when, you bathe the baby for the first time, you will more than likely be giving the baby a "sponge" bath--- meaning no tub bath for the immediate future. Until the umbilical cord stump falls off and the site heals, and— for male babies who have been circumcised and the penis heals, you should *not* place the baby directly into a bath. Both sites are portals for infection, especially the umbilical cord site which goes directly into the baby's circulatory system.

When giving "sponge" baths, you use really warm water, as the washcloth will begin to cool down as you go from the sink to the baby. You will start at the face and work your way down and around to the back, leaving the hair for last. By bathing the baby in this order, you decrease the amount of heat loss by saving the head for last, which for the baby is a large surface to be exposed.

The easiest way is to use two washcloths to bathe the baby— one to wash and one to rinse, and a dry towel to dry each section as you go. Wash the face (without soap the first few times) and dry it off, then move to neck and gently lift the baby's jaw with your fingers allowing access to the neck area. Wash this and the arms, fingers, underarms, and chest, then rinse and dry off. Move down below the waist and clean the groin area, legs, feet, and toes, then rinse and dry off. Turn the baby over onto his tummy turning his head to the side and wash his back and bum, then rinse and dry off. When finished, place a new diaper on the baby and wrap him in the towel you are drying him with, leaving only his head exposed.

Before washing his hair, turn the temperature of the water down to warm. You may have been given a soft-bristled scrub brush and a baby comb during your stay, so use these during the hair washing. Holding the baby tucked in like a football, and the baby's neck supported by your hand, run the top of the baby's head under the running water then place a dollop of baby shampoo (or head-to-toe body wash) on top of the baby's head. Use the scrub brush to gently clean the head all over. If there is stiff or sticky gunk in there still, use the comb to gently comb through the hair and remove the debris. Once it is thoroughly cleaned, then rinse and dry with the towel.

Once you start bathing your baby, it should only be about every 2-3 days for now, as your baby's skin is sensitive and daily bathing will dry it out. But if you choose to bathe daily, be sure and use lotion right after to help trap moisture and keep the skin hydrated. This soft, sensitive skin can dry out rather quickly, so take very good care of it.

Diapering Your Baby

With some parents, they can be "old hats" at changing diapers, but with others they either have not been around newborn babies *ever* or have never changed diapers at all. Whether you know what you are doing or don't, rest assured that your nurse will be there to assist you in tackling this feat.

For the "pros" out there who have "been there, done that," you may still need reminders of how to "start off at square one" again, or you have gone from previous baby's sex to the opposite with the new one, and have no idea how you need to do it. Don't be afraid to ask your nurse to show you how to do it again— that's what we are there for, so ask away!! And— don't let your nurse make you feel stupid if you do ask! You may have forgotten some of the "little details" in changing a newborn's diaper, and I would be surprised if you didn't. Remember, you only retained about 25% of the info from last time, so little reminders of how it's done *or* how it's done with the opposite sex baby is totally okay!!

As with all babies, you want to make sure you have your new diaper out and ready before you begin to change the diaper. That means unfold it completely and set it aside until you are ready to use it. These little kiddos really like to go some more when you start to change the diapers, so if you have it out and ready, you can switch out diapers quickly after you have cleaned your baby's nether region thoroughly. With little boys, you may want to place your hand or a diaper wipe or washcloth over their penis to keep from him spraying everything in sight— especially you, since you're right in the path of his aim. He may or may not do this every time you change him, but do you really want to find out the hard way?? (Just a little tip to help you avoid this, because I learned very quickly with my son— the hard way! He was notorious for doing this every diaper change.)

Next, you need to see what you have that needs to be cleaned. If it is just urine, then wipe the entire diaper area clean. *Do not* skip this step!! Some parents, for the sake of using less diaper wipes or just down right laziness, do not always wipe the urine off the skin. Even though disposable diapers are rather absorbent, that doesn't mean there isn't any urine residue still on the skin surface. If it is repeatedly not wiped away, the urine can cause skin breakdown in the form of diaper rash.

If there is stool (poop, feces, caca, whatever you call it), first use your dirty diaper to remove all the excess off the baby. You do not need to be overly gentle to do this. With the diaper, place is firmly against top of the baby's crotch where the stool starts and firmly wipe downward, lifting the baby's bottom off the bed to wipe further back. Usually, one swipe will remove the majority of stool, so you have a much cleaner surface to use your diaper wipes on for the remainder. This technique will change the need for diaper wipes from... say 10 to only 1-2 wipes.

With little girls, only wipe her off from *front to back*. You *do not* want to wipe from back to front, as this may cause some of the stool to be pushed into the vagina and urethra, possibly causing infection. With little boys, it is okay to place a finger or thumb on the scrotum and lightly stretch out the skin to make for an easier, more stable surface to wipe on. You may need to do this all around the scrotum to clean it thoroughly. Make sure to check in the creases of their hips and legs— also make sure the creases at the top of the bum are thoroughly cleaned as well.

Once you have him or her cleaned, place the new diaper under the baby, bring the front part up between their legs, and release one tape from the side and apply it to the *middle* of the diaper. Release the other tape with one hand and grasp the front top of the diaper in the other and bring the tape again to the middle of the diaper *or* over the middle, depending on how big or little the baby is. Make sure the diaper is around the waist snuggly, because if it is too loose, the diaper may fall off the bum and you may have quite a mess to clean up.

There— you have now changed your first of many diapers and soon you will become an expert!!

Some "Oddities" You Might Encounter Changing Diapers

This is a section where I will address "odd" things you might find while changing baby's diapers, and specific things you would find with girls and with boys, respectively. First, I'll address the features found with either sex, then approach the details you might find with each sex individually. This way you will know what to expect if you happen to see this when changing diapers and feel comfortable that they are "normal" features which may come up with your baby.

Small number of diapers

When your baby is starting his brand-new life outside your womb and is beginning to have wet and dirty diapers, we are expecting to see at least one wet and one poopy diaper in the first 24 hours of life, then two of each the next day, then three the third, and so on.

For breastfed babies, this is normal because the volume of colostrum is generally on the low side. When your baby starts to have 6-8 wet and 2-3 poopy diapers, it is when they are starting to get more volume of fluids, either from breast milk when it comes in *or* from formula, if formula-fed. Anything over and above what is expected for the first few days of life is just bonus. This is normal, so if your baby is not producing enough wet and dirty diapers expected of their age, then your nurse will address this and provide you with solutions to help remedy this.

Your nurse may provide you with a chart to help keep track of your baby's feedings and diaper changes. Watching the number of diapers is important as this is one tool we use to determine if the baby is getting fluids to prevent dehydration. If the baby is not getting enough fluids from his or her feedings, then the doctor may make an order for supplementation of formula for breastfed babies, or an increased amount of formula from what they are currently taking. I will be discussing supplementation later in the guide when I address the baby's feedings.

Pink-tinged spots on the diaper

You may notice when you go to change the baby's wet diaper that on the surface there is a little spot or a few spots that look pinkish in color, almost a salmon color. What this is— is Uric Crystals. If the baby is not getting a large volume to eat, the diaper might be very concentrated, and you might see this pink-tinged stuff on the diaper. This is normal for breastfed babies who get small to minute quantities of colostrum. The urine will be very dark, and these uric crystals may be present. As the volume of fluid increases, the crystals will go away.

When we get older and use the toilet to empty our bladders, if our urine is concentrated because we haven't had enough fluids, or you haven't urinated in a long time, you would see the darker color of urine in the toilet water. The uric crystals would be there, but you would not see them as the water would dilute the urine somewhat. In baby's diapers, the urine is *not diluted* in water, thus you will see these uric crystals when the urine is concentrated.

Sacral dimples

If you are changing a diaper or happen to have the baby on his or her tummy with the diaper off, he or she may have what we call a sacral dimple. These will be deep pits in the skin right where the tailbone (coccyx) is located at the base of the spine. Generally, these are considered common and do not have any effects on the baby or cause any problems. But if there is a tuft of hair present, a skin tag, birthmark, skin discoloration at the site, or it is very deep, the pediatrician may have testing done to determine if there is a need for further evaluation and treatment of any possible spinal cord abnormalities.

If the baby is moving the legs around in a normal fashion and the dimple is small or shallow, then more likely than not, the dimple isn't a concern for the doctor.

Lots of large stools at the beginning— and then nothing

When your baby has a lot of stools during the first day to day and a half, or they are very large stools that would equal several diaper stools, then he or she might suddenly stop having stools, *especially* if they are breastfed. The reason behind this is babies are born with meconium all throughout their intestinal tract and they have completely pooped out all the meconium.

If the baby is not getting much in the way of colostrum, then their system must wait and digest what little amounts of colostrum they have received, and it might take a day or two before they resume stooling again. This is normal and will correct itself once the baby is getting more volume of breast-milk. This can also occur with bottle-fed babies if they are not taking in much volume of formula because they refuse to eat or do not retain what has been eaten because they are throwing up the formula given. This too will resolve as higher quantities are eaten and digested.

Swollen genitals

When changing your baby's diaper, you may notice that their genitals are swollen and maybe even reddened. This is also a normal finding for either sex, as this comes from the hormones the mother passes on to the baby prior to birth. Also, the additional fluids the baby is born with may contribute to genital swelling. As the fluids or hormones decrease, the swelling will decrease as well.

Findings with Girls

There are other findings with girls, which follow along with the swollen genitals and additional hormones.

Vaginal discharge: The hormones past from mother to baby may also cause a thick, whitish discharge *or* it may be a pink or reddish bloody discharge, like a small "pseudo-period". This is called physiologic leukorrhea. These too will go away once the hormones have left her body.

Small outer labia: A small outer labia is common with baby girls born 37 weeks or less, and may be noted by parents when changing her diaper. Lack of fatty tissue in preterm or premature baby girls is a normal finding, therefore, the outer labia (labia majora) will be smaller and less prominent than the inner labia (labia minora) and clitoris. This will correct itself over time as the body starts growing and more baby fat is added.

Labial skin tags: Labial skin tags (also known as hymenal tags) are protrusions of skin coming from the inner vagina and visible when changing the diaper. These skin tags are benign and will resolve themselves over time. Only about 3-13% of newborn baby girls are born with these tags.

Findings with Boys

Besides possibly having swollen scrotums after delivery, boys have other genital issues which may not happen frequently but would be an entirely common finding.

Undescended testicles: At birth, one of the checks a nurse completes with male babies is checking if the testicles are descended into the scrotum. This is a more common finding in preterm or premature boys (~21%), but it can occur with even full-term infants (1-2%.)

It is not out of the ordinary for one or both testes to be undescended, but if it occurs, there will be regular assessments during the baby's hospital stay to check if one or both have descended or not. If they continue to be undescended, the pediatrician will continue to monitor the issue during follow-up office visits. If they remain undescended, which should occur by 3 months of age, surgical intervention may be necessary, but in approximately 99% of the cases the testes will descend on their own and no other evaluations are required.

Penile torsion: When changing the baby boy's diaper, you may see that his penis is looks twisted or rotated, generally in a counterclockwise direction (to the left.) This can be mild to severe, and in most cases surgery does not have to be done if it is 90 degrees or less.

Approximately 1 in 80 boys are born with penile torsion. It is not known to cause issues with urination or sexual intercourse unless it is accompanied by either hypospadias or congenital chordee. (*See below.*) Some parents may opt to have surgery to correct this defect for cosmetic reasons, or if they feel this might have psychological effects later in life from being tormented by other males who see it.

Hypospadias: Hypospadias happens in about 5% of male infants born, making it the most common birth defect in baby boys. This defect is noted as a urethral opening on the lower segment of the penile shaft anywhere from the head to the point where the shaft and scrotum meet. This can cause the penis to curve downward, making urinating standing up in the future difficult and/ or sexual intercourse difficult.

In most cases, this will need be corrected by a urologist by the age of 18 months and these boys will not be circumcised due to this defect.

Congenital chordee: This is where the penis curves downward, and would be especially noticeable during an erection. The cause is due to more elastic tissue on the top side of the penis than the bottom. This may not be noted at birth, but in years later when an erection takes place. Again, only surgical intervention can correct this defect.

Natural circumcision: A natural circumcision is where the prepuce (or fore-skin) does not completely cover the head of the penis— only partially _or_ not at all. Pediatricians do not generally circumcise these boys when this is a natural occurrence.

Other Newborn Observations

In this section, we'll go from head to toe discussing other occurrences that are found on a routine basis with newborns. Some will normally occur on a frequent basis and some will not, but we will discuss each one, and if anything needs to be done to correct the issue or whether it will resolve on its own.

Findings on the Head

Caput succedaneum (swollen head): When the baby has been engaged deeply in the pelvis for a long time prior to and during labor, the mother has been pushing for an extended period, or the doctor needed the use of forceps or a vacuum extractor to get the baby delivered quicker, fluid and/or blood will gather between the layers of the scalp due to pressure on the head during delivery. This causes swelling and possibly bruising, and is a very common occurrence which will resolve itself in the next few days as the body reabsorbs this additional fluid.

You may notice that when your baby lies with her head to one side or another that the fluid will shift under the scalp. This is what we call "dependent drainage," where the fluid falls by gravity to the lower side of the head the baby is lying on.

You may want to avoid touching or holding on to the head where this fluid is located, as the baby more than likely has a "little bit of a headache" from this trauma. He or she will probably cry every time you place your hand or arm against it, or even when the baby is lying in the crib face up. So, to support the head until the swelling resolves, place your arm or hand against their neck only— and no fingers placed on the head anywhere. If the swelling is substantial, and the baby cries every time you lay him or her down in the crib, the nurse might place a small roll under their neck to elevate the head a little and relieve some of the pressure off it. (This would only be a temporary solution until the swelling goes down and should _not_ be customary practice when you go home.)

Cephalohematoma (blood-filled, swollen head): This is different from the caput succedaneum in that it's the collection of blood from broken capillaries between the periosteum and the bone, but does not cross the central suture line on top of the head. This is commonly caused by the same issues during delivery as the caput succedaneum, it's just that the fluid/blood is in a different location and will possibly take a month or so to totally resolve.

(Just to eliminate repeating the same information, if you are holding the baby or feeding the baby, use the same techniques suggested above in the *caput* section.)

Both issues will resolve on their own over a short or long period of time, respectively, without any further health concerns, but one issue that might occur with either one of the two during your hospital stay and that would be the increased risk for jaundice. When the body breaks down excess red blood cells, this makes bilirubin— and when there is bruising or trauma such as this, the body must break this down as well, therefore creating excess bilirubin. If the baby does not successfully eliminate the excess bilirubin, then the bilirubin backs up in the liver causing jaundice. (See section below on *Skin Color/Conditions* under *Jaundice* for information on bilirubin and treatment)

Sutures of the skull: When you feel along the baby's head, you will notice several ridges: around the front, along the sides and top, and around on the back of the skull. Some parents wonder or worry about these ridges they feel, thinking there may be something wrong with their baby's head. I can assure you that is not the case.

The baby's skull is in separate sections: six skull bones to be exact. The *Frontal* bone, where the forehead is; the *Temporal* bones, on each side of the head by the temple; the *Parietal* bones, on each side of the head above the Temporals; and the *Occipital* bone, in the back of the head. To allow the baby to pass through the birth canal, the head needs to "mold" itself to the pelvis and cervix enabling it to come through the vagina. If the bones were completely fused, this would make birthing the baby very difficult this way. Since the bones are not fused, this allows the skull bones to overlap and mold itself to deliver more easily.

After the baby is born, you may periodically notice some of the skull bone edges protruding a little more or a little less. This is dependent on how the baby is lying down in the crib, and in what position the baby is laying their head. Those bones will keep moving around a little, and at times you may notice them more than others. As the baby gets older, the suture lines between the bones will begin to fuse and eventually the ridges will no longer be noticeable.

When assessing the baby during your stay, you will see the nurse run her fingers all over the head. This is where she is feeling those suture lines to determine at that point if the suture lines are overlapping, spread apart a little or separated, and fitting together like a puzzle or approximated. That, like all other assessment information, is documented in the chart.

Fontanels ("the soft spot"): Your baby will have several of these "spots" on the skull, but there are two main ones used for observation. One on the top front of the skull and one on the crown of the head. These are the main ones that are observed during the baby's assessment. The posterior one at the crown will close completely at about 1-2 months of age, where the anterior (front) fontanel will close somewhere between 7-18 months.

The fontanels have a tough membrane that helps to protect the brain during the baby's 1st year, allowing room for brain and skull enlargement. It is not dangerous to touch this area of the head because the membrane is durable and will withstand normal pressure from touch. In fact, your nurse will be assessing the fontanels regularly for signs of dehydration or swelling.

Dehydration in babies can be detected by a sunken-in fontanel, along with other signs, such as decreased or no urine output and dry membranes in the mouth. This finding can help the nurse know that intervention is needed to increase the baby's breast milk or formula intake to correct this problem.

A raised or bulging fontanel, only when the baby is quiet and head up, can be serious indication of some type of brain or fluid swelling inside the skull or indication of infection. Immediate additional testing would be needed if this is observed from the assessment to rule out hydrocephalus (fluid build-up in the skull), encephalitis (swelling or inflammation of the brain), increased intercranial pressure, or meningitis (infection of the brain tissue.) Any one of these can be life-threatening if not found and treated quickly.

Bruising on head or face: When a baby comes out of mother forcefully (forceps or vacuum extraction) or delivers very quickly, the head and face may sustain surface bruising on the skin. Any part of the baby's head or face that bumps against the vaginal wall or ischial spines in the pelvis can become bruised due to the rapid delivery. Forehead, nose, ears, cheeks, and head are all susceptible to this trauma. If your baby does sustain this trauma, generally the bruising will begin to subside within the next few days and resolve on its own.

Birth trauma can also affect other body parts as well, including shoulders, arms, legs, hips, and feet. The bruising in these other regions will also resolve on its own.

Abrasions, scratches, and lacerations: Again, with rapid or forceful births, the scalp and face may sustain what appears to be scratches or abrasions. Most of the time, this will be more prevalent on the scalp as the head passes through the pelvis and scrapes against the ischial spines of mother's pelvis.

Lacerations may be noted upon cesarean deliveries, due to the scalpel nicking the head sometimes during surgery, especially if the doctor is moving quickly to get the baby delivered due to fetal distress. There may also be lacerations located on the buttocks or upper legs if the baby is in a breach or side-lying position at the time of surgery.

Another laceration on the back of the skull can be from internal monitors that are screwed into the surface of the scalp to monitor more accurately baby's toleration to labor.

There also may be facial abrasions or lacerations from the baby himself due to long fingernails at birth. When the baby extends and flexes their hands close to the face, these sharp nails will score the skin and cause surface scratches. Any of these abrasions or lacerations are evaluated by the pediatrician, and topical antibiotic ointment or steroid cream may be ordered to heal the site if needed.

Findings on the Eyes, Ears, and Face

Petechial hemorrhages: Due to the ocular pressure in the eyes and face from a tightened nuchal chord or facial presentation during a vaginal birth, petechial hemorrhages may be found in the eyes, face or scalp. Petechiae are little blood-filled spots on the surface of the eye or skin that will resolve themselves over time as the body breaks down these red blood cells and eliminates them.

Swollen eyes: Tightened nuchal chords and antibiotic eye ointment are the two common causes of swollen eyes or eyelids. Over the next few days the swelling will subside and resolve on its own.

Eye color: Most parents are already aware of the eye color of babies when they are born, which is usually a slate blue-gray color. But some darker-skinned babies, especially those with African, African American, Middle Eastern, Micronesian, Asian or Mexican/Spanish descents may present with dark-brown or brown-black eye color. Most lighter-skinned parents are usually guessing what the eye color will eventually be with their newborn, but that can continue to be a guessing game for some over the next several years.

It's hard to predict what the final eye color will be for the newborn, as eye color can change anywhere up to 6 years of age, but generally the permanent color of the newborn's eyes will be determined by the age of 1 year. And— just because mom has brown eyes and dad has brown eyes, that doesn't mean the baby will too. Eye color is determined by genetics, so depending on the grandparents or even great-grandparents, the eye color may have come from one of them.

Milia: Milia are white spots on the face and nose that look like little white-heads and are made up of keratin and sebaceous (oily) materials in the facial skin. These are benign and will go away on their own without any additional treatment.

Preauricular pits: These are small, pinpoint pits that are located on the upper front of the ear. They may be on one side or on both sides and mark the location of the sinus tract. Generally, these pits are benign and do not cause any problems, but can produce cysts or become infected later, or be associated with potential hearing deficits. Your baby will have a hearing screening done prior to discharge.

Preauricular cysts or tags: These are small mounds of tissue attached to the tragus, the little ear flap in front of the ear canal, or any part of the ear around it. They are also generally benign and do not cause any problems.

Either of these malformations may be found along with another abnormality during an assessment, therefore, a congenital workup may be in store to rule out potential congenital defects. But— if the cysts, tags, or pits are the only anomaly noted, then they are considered mild cosmetic abnormalities.

Skin Color and Conditions

Pink or pink undertones is the color we a looking for in a newborn when assessing their well-being. For the most part, this tells us that the baby is providing sufficient amount of oxygen needed for their body. There are also some other normal findings that are benign and cause no other concerns during assessments and are just noted. However, at various times the skin may tell us there is some underlying issue that may need to be addressed and further evaluated. Follow-up care with a specialist or additional treatment may be necessary to help correct the problem.

Here we will address the color of the skin with various changes and what they mean, then follow with visible deviations on the skin surface and define what they are. Remember, some are normal or routine findings, but others may be concerning or even need prompt medical care.

Acrocyanosis: This finding is normally observed occurring in newborns from the time the baby is born and only lasts a few days after birth. When the hands and feet take on a purplish or bluish tinge, the extremities are generally cold from exposure to lower temperatures in their environment, or when the baby is held tightly around the arms and legs during breastfeeding. This causes the baby's capillary bed in these extremities to constrict and shunt blood to the major organs. Covering up the feet and hands can help to correct this issue by providing warmth around the extremities.

When it's cold outside we normally wear gloves, hats and warm socks to keep our head, feet, and hands warm— for our extremities would get cold otherwise. This is the same principle for infants. Even though this phenomenon is common, it's important to keep those extremities warm for good circulation.

Circumoral cyanosis: Circumoral cyanosis is where there is a visible bluish tint to the skin around the mouth region, but not actually on the lips, and is a key concern for your hospital staff. Although this finding may be benign in most cases, this is a sign that there might be a hidden cardiac or pulmonary issue that needs immediate medical attention and intervention. If it is not evaluated and there is a health issue with your baby, it could be serious or even life-threatening if not treated.

If this is a temporary issue and the cyanosis around the mouth goes away, it may be due to an apneic (stop-breathing) episode or airway obstruction that is or can be resolved. If the baby continues to show circumoral cyanosis and is lethargic, limp, not feeding, irritable, or having breathing issues, then let your nurse know *immediately* so close observation and testing can be started.

Central cyanosis: This observation is one where quick intervention is necessary for the well-being of the baby. Cyanosis is where not only the extremities take on a purplish or bluish tinge, but the rest of the body takes this on too. This is an indicator to any healthcare worker that the baby is not breathing well or at all, and respiratory intervention is needed immediately.

This may indicate a cardiac, respiratory, metabolic, or neurologic disorder, and further testing and intensive care would be necessary to find the underlying cause of the cyanosis. If you observe this with your baby, let your nurse know *STAT!!*

Skin mottling: Cutis Mamorata is bluish, reddish or purplish marbled (blotchy) skin, which is noted with mottling, and can just be an indication the baby is cold, or circulation is beginning to increase along the surface of the skin. Wrapping the baby up in a blanket, if the baby is unwrapped for some time, or increasing the room temperature can most times remedy this issue. However, it can also be an indication, along with pallor (paleness), that there is an underlying infection, cardiac issue or poor circulation. Let your nurse know if you observe this in your baby so that additional medical diagnostic testing can be started if necessary.

Pallor: This is one that is not seen very often, but when it is observed then immediate medical attention is needed. This can be due to a maternal hemorrhage at delivery, an abrupting placenta (placenta pulling away from uterus while pregnant), placenta previa (placenta covering the cervix), and various other issues. These can cause anemia in the infant (low blood count, decreased hemoglobin, etc.) which can be life threatening to the infant. Generally, when it is known prior to delivery there is a maternal issue which may threaten the well-being of the baby, these newborns are immediately observed and tested quickly after delivery to determine what care is needed for a positive outcome.

Dusky skin: Generally, dusky skin is observed in premature newborns or infants whose brains are "forgetting to breathe" frequently or for extended periods of time. When this happens, babies need to be monitored by neonatal nurses continuously until the issue resolves on its own and close monitoring is no longer needed. This usually resolves when the immature breathing centers of the brain fully develop and start to function regularly on its own.

Bruising on body: Like bruising on the head and face, there can be some bruising on other body parts; most noticeably on the shoulders and forearms, but there can be some on the back, legs, or feet. Again, this can be from birth trauma: the forceful pulling or pushing down on the arms and shoulders during a shoulder dystocia (shoulders not wanting to deliver after the head is delivered) or pulling and tugging baby out during a cesarean section. Babies will sometimes have presenting body parts which may be coming out along with the head, such as a hand or arm, which tightens the space even more during delivery.

Any bruising from birth trauma with the head or face (discussed earlier) or with any other extremity will usually resolve rather quickly within the next few days.

Plethora or ruddiness: This is the medium to dark beefy red color of the infant's skin when they are not crying, and can affect 1-5% of infants born. Babies who are ruddy or plethoric may indicate the baby has too much blood volume and increased hematocrit counts (too many red blood cells). This can be due to delayed cord clamping, prematurity, LGA babies, infants of diabetic mothers, endocrine abnormalities, uterine hypoxia (decrease in oxygen to baby), and several other issues. The increased amount of red blood cells greater than 65% is called polycythemia.

Most babies (79-90%) will show no signs or ill effects of having this increased blood volume, but babies who are vomiting or feeding poorly, lethargic, tachypneic (continuous fast breathing), tachycardic (increased heart rate), hypoglycemic (low blood sugars), and/or jaundiced, along with other issues will need to be evaluated and monitored closely for complications that need intensive treatment.

With this finding, expect ahead of time that your baby will more than likely become jaundiced and require phototherapy to correct it. With having too many red blood cells the body does not need; the excess will need to be broken down and eliminated from the body. (*Read the information below regarding jaundice.)

Jaundice: Here is a condition that most parents have heard about at one time or another. This condition is common in newborns and is evaluated and tested in each newborn in our hospital, but some other hospitals or birthing centers may only test newborns who are observed to be greatly jaundiced from head to toe and in the whites of the eyes. Darker skinned babies are harder to make a visual observation with, and testing should be done routinely to prevent these babies from "slipping through the cracks." Since this is a common condition that is observed frequently in newborns, this will be discussed in greater detail than the previous findings.

Jaundice is the condition where the body breaks down red blood cells, turning it into bilirubin, which is filtered by the liver to be eliminated from the body mainly through the stool. If the baby has too few or no stools in the first few days, then the bilirubin backs up in the liver and causes the skin to begin turning yellowish in color. (Here's a _real_ widdle pumpkin!) Gradually, the baby will begin to look jaundiced in the face first, then it slowly moves down the body and increases in intensity and color. If the color gets darker yellow on the skin, then the whites of the baby's eyes will begin to turn yellow as well. When this happens, it is a good indication that the bilirubin levels are too high and needs to be treated. This is called hyperbilirubinemia.

Lab testing is the first step in evaluating the intensity of the jaundice and helps to determine if further treatment is necessary. Blood is collected and tested for bilirubin, and the results, along with the age of the baby (in hours), are calculated to see if they fall in the treatment category, if they need a recheck of the bilirubin levels again soon, or if nothing at all needs to be done.

If treatment is needed, then the baby's eyes will be covered with a mask to protect the eyes, be placed under phototherapy (ultraviolet) lights continuously, and have bilirubin levels re-checked at intervals to determine if phototherapy is to be continued or stopped. The baby is placed under the light after they are stripped down to their diaper and eye covers are placed on him or her. This is to protect the baby's eyes from the phototherapy lights which can be damaging to them. The baby will only be removed from the lights when they are feeding, which is usually limited to 30 minutes at a time, so the baby can get the maximum exposure to the lights during treatment.

If the baby is breastfeeding, then usually supplementation of formula is ordered along with breastfeeding to increase fluid volume and help with increasing stool production. (Unless mother's milk is in, then supplementation may be needed.) With increased stool production and phototherapy, the bilirubin will begin to be eliminated from the baby's system and decrease the levels of bilirubin quicker. When you see the baby's stools after beginning phototherapy, they usually have a glowing *green* cast to them. So, do not be alarmed when you see this.

The treatment method for hyperbilirubinemia through phototherapy is a quick and easy fix for this condition. If a baby is jaundiced and bilirubin levels are high, but are not treated, then this puts the baby at risk for kernicterus. This is when very high levels of bilirubin are deposited on the brain tissue and may cause irreversible damage. If treatment is not initiated in a timely manner, hyperbilirubinemia can be toxic to the nervous system and can lead to brain damage or death.

Hyperbilirubinemia usually is detected and treated while in the hospital setting right after birth, but the condition can be slow to develop and happen after discharge. Keep an eye out for any of the symptoms noted above and contact your pediatrician immediately for further evaluation.

If the bilirubin levels are not high enough to be treated, but the baby is visibly jaundiced, the pediatrician may have you place the baby in an area of indirect sunlight to help break down the bilirubin they have, and eliminate the need for phototherapy. Babies can develop jaundice up to 2 weeks after discharge from the hospital, so keep an eye on this and contact the pediatrician if it worsens.

Harlequin color change: This is noticed when a baby is lying on his or her side and the visible side of the skin is lighter or paler than the side to which the baby is lying on, and a demarcation line is in the center of the baby. This is a benign condition that is unknown why it happens, however, it can occur in 10% of newborns and generally resolves on its own.

Surface Skin Conditions/Lesions

Here is where we discuss the more common visible surface skin conditions which are noted during the head-to-toe assessment at birth, or that develop over the next few days. Again, some of these findings are benign and need no treatment, but others may need further evaluation or follow-up care with a specialist after discharge.

Skin Conditions

Newborn rash: Erythema Toxicum Neonatorum or newborn rash are the formation of small reddened papules (with a lighter or whitened center) on the body of the baby usually found on the back, trunk, arms, and legs, but may also be found on the face as well. This occurs in up to 72% of newborns and can range from mild to covering most of the body. (Some parents are concerned their baby may have contracted chicken pox when they see this.) It is thought that it occurs from the immature pilosebaceous glands (hair follicles and oil glands) activating, but it has not been proven. This is a benign condition which usually resolves within 5-7 days without further treatment. I would recommend not putting baby oil on the skin as this might make the problem worse.

Sucking blisters: You may notice on the baby's hand or forearm it looks as if there is a blister or had been a blister, but it popped and is drying. It is not found on any other part of the baby's body, just in these areas. While the baby was still inside the womb, they have been sucking on their hands or forearms, creating sucking blisters. If they break open in the womb, the blisters will begin to heal, which is why you might see what looks to be a drying out blister at the site. Generally, these areas will resolve on their own without any treatment.

Dry, cracked, and/or peeling skin: Newborns who have been "overcooking" in mom's oven (more than 40 weeks), the vernix is beginning to disintegrate prematurely as a protective barrier. These post-term babies, or even darker-skinned term newborns are at greater risk for having dry, cracked, and/or peeling skin.

When the baby has been inside the womb for too long, the vernix begins to disintegrate or break down. As this occurs, the baby is exposed to the amniotic fluid which begins to dehydrate the skin, causing the dryness, skin cracking or peeling. Use lotion frequently on the exposed skin to help rehydrate it.

Lanugo (large amount of body hair): Babies are born with soft, downy unpigmented hair covering their bodies, but some darker skinned babies will have a larger than normal amount of this hair and it will be darker. The function of this hair is to aid the vernix by allowing it to "cling" onto the hair and help protect the skin. This hair most often will slough off within the next few days to a few weeks after birth.

Birth Marks and Lesions

There are several types of birth marks, which are noted after delivery during the head-to-toe-assessment. Stork bites, port-wine stains, Mongolian (slate-gray spots), nevi, and freckles are some of the main birthmarks found. Some are pigmented (having color), others are vascular (from blood circulation) or from abnormal skin development. Here we'll go over each one and discuss what, if anything, needs to be done to correct it.

Stork bites: Nevus simplex or stork bites are pinkish red blanchable patches on the skin surface. They occur in 40-60% of newborns, and may be singular, or found in multiples on the baby. Common locations where found are the eyelids, forehead, and nape of neck. Less common are the nose, lip, scalp, and back. These are largely benign and will fade within the next couple years, however, the nape of neck may remain permanently.

Slate-gray spots: Congenital Dermal Melanocytosis or slate-gray spots are generally found on dark-skinned newborns: Asians – 85 to 100%, Blacks – greater than 60%, and Hispanics – 47 to 70%. However, less than 10% of white newborns can also present with this finding. (These were previously known as Mongolian spots, but the term has been changed for political correctness.)

These slate-gray spots can also appear to be more greenish-blue or brown in color, and be located most commonly above or on the buttocks. In some instances, they may appear on the shoulder area as well. Mistakenly, these spots may look to an observer as bruising, which is not the case. However, there have been false reports of child abuse when seen in these areas of the body.

Congenital Dermal Melanocytosis usually fades away within the first year or two of life, but some remain up to the age of 10, and approximately 3% remain through adulthood.

Congenital melanocytic nevi: Occur in 0.2 to 2.1 % of babies and appear as brown or black flat areas on the skin, although they may be raised areas as well. This type of birthmark has the potential for malignancy. Pediatricians will monitor these areas closely if they are small (0.5 cm or less) for additional growth in size. Medium sized (0.5 to 7 cm) will be referred to a dermatologist for evaluation, and large ones (7 cm or above will be removed by a dermatologist and be evaluated for recurrence.

Nevus flammeus or port-wine stains: Occurs in 0.3% of babies and are dark red to purple in color and are flat on the skin. These are readily noticeable and do not fade over time, in fact they may deepen in color. Pulse dye laser therapy may help to eliminate or reduce the visibility of these birth marks and are best if treated by the age of 12 months.

If these port-wine stains affect the area of the eye (ophthalmic distribution of the trigeminal nerve), these babies are a risk for glaucoma. This might occur alone or with Sturge-Weber syndrome, which might cause mental deficits and need to be further evaluated. For babies not affected by Sturge-Weber syndrome, they are referred to an ophthalmologist for testing and monitoring.

Hemangiomas: These are referred to as strawberry hemangiomas, which are lesions that may only be noticed as unmarked pale patches of skin, and occur in 1.2 to 2.6% of babies. These are generally benign and require no further treatment. They may enlarge, or become blood-filled raised areas on the skin, but are usually still benign and will resolve on their own over time.

If they compress the eye, airway or vital organs, then immediate evaluation is needed in the newborn period. Rare large or multiple hemangiomas can be life threatening, and would be immediately evaluated and treated by the care team at birth.

Immature Body Systems

When babies are born at term most parents believe their bodies will function just like they should, which is why they are surprised when certain things happen or come up in the days or weeks after birth. Just because they are good enough to come out of the oven doesn't mean they are "fully cooked." So here we will go over some of the more common systems that are affected and are not at full functionality.

Eyes: These take a long time to complete their transition. From changes in eye color to seeing the entire world as we see it, they have months and sometimes years to make necessary changes. For the most part, the eyes will be fully functioning and sending appropriate signals to the brain by 6-8 months of age.

For the newborn, they can only see things in black, white and gray as well as only see approximately 6-10 inches away from them. They also see things blurry because their brain hasn't yet fully processed what they are seeing. Light, shapes, and movement are about all they can detect at this time, so bring your baby in close range with your face. Up close time is very good for your baby's eye development and facial recognition.

The muscles in the newborn eyes are not coordinated enough to control movement early on. You may see her cross her eyes or roll his eyes up into the back of his head. This uncoordinated eye movement will improve over time as the muscles strengthen. You will notice this when he starts tracking things and reaching out to them. This eye/hand coordination starts developing within two to three months of age.

Liver: One of the main causes of newborn jaundice is the immature function of the liver. The function of the liver is to filter out toxins and remove waste from our bodies, among other things, but the newborn liver cannot filter out things quickly enough. This puts them at risk for developing newborn jaundice, as the liver cannot remove the bilirubin fast enough and transfer it to the intestines for removal.

There are several common factors that put the newborn at risk for developing jaundice:

- premature or preterm births
- significant bruising on the head or body
- breastfeeding (smaller quantities of milk causing decreased or lessened intestinal movement and stooling)
- differing blood types in mother and baby
- infections.

Nervous system: Babies tend to jerk or startle easily, whether they are awake or asleep, and do not have full control over this. It is a common occurrence in newborn's response to stimuli around them.

Benign sleep myoclonus is where the baby jerks or flails their arms or legs during sleep, but does not show signs of this when awakened.

Jitteriness is when the baby is awake and reacts to a sudden noise or their crib or car seat is bumped and is usually very brief in duration. They may also appear jittery when in a full out crying jag, such as when you change a diaper or bathe the baby. Whether awake or asleep, if you hold down the flailing limb gently and the jerking or flailing stops, then this indicates immature nervous system. If it continues, along with eye rolling, when you hold them down then this can be an indication of some neurological issue that needs to be further evaluated.

Newborn babies may also be jittery for another reason, but this is usually a little more prolonged in duration and is noted when they are quiet or sleeping. This may be an indication the baby is having low levels of blood sugars (hypoglycemia), in which jitteriness is a sign. If this happens, let your nurse or doctor know, and if you are unsure whether it is immature nervous system or jitteriness from hypoglycemia go ahead and ask.

Gastrointestinal system (gastric reflux): One of the most common occurrences with newborn babies is spitting up, whether it's formula or breastmilk it doesn't matter. The immature esophageal lower sphincter is associated with frequent relaxation, thus allowing for the formula or breastmilk to come back up easily. The newborn may spit up or vomit when they are burped, or they may just "spit up" on their own without any warning. As long as baby is gaining weight, feeds well, and is not irritable, then there is no cause for concern. Some babies are just "happy spitters" and will continue to do this for several months, usually resolving around 12 months.

Spitting up or vomiting substantial amounts of breastmilk or formula can be associated with overfeeding. If we are eating food, it takes 20 minutes for our brain to realize we are full and to stop eating. If a baby sucks down a bottle way too fast or continuously breastfeeds on a full breast without taking a break, he or she will over distend the stomach and it will regurgitate because it is overly full, thus vomiting up what was taken in. One way to eliminate this from happening is to slow down the feeding. That means taking the bottle out of the baby's mouth or disengaging the baby from the breast periodically to slow the feeding down. Take this time to burp the baby well (it may take several minutes to relieve all the air— as they may take in a large amount of it because they are "snarfing" it down fast— so give it a little time.) By slowing the feeding down, the brain and stomach connection will kick in, and the baby will become full and not overfull.

If your baby continues to have gastric reflux issues, your pediatrician may suggest sitting the baby in a more upright position, say in a car seat, non-moving bouncy seat, or unmoving swing for 30-45 minutes. This will allow the stomach to begin gastric emptying, and reduce some reflux issues your baby may continue to have. If this doesn't help, there may be other underlying causes to this problem, and further evaluation by your pediatrician may be necessary.

Preterm or Premature Newborn

If you think the normal term newborn has immature body systems, it even more so with ones born too early. Premature newborns are those delivered before 37 weeks, usually due to maternal issues such as:

- infection of amniotic fluid or lower genital tract;

- preeclampsia;

- pregnancy of multiples;

- previous preterm delivery;

- problems with the cervix, uterus or placenta;

- poor nutrition;

- smoking, drinking, or illicit drug use during pregnancy;

- diabetes (gestational or chronic);

- interval of less than 6 months between pregnancies;

- underweight or overweight during pregnancy;

- multiple miscarriages or abortions;

- life trauma such as death in family or domestic abuse;

- physical injury or trauma, such as a car accident.

The earlier the baby is born before its due date puts them at higher risk of the previous mentioned issues, but also a host of others. So, keeping the "bun in the oven" as long as possible would be the goal of your obstetrician for a better overall outcome. 39 weeks or greater is the goal, but we all know that is not always possible, as some women's bodies just cannot or will not do it.

For those out there who are still pregnant and reading this, please *do not* be tempted to force your doctor to deliver you earlier than you should deliver. I know that there are some that are "tired of being pregnant" or want to plan the delivery around their own schedule, but look at all the possible issues your baby may have to deal with if born too early. Just continue to read and it might quickly change your mind.

Respiratory (breathing) difficulties: The most common issue for preterm or premature infants is breathing difficulties. Term babies are born with a substance called surfactant in their lungs. The earlier the baby is born, the more likely they will not have this substance, causing a lack of expansion and contraction of the lungs to move oxygen throughout their system. This causes Respiratory Distress Syndrome (RDS), and the earlier they are, the more likely this will cause further respiratory complications as they get older.

If the neonate is 34 weeks or less gestation, and if the doctor has enough time prior to delivery or the labor can be stopped or postponed, the mother will be given one betamethasone injection and another 24 hours later. This steroid helps speed up the baby's manufacturing of the surfactant and to help decrease respiratory issues once the baby is born.

For those over 34 weeks, the baby is more likely to have some or most of the surfactant production, but they are still at risk for respiratory issues. For each week of delayed delivery, the risk for respiratory distress issues goes down, thus less treatment or intervention and less long-term effects.

Another factor at play is the risk of apneic episodes (delay in breathing for more than 20 seconds). The brain centers which control breathing are also premature, therefore, not functioning as they would with a term infant. The delay in neurologic synapses (brain communication) does not signal the lungs to "take a breath", therefore, decreasing oxygen supply to the body. Again, the earlier the baby is born, the greater the risk for apneic episodes and longer duration.

Respiratory issues for preterm babies also puts them at higher risk for SIDS (Sudden Infant Death Syndrome), which we will discuss at length under the section, *Other Topics for Discussion*.

Feeding difficulties: When the preterm or premature baby is born, they are not driven to eat any time soon (as they are not supposed to eat yet) or if they do, they get tired quickly from exerting energy to feed. Also, they have problems with sucking and swallowing coordination due to immaturity. This can make breastfeeding difficult, so in those cases pumping and providing breast milk for feedings would be beneficial.

For those who can breast or bottle feed, limiting the feeding to 30 minutes can reduce fatigue and lessen the calories burned up by feeding. If a baby is unable to breast or bottle feed and is needing nutrition, they may have a nasogastric tube placed through the nose and into the stomach to give feedings. When the baby is ready to breast or bottle feed, then these babies will be weaned slowly until they are able to take all feedings by breast or bottle.

Gastrointestinal (stomach/intestinal) issues: Since premature babies are not supposed to take their feedings by mouth yet, the immature stomach and intestinal tract may have issues as well. NEC (Necrotizing Enterocolitis) is one of the more possible serious complications. The cells lining the intestines can become injured from the feedings and cause intestinal cells to die off, therefore, causing the intestinal tissue to die. Babies receiving breast milk have a decreased chance of having NEC or other complications, but are still susceptible to this very serious one.

Hypothermia (low body temperature): Due to the decrease in brown fat stores for heat production and the decrease in white fat for insulation, premature babies are at higher risk for decreased temperatures. They also lose heat more readily from the skin surface due to greater surface-to-body weight ratios. The more calories the baby uses during feeding, crying, breathing, etc., the greater chance for hypothermia, and lead to hypoglycemia (low blood sugars).

Because of the expending of calories to try and maintain adequate body heat, premature babies do not tend to gain weight very well, which is why they are kept in a warm environment such as an incubator or warming bed.

Hypoglycemia (low blood sugar): Preterm or premature babies are at three times greater risk of developing low blood sugars. The abrupt loss of maternal-provided glucose during pregnancy is the main factor in hypoglycemia in preterm babies. Preterm babies also have decreased glycogen stores due to the abrupt loss, along with impaired ability to make glucose because of an immature pancreas. Due to quickly using up glycogen stores for energy, preterm babies can become hypoglycemic very quickly, so monitoring of this is begun within the first hour of birth and continually monitored until glucose stores are adequate and remain so with feedings. (This means the baby will be subjected to heel sticks frequently to draw a small amount of blood each time to check glucose levels.)

If a preterm or premature baby cannot maintain adequate glucose levels, they will be given an IV, and glucose will be administered until they can wean off with feedings and maintain adequate levels on their own.

Cardiac (heart) issues: One of the most common heart issues for premature babies are PDAs (patent ductus arteriosus), which is the persistent opening of two major blood vessels leading from the heart. This often closes on its own with term babies, but with premature babies it may not, which can cause too much blood to flow through the heart and cause complications, including heart failure if left untreated.

The other common issues along with a PDA is low blood pressure. Medications, changes in IV fluid amounts, and possible blood transfusions can help correct this.

Brain issues: If a baby is born too premature, they are at greater risk for brain bleeds, especially if vaginally delivered. The additional intercranial pressure (pressure in the skull) during vaginal deliveries and the delicate brain structures of the early baby make them at risk for this.

Even if delivered by cesarean, these delicate brain structures and vessels can break, leading to what's called an intercranial hemorrhage. Most will resolve on their own, but others may have larger brain bleeds which can cause the cells in the brain to die, causing permanent brain injury. The large fluid accumulation would require surgery to relieve the fluid, thus decreasing potential brain damage.

Blood issues: Anemia and jaundice are two of the most common blood issues with premature babies. Anemia can be caused due to lower blood volume and repeated blood draws for labs or glucose checks, thus putting them at risk.

Jaundice, in the premature newborn, which discussed previously under the section *Skin Color and Conditions*, is caused by the very immature liver not transporting the bilirubin to the intestines for removal through the stools. This causes the bilirubin to back up which causes jaundice. Phototherapy would be necessary to help the body rid itself of the excess bilirubin, as their system will not be able to correct this on its own.

Immune system: Due to the underdeveloped immune system in prematurity, these babies are at higher risk for acquiring infections. With the inability to fight infections, preemies are at risk for developing neonatal sepsis, which can be life threatening.

Visitors in the Neonatal ICU will be limited to parents, and only if they are not sick. Strict hand hygiene and gowning will be required during visits. Only with preterm babies at lower risk will grandparents and siblings be allowed to visit, and again if they are not sick and also follow hand hygiene protocols.

Q & A on Your Baby

Here are some frequent questions or concerns parents have with their new-borns in the post-delivery period. (And some are just thoughts that the parents had, but were not correct on their own assessment.) Again, most are normal and will resolve on their own and are nothing to be concerned with, but if you just aren't sure or your gut feeling is telling you there is something wrong, *do not* hesitate to ask your nurse to check for you.

Q   *My baby's breathing is really fast, but it slows down again… Why is that?*

A   Babies do not breath regularly like you and I do— *yet.* They will breath fast, then slow down, then speed up again. This is normal, and is also why your nurse assesses the baby's breathing for a full minute, instead of only a few seconds like they do with you. We want the respirations to be between 40-60 per minute, but if you are not sure if they are breathing too fast just ask your nurse to check. It's better to be sure everything is fine than to worry about it. If it continues to be fast and doesn't seem to slow down, this could be an indication your baby is having some respiratory distress or infection and may need to be fur-ther evaluated. So, again ask if you are not sure.

Q   *I worry that my baby might stop breathing while he sleeps… How can I check on him without disturbing him?*

A   There are two things you can check without disturbing your sleeping baby. One is to place your hand on your baby's stomach. Babies are tummy breathers, and this is how you can feel if your baby is breathing. Another thing is to look at your baby's skin color. If baby is *pink*, not pale, dusky, or blue— but *pink,* then your baby is breathing. I always tell my parents, *"A pink baby is a breathing baby."*

Q   *Oh… isn't that a cute little noise my baby is making… It sounds like she/ he is humming or singing…*

A   This is not necessarily the case if your baby is "singing" or "humming". Sometimes babies might "hum" or kind of "whine" while they are breathing out. This may be due to a couple of things. The first may be due to the baby having a belly ache. Too much food or amniotic fluid in the gut may make your baby kind of lightly "hum" or "whine" like you or I would with a belly ache. It hurts— therefore, they make a little noise. But if the noise is like a loud "humming", where you can hear it pretty well, it's a good chance your baby may be having a little respiratory distress. It's a good idea to ask your nurse to check this out for you any time you hear it. It's better to be sure your baby isn't having difficulty breathing, rather than ignoring it.

Q   *My doctor/nurse said my baby has a heart murmur, but didn't explain it… What does that mean?*

A   When your baby is born, the circulation in the baby's heart changes and the *ductus arteriosus* starts to close-up. As it is closing, the blood "swishes" through the hole causing what we call a murmur. In most cases, this will resolve within the next day or two, and the murmur will no longer be detected with a stethoscope.

Sometimes the ductus does not close all the way, and the baby may have a murmur for months or possibly years. Usually, this is benign and doesn't cause any additional problems.

If the murmur is loud and is noted at every assessment by each nurse and doctor assessing the baby, blood pressures will be checked to make sure they are within normal limits. If they are high, this can indicate there may be an underlying problem with the structure of the heart and further evaluation with a pediatric cardiologist would be necessary.

If your nurse or doctor did not explain in detail what to expect with the heart murmur, it is likely this was a benign murmur, what we call a "soft" murmur, which will resolve on its own. With these "soft" murmurs, some nurses and doctors have difficulty even hearing them, so you may not be informed by every care provider that there is one.

Q   *I'm afraid I'll hurt the baby if I move the umbilical cord...*

A   The umbilical cord does not have any nerve endings within the cord itself. It consists of a gelatinous substance called Wharton's Jelly and two arteries and a vein. As the cord dries it will fall off, so there is no concern in moving the cord out of the way, like during a diaper change. The only surface where your baby would have nerve endings would be the pink skin area around the umbilical cord, and this isn't moved much.

Q   *Why does my baby's belly button around the cord pop out when she/he cries? My baby's belly button area is sticking out!!*

A   When you baby cries, sneezes, or pushes during a bowel movement, the umbilical cord area may pop out a little farther than most, due to increased inter-thoracic pressure and a separation in the rectus muscle on the abdomen. This is common and usually resolves on its own by age 4, but may need corrective surgery if it becomes tender, swollen, reddened or your baby is in obvious pain or is vomiting.

This is more common in African-American, premature, or low birth weight babies.

Q   *Why does my baby lose weight after delivery?*

A   When your baby is born, there is additional fluid along with all the meconium (stool) that has accumulated throughout the intestinal tract. When your baby begins to urinate and stool they start to lose weight. Babies that are formula fed generally lose less weight than breastfed babies, due to the volume of nourishment they receive during feedings. Breastfed babies may only get a few drops to few teaspoonfuls of colostrum verses the 10-30 milliliters of formula at any given feeding.

As long as your baby is *not* losing more than 10% of their birth weight, he or she is doing well. The weight loss will begin to slow down, stop, and then gradually begin trending upward again. By the time your baby is a week old, he or she should be back up to his or her birth weight or higher.

Q   *Why does my baby sound "congested"? Is she/he getting a cold? Why is she/ he sneezing a lot?*

A   No, your baby is not getting a cold so soon after birth, but the congestion is due to all the amniotic fluid she/he has been surrounded by in the uterus. Your baby sucks and swallows this fluid as well as "breathing it in", so its normal to have some retained fluid in the nasal passages and upper airways. Your baby will sneeze frequently to help clear out the nasal passages, and the congestion will resolve over the next few days.

If the nose is clogged up, your baby cannot sneeze well enough to get rid of the congestion, and it is interfering with feeding, it might help for your nurse to administer some saline nasal drops to help soften up the mucus and then remove it with a nasal aspirator (the little "sucky-thing").

Q   *Why is my baby gagging and spitting up stuff? I'm really concerned with my baby choking.*

A   Again, your baby has been swimming in amniotic fluid for a long time, and while inside she/he was practicing sucking and swallowing to get ready to feed after birth. There may be some amniotic fluid still in the stomach after delivery, especially if they deliver very fast vaginally or deliver by cesarean section. This is due to not getting "squeezed" enough during birth which helps to push out the excess fluid. And sometimes babies take a gulp of fluid as they deliver, which adds more fluid to the stomach.

This amniotic fluid does not digest. It sits on the stomach, turns to mucus, and upsets the stomach, causing your baby to throw up this fluid. It may be thick or thin, clear, whitish, yellowish, and may even have red or brown (old) blood mixed in. Some indicators of your baby getting ready to throw up this fluid would be getting frothy or bubbly around the mouth, gulping like they are about to throw up but don't want to (just like you or I would if we were going to vomit), or gagging like they are choking on the fluid in the back of the throat. Any time after you start seeing any of these indicators, there's a good chance the vomiting will begin. If you see anything that might be concerning to you, just ask your nurse.

The scariest thing for parents when the baby starts to spit up this fluid is when their baby starts choking on it. Sit your baby upright or leaning forward and pat his back. *Do not* be overly gentle on this as you want to help them spit up the fluid easily, but you also don't want to pound on the back hard. Keeping the baby in an upright position for a little while, say on your shoulder or chest, will also help to get your baby through this choking episode.

If there is any fluid still in the baby's mouth or nose, gently use the nasal aspirator bulb (the little "sucky-thing") to remove the fluid. Depress the bulb first with your thumb, place it in the baby's mouth around the cheeks and front of the mouth, then slow release the bulb as you move the tip around in the mouth. Once you have removed some fluid, depress the bulb quickly into a blanket or burp cloth to remove it from the aspirator and repeat if necessary. Always do the mouth first, then the nose, as you want to move from a "clean" area to a "dirty" area.

Then be sure to clean the aspirator out with warm soapy water to be ready for the next time.

Sometimes when the baby is choking *he panics*, because he has spit up fluid not only in his mouth but through his nose as well. When he cannot breathe, he might stiffen up his body or go rigid, clamp his mouth tight, and get a panicked look on his face. If you cannot get him to open his mouth to take a breath, use your emergency call light to summon help quickly. The longer he goes without taking a breath, he will be deprived of oxygen and will quickly start turning blue.

Once parents experience this, they get very nervous about keeping their baby in the room with them when they are sleeping. If your hospital will allow you to send your baby to the nursery to be watched while you are getting some sleep, you may rest more comfortably. However, if your hospital follows strict "rooming in", you will have to keep your baby with you. Or, if you prefer to keep your baby with you and don't want to send your baby to the nursery, that is okay. Have your spouse or significant other stay with you so you can switch off watching your baby while the other sleeps. This way your baby is continually being monitored and you can call at the first sign of hazardous choking. Rest assured this issue should resolve itself completely prior to your discharge, or within the first 24-48 hours after delivery.

Q   *Why is my baby wide awake at night when I want to go to sleep?*

A   Think back to when you were pregnant and the time when your baby was the most active. Usually when you were settled down and resting, especially at night, is when your baby would start doing summersaults.

When you were up moving around during the day, you were lulling your baby with your movement. When you were resting, your baby woke up and started moving. This is your baby's wake-sleep cycle, and it will continue for some time after birth.

If you mistakenly think you will get your baby on a schedule more in tune with yours, good luck with that! You will find your baby has other ideas when it comes to play time— possibly for a long while. If you do manage to make this work, then you are very lucky indeed, but— in reality— this does not happen very often.

Q   *Why is my baby crying so much? I don't know what he/she wants…*

A   There may be several factors which can explain why your baby is inconsolable and won't stop crying. Here's a list of several things which might be the cause of your baby's crankiness:

- I'm hungry, so feed me!

- My diaper is "dirty" and I don't like sitting in a mushy mess!

- I'm too hot, so take off the extra blanket!

- I'm too cold, so wrap me up!

- Something is poking me! (check the diaper area, umbilical cord stump, and clothing)

- I'm about to explode, so burp me!

- I'm overstimulated from all the visitors passing me around!

- I don't want to be put in the crib, so hold me!

- You are acting very nervous around me and it's making me nervous!!

- I just scratched myself with my sharp nails… and it *hurts!*

- It hurts to pee since my "weenie" was whacked (circumcised)!

- I just want my mommy!!

This is a list of the most common reasons for babies to cry, until your baby gets what she/he wants or needs. This is the only method of communication your baby has to "tell" you what is upsetting him or her, you just need to interpret what it is. Usually, if you work your way down this list you will find what the cause of the crying is about, and your baby will begin calming down.

But there may be other factors that play into this as well. If the mother was a smoker or used drugs (this is unfortunate, but it does happen) the baby has now been cut off from receiving this on a continual basis, so they get irritable and cry on a frequent basis until they finish going through "withdrawal." This may require medical intervention if this is a matter of concern for the pediatrician.

Q   *What are some of the ways I can try to quiet my baby when she's crying and won't calm down?*

A   There is a method which has been successful in calming crying babies, and that is *"The 5 S's"*. These are swaddling, shushing, swinging, side or stomach position (not during sleep time), and sucking. Each one can be very affective in getting your baby to relax and calm down.

Swaddling is the next best thing for babies to feel like they did when they were in the womb: all warm, cozy and safe. By swaddling, your baby is wrapped tightly, which keeps arms from flailing around and startling him or her.

Wrap your baby tightly in a blanket, as shown in the hospital. Once you go home, just do this when your baby is fussy or during sleep time to help soothe your baby. Your baby shouldn't be wrapped like this all the time; your baby needs to get used to being free from binding and relax in their surroundings. And remember— to lay your baby on his or her back for safe sleep.

Side or stomach position is a terrific way to soothe your fussy baby, but not during sleep time. Back sleeping is the only safe way for that. Holding your baby on their side or over your shoulder or on their stomach across your arm will help to soothe your baby in no time.

Shushing is a great way to quiet your fussy baby as well. The baby is used to hearing the shush of the blood flow around him or her while in your womb, so naturally the white noise will help with that.

Placing your mouth close to your baby's ear and using a continual "*shuuuuush*" sound will help to quiet him or her. Also, any other "white noise" with a continual sound will help to soothe your baby as well. There are some CDs, MP3 products, or phone apps out there which produce white noise specifically for babies, but if you don't want that, then the "*shuuuuuuush*" by his or her ear will work just as well.

Swinging your baby back and forth is another great way to calm your baby. For months, he or she has been swung back and forth when your body was moving during the pregnancy, so naturally swinging your baby back and forth will make it like he or she is in the womb again.

Supporting his or her head and neck, swing your baby and inch or two side to side, back and forth. This will mimic the movements in the womb and help soothe a fussy baby.

Sucking is another way to help calm your baby when he or she is fussy. It is relaxing for some babies to continually suck, which helps to soothe them. It is obvious you cannot put your baby to breast or put a bottle in his or her mouth every time your baby gets fussy, so the alternative is to use a finger or pacifier if continual sucking is what she or he is craving.

These methods all work well, but some may work better than others. You just have to try them to find the perfect fit for you and your baby, and you can continue to use them when you go home from the hospital. But— be sure during this trying time of fussiness *not* to shake your baby in anger or frustration!! Try remaining calm while trying any or all these methods, as your baby will pick up the calm vibe from you and will attempt to calm down as well.

Q   *Why does my baby cry every time I put him/her in the crib?*

A   Babies know what they like and if they haven't really been put down in their bed since they have been born, they generally don't want to be put down. They like those *"nice warm arms"* versus that *"cold, hard bed."* This is what we fondly call… "a bed allergy."

This doesn't mean you can never put your baby down, in fact, it's a good idea if you do. Let your baby cry for a little while in the crib and see if baby can soothe his or herself and fall asleep. Don't be tempted to pick him or her up at the very first whimper, otherwise, they will quickly learn *that* is all he or she needs to do for you to pick him or her up. Give baby a few minutes, and if he or she do not seem to be relaxing and the crying is starting to escalate, then go ahead and pick your baby up. This may be a battle for a while, even after you go home, but babies will learn if given time.

Also, when your baby is rooming-in with you in the hospital, he or she is in close proximity to you. Your baby can hear you talking to others and can smell you, so baby knows you're near, and then what does he or she want— MOMMY! So, your baby will cry because baby wants to be near you and held by you, or wants to be fed by you. That mother-baby bond is very strong (since you've been constantly together for the last nine months), so dad— don't be upset if baby doesn't necessarily want you. This is a natural survival instinct with baby.

When you go home, if your baby is placed in a room and you walk away, sometime this makes it easier for your baby to relax and self-soothe. Once mom is no longer within range of smell or sound, your baby can sometimes relax and fall asleep once all his or her needs are met.

Do not be tempted to put your baby in bed with you to co-sleep just to calm him or her down. This is a dangerous practice to get started as it has been shown that co-sleeping with your baby puts them at risk for SIDS (Sudden Infant Death Syndrome). It is best to have a crib or bed to place baby in, and it can be placed beside the bed, if needed, for easy access.

Q   *My baby has very long nails... do you have nail clippers to clip them?*

A   I believe most, if not all, hospitals are like ours, in that we do not have clippers or scissors to cut babies nails. Cutting or clipping nails are considered a "surgical procedure" because of the potential for skin breakage and/or infection, so we do not provide this service.

However, if you have your own set or someone brings you a set while you are in the hospital, you can do this one on your own. Catch your baby while asleep, as the hands are more relaxed during this time. While holding the hand, take your thumb and place it on the baby's finger or thumb by the nail bed and gently pull the skin away from the nail. This will keep you from clipping the end of the finger or thumb. If you are too worried about clipping the nails, you can use an emery board (usually comes with nail clippers) and file the nail down. Use the same method described above to do this.

If this is not possible while in the hospital, most of the gowns or t-shirts provided for your use have hand covers built-in to them. This will help keep your baby from scratching themselves until you are able to do this at home.

Q   *If I need to check my baby's temperature when I go home, how do I do that safely?*

A   Checking a rectal temperature is not recommended anymore since there is a potential for perforating the bowel if not careful. After our first temperature check at delivery, which is rectally, we switch to checking the baby's temp axillary (under the arm) for all future temperature checks.

When you check your baby's temperature this way, place the thermometer in the baby's arm pit in the center, and press the shoulder down snuggly to the body. This helps to make a seal and get a more accurate temperature reading. Your baby may fuss when you do this because it's either uncomfortable or he or she just might not like the shoulder being held down. This is okay, since you are only doing this for a few seconds until the thermometer gives you a reading. If your baby is running a temperature of at least 100.4 and you call the doctor, be sure to tell them how you took the temperature.

If your physician wants you to take a rectal temperature instead, here are the steps you need to take:

- Make sure your thermometer is clean. Either use alcohol and a cotton ball or wash with soap and water first;

- Use some petroleum jelly on the end to make the entrance into the bottom easier;

- Remove the baby's diaper and push the legs up towards the ears, like you do during a diaper change, and hold them during the check to keep baby from wiggling around;

- Place the tip of the thermometer in the rectum only about a half inch to ¾" or until the metal tip is no longer visible;

- Once you have a reading on the thermometer, remove and replace your baby's diaper;

- Give the information to the doctor of the reading and method you took for the temperature

If your taking your baby's temperature to check for a fever and your baby is wrapped in a blanket or has several layers of clothing on, be sure to unwrap the baby or remove a layer or two and wait about 20 minutes before taking the temperature. The baby may have been just overly heated from this and not actually running a fever. If your baby is running a temperature, then the removal of clothing or blankets will not cool the baby down much and you will get a more accurate temperature for the doctor.

It is not recommended for you to use the auditory (ear) thermometer on your newborn, in fact it's not recommended until they are at least 6 months old, as the ear canal may not be big enough for an accurate reading. Also, temperature strips for the forehead and pacifiers with built-in thermometers are not accurate, so do not rely on these.

Feeding Your Baby During Your Hospital Stay

Nutrition and nourishment is essential for optimal growth and development for your newborn. To achieve this, you must start by feeding your baby on a routine basis— and around the clock. Most parents already know this before the baby is born, so mental preparedness for routine lifestyle changes are already in place. But for those of you who are not aware, babies need to be fed every few hours--- 1 ½ to 3 hours or on demand for breastfed babies, and every 3-4 hours for formula fed babies. This will continue for several months after you have returned home, so resting in between feedings is essential for your health and wellbeing. You're in for the long haul, but parents do manage to make it through until the end— when babies start sleeping through the night, getting introduced to solid foods, and start getting older.

Exclusive Breastfeeding is BEST... but It's YOUR Choice

Since breastfeeding help and education will be provided during your hospital stay from nurses and/or lactation consultants, we will discuss the benefits for mother and baby, and what can be done to make exclusive breastfeeding a reality, or provide alternatives if this is not possible for you and your baby.

There is a lot of valuable information out there about breastfeeding and how breastfeeding is *best* for your baby. Studies demonstrate that the pros of breastmilk far outweigh the cons. There are essential nutritionally balanced meals for each stage of your baby's growth cycle, and antibodies are passed on from you to baby for protection against many diseases your baby cannot fight on their own. Other benefits are better survival during the first year of life; a decreased risk for SIDS (Sudden Infant Death Syndrome); reducing risks for allergies, obesity, and asthma; and improving baby's cognitive development, among many others. Mother's benefits include decreased risk for Type

2 diabetes, ovarian cancer, and certain types of breast cancer. Benefits for both mother and baby include skin-to-skin contact which promotes bonding.

The Centers for Disease Control (CDC), American Academy of Pediatrics (AAP), the World Health Organization (WHO), American College of Obstetrics and Gynecology (ACOG), the U.S. Surgeon General, and many others agree that breastfeeding is *best!* So, hospitals across the country are putting protocols and procedures in place to make "baby friendly" a top priority to support breastfeeding. They are providing information and education, along with breastfeeding support from nurses, pediatricians, and lactation consultants.

The World Health Organization (WHO) and UNICEF joined together in 1991 to promote the worldwide initiative "Ten Steps to Successful Breastfeeding", where hospitals are launching the baby-friendly initiative, and it has been demonstrated to increase breastfeeding initiation, duration, and exclusivity. Since the initiative began, over 152 countries have adopted this practice and it continues to grow.

Introducing breastfeeding exclusivity for at least 6 months, and onwards up to a year and beyond, has improved with this initiative and have proven impacts which are measurable. Costs are reduced and can be reduced even more nationally, up to $13 billion per year in health-related costs. This does not include the long-term future benefits in reducing potential adult diseases which were acquired in childhood, or a decrease in parent-related work absenteeism. The benefits for exclusive breastfeeding are there in the *"Ten Steps to Successful Breastfeeding"*, utilized by hospitals world-wide that are making this happen, are:

"Ten Step to Successful Breastfeeding"

- Written hospital breastfeeding policy that is routinely communicated to staff;

- Train all staff in the skills necessary in implementing this policy;

- Educate all women in the benefits and management of breastfeeding;

- Help mothers initiate breastfeeding within the 1st hour of birth;

- Show mothers how to breastfeed and maintain lactation, even if separated from their babies;

- Give no other food or drink other than breastmilk, unless medically indicated;

- Practice "rooming-in", allowing mothers and babies to remain together 24/7;

- Encourage breastfeeding on demand;

- Give no artificial nipples or pacifiers to breastfeeding infants;

- Have established breastfeeding support groups available and provide referrals to mothers upon hospital discharge.

Breastfeeding education is essential in providing information to parents with regards to all the potential benefits for exclusive breastfeeding, along with ways to make this an important part of their lifestyle. Some mothers, at least here in the U.S., may feel overwhelmed with the thought of exclusive breastfeeding due to having other children to care for, a return to work after maternity leave, single parenting issues, fast-paced lifestyles, etc. Fathers may feel "left out" because of the continual bonding between mother and baby, wishing they could get in on the action. But there is help available to make this a positive experience for all involved.

Lactation consultants are becoming more common place in the hospital setting and pediatrician's offices to provide education and help with breastfeeding, and to maintain continued exclusive breastfeeding. Nurses in the hospital setting are provided with educational opportunities to learn how to help mothers and babies initiate and establish breastfeeding, and provide effective ways to make this work with most of their patients.

However, there are obstacles for some mothers who may have breast issues which will not allow them to breastfeed exclusively. Breast augmentation (enlargement) or reduction may affect breastfeeding with decreased milk supplies or scar tissue, not enabling them to provide enough or any milk for their infant. Inverted or flat nipples may never allow a woman to latch baby correctly onto the breast. Shape or size of the nipple may make this difficult as well. Pain from sensitive, sore, or damaged nipples can be another factor. But there are ways around some of these issues which will allow babies to receive their mother's breast milk (or even tiny amounts) which is still beneficial for them. Do not despair— help is out there for these issues!

Breastfeeding, throughout the ages, has provided nourishment and nutrient to babies— and for those who could not or would not breastfeed there were "wet nurses" used to ensure their baby's survival. The old adage, "… it takes a village to raise a child…" could not be any *truer* here, and today it's the same. Breastfeeding is "natural", however, the caveat here is that breastfeeding does take time, patience, and quite a bit of effort. And it may not be easy!! With adequate breastfeeding education and support, mothers can be successful in exclusive breastfeeding.

Even after being educated about the benefits of breastfeeding and ways to make this successful for the long haul, some mothers still do not wish to engage in breastfeeding or even pumping and bottle feeding. To those who choose to still formula feed your baby— it is *okay!*

Your baby will still thrive and undoubtedly do just fine, many have throughout the years, but the protection from diseases by providing immunities, and various other potential health risks will still be there. They will be prone to more illnesses during infancy and childhood, and possibly into adulthood, but like anything— *there is no guarantee this* will *happen*— only that the risk is greater. It is ultimately *your choice* for you and your baby!

For those who choose *not* to breastfeed, you may run into nurses or lactation consultants who may actually *bully* you into breastfeeding, make you feel that you are not being a good mother— a failure because you choose not to breast-feed, or tell you downright lies because you are not breastfeeding. Being made to feel guilty and belittled when you cannot or will not breastfeed— is... *outrageous and unacceptable!!...,* but unfortunately it does happen to some mothers out there. There should be less judgment for these mothers and more support, but with the big push for hospitals to go "baby-friendly" and promote exclusive breastfeeding, this has become a problem for some. There are those nurses and lactation consultants who have been called "Breastfeeding Nazis" or "Breastfeeding Mafia" because of their bullying ways. *This must stop!!* This sheds a bad light on those who properly educate and support mothers who breastfeed, but who are willing to support the mother who decides this is not the way she wants to feed her baby.

I will be the first to tell you that breastfeeding is best for your baby. I breastfed my babies, but only for "a short time" because the support and education were not available to me back when my older children were born. Circumstances with my last one prompted me, at the time, to stop breastfeeding too soon. I wish it could have all been different for me, but *I do not* and *will not* ever make a mother feel inadequate, or bully or belittle her just because she chose not to breastfeed. I want all mothers to love and enjoy their babies, and to me, that is the most important part! I do not want them to dread feeding their babies because their nipples are so sore or torn up from breastfeeding a "Hoover" vacuum that their toes curl, they stiffen up, and/or cry throughout the whole feeding time. One registered dietitian said it best in a September-October 2014 article for *Food and Nutrition* magazine, titled "Besting Breastfeeding Bullies: A Case for Supporting, Not Shaming".

> "Using formula to feed a baby is sometimes a conscious choice and other times a decision that's out of a mother's control. Either way, health professionals' roles are to provide less judgment and more support and encouragement— and, of course, science-based nutrition education free from personal bias."
>
> --*Kerry Neville, MS, RD*

Whether your choice is to exclusively breastfeed or not, the ultimate choice is *yours*. And for those who decide to breastfeed— if you feel you are not providing enough nourishment for your baby until your milk comes in and you choose to supplement with formula, it should not be *only* up to the doctor to deem it "medically necessary". You can do both if *you choose*. The most important part is feeding your baby— shouldn't it be "*Fed* is Best?"

Starting to Breastfeed

Feedings will begin with "on demand", meaning whenever the baby wants to nurse. The longest you should ever go is 3 hours before feeding again, even if it means having to wake up your sleeping baby to do so. This is one of the hardest things for parents to do— is wake a sleeping baby, but babies must be fed to avoid potential issues down the road. If your baby is not getting adequate nutrition from feedings, he or she can have issues with hypoglycemia (low blood sugars), decreased temperatures from expending calories to keep warm, decreased stools which can lead to jaundice, decreased wet diapers which can indicate dehydration and various other issues. Suffice it to say, waking a sleeping newborn is important— even if you are interrupting their sleep.

Colostrum and breastmilk are easily digestible food for your new baby. Because it is easily digestible, it digests *quickly* which is why breastfed babies need to eat every 1 ½ to 3 hours— *and* on demand, especially in the first few days. Colostrum comes in very small quantities, and it's richer and thicker than breastmilk, but because of the small quantities your baby may want to eat more frequently or on demand. When your breastmilk comes in, 3 to 5 days for first-time moms and 1-4 days for subsequent babies, your baby will fill their stomach and be totally sated and satisfied. Once this happens, generally feedings will be every 2-3 hours and frequent demand feedings will be few and far between.

While you are in the hospital, your nurse or lactation consultant (if available in the hospital) will assist you with breastfeeding. They will show you how to properly latch your baby to the breast, making sure the mouth is wide, tongue is down, and lips are flanged out (like "fish lips"). Your baby must also get a deep latch, meaning they must take in not just the nipple but all or a lot of your areola as well, depending on its size. This is important because your lower milk sinuses are right behind the areola and the baby needs to "massage" those sinuses to bring down the colostrum or milk from the upper milk ducts and stimulate milk production. If your baby isn't latched on deep enough, you won't get optimal stimulation or proper removal of colostrum or milk— and you will get nipple soreness and trauma to the nipple as well.

Comfortable Breastfeeding Positioning

When working with breastfeeding mothers, I will have them get into a comfortable position for breastfeeding. I will tell them or remind them to always bring the baby up to your breast, not lean over to get the breast in the mouth. This way you remain comfortable during the feeding and not find yourself in an awkward position you are stuck with for 20-30 minutes. You always want to position the baby in a "tummy-to-tummy" position with you so the baby will be straight on the nipple. If the baby has his or her head turned to the side, the baby cannot stay in a straight line with the nipple and will "pull and twist" the nipple to keep it in his or her mouth.

Latching Baby On

I will then have them cup the breast in one hand— in a "C" shape— and move their thumb on top— close to the nipple on the areola— with the fingers back close to their chest wall. Using their thumb to gently draw the nipple upward (toward what will be the roof of the baby's mouth), and once the baby opens the mouth wide, I have them "roll" the nipple and breast tissue into the baby's mouth, pressing it down on top of the baby's tongue and holding it into that position until the baby latches on and begins sucking, then remove the thumb and support the breast in a relaxed "C". This helps to ensure a good deep latch and help the baby know exactly where the breast is in their mouth.

By pressing the breast tissue and nipple down on the tongue, this gives the baby more surface area of breast to latch on to, instead of "finding" the nipple with their tongue, place the tongue underneath it, and get a hold of it! If you just place the nipple in the mouth, the baby will "search" around for it with their tongue and mouth, bobbing and fussing because they know it's right… there… they can smell it… they just… can't… get… a hold of it… and trust me when I say they can get *really* frustrated when they can't find it.

This also helps with getting that "baby fish mouth" you want the baby to have when latching on. By rolling the breast tissue and nipple in on top of the tongue, it automatically helps to bring the bottom lip down. If the breast is just placed straight in the mouth, you run into the problem of having the bottom lip curl inward and not getting a proper latch— then having to reach under your breast and try and pull the lip down in those "tight quarters."

Positioning Baby Against the Breast

Once you have the baby latched on correctly, make sure that the tip of the baby's nose, chin, and *both* cheeks are just touching the breast and not pressed in too tight. Don't be afraid to hold your baby in this position during the feeding— and don't relax this firm hold. Your baby's nose is curved enough on the sides to allow him or her to breathe while latched without the worry of suffocation. This keeps the baby in a deep latch and does not let him or her "slide" down to the end of the nipple and lose the correct latch.

Positioning Baby Against Large Breasts

For some women, if you have an over-abundance of breast tissue which can form around the nose and mouth (even if just touching with nose, chin and cheeks), you can use your finger to *lightly* press downward on the breast tissue up against the baby's nose. This will allow airflow to the baby during feeding. But, be sure not to press down too hard into the tissue. By doing this, you may block off a milk duct and not allow it to drain properly. Improper drainage of one or more of the milk ducts can lead to mastitis. And— if you pull back on the breast tissue instead of pressing down, you may stretch the breast tissue out, relieving the baby of some of that breast tissue and either pop the baby completely off or cause him or her to slide down to the end of the nipple, which in turn can cause an incorrect latch.

**_Mastitis:_ is an infection of the breast which can cause fever, pain, redness, and swelling and will need to be treated by your physician. You will still be able to breastfeed if you have mastitis.

Taking Baby "Off" the Breast

If you need to remove your baby from the breast, take your pinky finger and slide it in the corner of the mouth. Place it between the baby's gums and twist your finger. This will help release the suction and baby will come off the breast easily. _DO NOT_ try pulling your baby off the breast without doing this first. Your baby may not want to release the nipple and will continue to apply suction to the breast to maintain attachment. This can cause soreness and even tissue trauma, which can make future feedings difficult for you.

Establishing Breastfeeding

It takes approximately two weeks to establish successful breastfeeding between you and your baby. Some think that breastfeeding should be simple because "it's natural… so therefore it must be easy." I can assure you this is not necessarily the case. In fact, it is pretty rare for breastfeeding to be easy right from the get go! You may have difficulty latching your baby to the breast because of flat or inverted nipples, or you may have very dense breast tissue which does not make it easy at all to compress it down to get it into your baby's mouth. You may also have a baby who does not get the tongue down, and want to suck on the nipple as if they are "sucking on a straw." This can be very frustrating not only for you but also your baby.

Sore Nipples

Sore nipples are a problem for breastfeeding mothers, and— yes, your nipples will get sore at the beginning and for a while, until the tissue toughens up. Even if the latch is correct 100% of the time, this is a very common occurrence. This soreness can make it somewhat painful putting the baby to breast— even make some mothers dread it. Because your nipples have not been subjected to continuous suction for extended periods of time, possible frequent latching off/on, and incorrect latching; your nipples can get sore, dry, cracked, blistered, and/or bleed. Some mothers have overly-sensitive nipples that might become severely damaged, like turning to "hamburger", which can make breastfeeding for them very difficult— but this is uncommon. It may even cause them to stop because it becomes excruciating for them.

(**Think of the tissue on your lips. It's just like what you have on the nipple, making it also easily prone to drying, cracking, bleeding, etc.)

Be Proactive with Your Nipples

One way to tackle the issue is to be proactive. If you can express some colostrum after you finish breastfeeding, you can rub this into the nipple and areola, and allow it to air dry before replacing your bra. There are healing properties in colostrum and breastmilk, so use whichever one you have at the time. If you are unable to express colostrum after a feeding, you can use a nipple cream after breastfeeding, such as Lansinoh® or Medela® Tender Care Lanolin. Neither one needs to be wiped or rubbed off before starting the next feeding. It is safe to put the baby directly to the breast without doing so, as it will not harm your baby.

Poor Breast Attachment

Other difficulties with breastfeeding can be poor latching, tongue sucking or thrusting, not keeping the tongue down, not opening the mouth wide enough, wanting to suck like they are sucking on a straw, or wanting to push out all the extra breast and just take the nipple. Approximately 80-90% of newborn babies need some assistance or repeated assistance getting them to latch on properly, and some more than others. Unfortunately, babies did not read the breastfeeding manual before delivery, so they are trying to figure it out once they get here. I tell my mothers whose baby gets latched on correctly right off the bat that this is ¾ the battle with breastfeeding. The rest will make it a lot easier.

But when a baby has been worked with by the mother and nurse or lactation consultant, and they finally "get it right", doesn't mean the baby will continue to "get it right" every time now. For every two steps forward there may be one step back. Nursing is a learning process for both the mother and the baby, and any forward progress is progress in the right direction.

Positions for Feeding Baby

Positioning during breastfeeding is another obstacle for both mother and baby. Placing the baby on one breast may be awkward because the hold "feels" awkward. If the mother feels uncomfortable with the hold, the baby may sense this and may not want to latch on that side.

Cradle hold: The "cradle hold" is the most common position people are familiar with when they picture babies breastfeeding, but this is not the only possible hold to be used, in fact, it's more difficult to learn breastfeeding for both mother and baby. This position makes it difficult for getting a proper latch during the learning process. It also makes it difficult to visualize the baby's latch fully to make sure it is correct. (**This one should be used only after baby is more adept to latching onto the breast.)

There are three other possible holds to use while learning to breastfeed: the "football hold", the "modified cradle hold", and the "side-lying hold". The easiest by far is the "football hold".

Football hold: This is a really good hold to use to get full visualization of the baby's position and latch with relation to the breast. It is also a great hold to use for mothers who had a cesarean section, because it keeps the baby from lying on top of her already sore stomach. With this hold, the baby is placed in the mother's arms, like a football, with the head and neck in her hand and the baby's feet tucked under the arm. When the baby is placed at the breast, you can visualize the baby's whole face and latch, versus half of the face with the "cradle hold".

Modified cradle hold: The "modified cradle hold" is like the "cradle hold", except you are holding the baby with the opposite arm in relation to the breast being used— instead of the same side. The baby is place across the stomach, tummy-to-tummy with mom, and your arm is wrapped across the back and the head is held in position with the hand. You use the hand on the same side of the breast used to "cup" the breast and latch the baby on. You can see more of the baby's face and position with this hold versus the "cradle hold", but not fully like the "football hold".

Side-lying hold: The "side-lying hold" can be used when you are lying down, especially if you had a very extensive repair to your "hoo-ha" after a vaginal delivery and it's too uncomfortable to sit on your bottom. The baby is placed on his or her side facing you and can be latched on to the breast from this position. The downside to this position is you *do not* want to utilize it when you are very tired— *even just a little.* Breastfeeding is very relaxing, and if you are tired you run the risk of falling asleep during the feeding. This puts your baby at risk for suffocating up against the breast when you fall asleep and cannot monitor the feeding and position. So, use this position with caution, and only when you are fully awake and not in danger of falling asleep.

Nipple Shape and Size

Nipple shape and size can also play a role in making latching the baby difficult. If the nipple is very large or wide in relation to the baby's mouth, the baby may not be able to latch on to the whole thing or the nipple may be all they *can* get in the mouth because there is no more room. If this becomes an issue, work with your nurse or lactation consultant. You may need to pump and feed for a while until the baby gets big enough to latch on correctly, or they may have other alternatives for you.

If the nipple shape or size on one side of the breast is easier for the baby to latch on to than the other, the baby may resist being placed on the side that is more difficult for him or her. If the baby refuses to latch on the unwanted side, place the baby on the other side for a few minutes to calm him or her down if agitated, then remove the baby (release the baby's latch first with your pinky) and place them on the unwanted side again. This might calm the baby down enough to get baby to latch on and get a good feeding on the side he or she doesn't like.

Instant Gratification

If your baby has been latching on well for a while and suddenly with this next feeding, he or she gets latched on— sucks a few times— then pops off (and possibly start fussing); then the process starts all over again a second, third or fourth time, you may wonder why this is happening. When your baby gets latched on and starts sucking, he or she is expecting to "get something" for the effort. Even if the colostrum is in small quantities at the moment, they are thinking in very *simplistic* terms "I suck… I get something." They don't think like you or I would in *complex thought*, like "I have to suck for 2-3 minutes to get the colostrum to come down… and *then* I get something." This is why they get frustrated. And, this is called "Instant Gratification." So, read on and see what you can do to help "fix" this problem.

Breast Massaging

One thing you can do to help remedy this would be to massage your breast prior to baby latching on. By massaging your breast, you will move the colostrum down from the upper milk sinuses down to the lower sinuses and out through the nipple. Take one or both your hands and place them at the top of the breast by your chest. Press downward on the breast to help compress the milk sinus and stroke downward toward the nipple. Repeat this process over the next several minutes in different areas on your breast to move the colostrum down.

Expressing Colostrum

After the massage is complete, place your thumb and forefinger on your areola by the nipple, press in toward your chest while spreading out your fingers about 2-3 inches, then grasp the breast where your fingers stopped and squeeze your fingers slowly together as you are pulling the nipple forward. You may need to do this a couple times before you start seeing the colostrum bead at the end of the nipple. If after this you haven't managed to work any colostrum down, repeat the process of massaging your breast for a couple more minutes and then working the nipple and areola again. This is very effective in getting the colostrum down to the end so when baby latches on again, he or she will immediately "get something".

Some babies will just keep popping off and re-latching onto the breast repeatedly, and others will show their displeasure when they don't "get something" immediately— either screaming or crying really loud or pushing off the breast when flailing their arms— or both. Once the baby latches on after the "massage and squeeze" and "gets something", the sucking will get rhythmic and the baby won't pop off the breast until done— and you and baby will be happy again.

You may need to repeat this trick for each feeding, at least until you notice the colostrum (or breastmilk) is already at the end and ready for them to nurse.

When Your Milk Comes In

With some mothers, who have had previous children, their milk may come in during their hospital stay. This will be the engorgement period. For 1st time mothers, this will probably occur after you have returned home, but may occur in the hospital. Remember, the average for colostrum to change over to milk is 3-5 days for new moms and 1-4 days for the pros. Your breasts will rapidly change, and you will now be in the engorgement period.

The Engorgement Period

During this engorgement period, your milk production starts to increase greatly, which causes an overabundance of milk. This engorgement period is the timeframe where your body is trying to determine how much milk to make based off your baby's feeding habits. This period lasts approximately 48 hours, and you may become *very* uncomfortable during this time. Your breasts will swell, get hard, heavy, feverish-feeling, and very tender to the touch. It will feel like you have a couple of "boulders" on your chest and it can be uncomfortable for you. But as previously stated, this only lasts for about 48 hours, and then you will start getting some relief.

When the engorgement happens, sometimes this becomes very difficult for your baby to latch on to the breast. The breast tissue all around swells and tightens up, and may even flatten out the nipple more, making it difficult for the baby to get a good latch. If this does occur— don't panic! You may have to hand express or pump "*a little off the top*" to make it easier for your baby to latch on again.

Your nurse or lactation consultant can work with you to show you hand expression or set you up with a pump in the hospital to make this happen. If you are using a pump, just pump for a minute or two to remove some of the milk, enough to allow softening up of the nipple and areola which will allow the baby to latch on. *DO NOT* be tempted to pump or hand express the milk until you get complete relief. Remember the reason for the engorgement period— your body is trying to judge how much milk to make based off what the baby takes. Then over next two days of engorgement your body will adjust and produce only the amount the baby is removing from your breasts. If you breastfeed *AND* pump your breasts dry, then your body decides "Oh… I guess I need to make *THIS* much milk" — and it will. Then you will continue to produce the larger amounts of milk right from the start.

During your engorgement period, when you start feeling very uncomfortable and want to get some relief, just put the baby to breast and let him or her remove some of the milk for you. This way the body is still making what the baby is taking away, and not more than what they need for the time being, plus your baby is getting the benefit of the milk's nourishment.

Down the road, in a few weeks, when your baby goes through growth spurts, he or she will demand to eat more frequently again, and you need to let them. With the growth spurts comes the need for your body to produce more milk for your growing child. And when more milk is needed, then more breast stimulation is needed to produce a larger amount for your growing baby. This may continue for about 48 hours, just like during the engorgement period, so your body will adjust to manufacturing the newer amount. Then your baby will slow the frequency of the feedings down again when he or she starts receiving the amount of milk they now want. This will continue with each growth spurt they encounter, until they start to take in more "solid" baby food and you start to nurse less frequently.

I so wish I knew then what I know now about breastfeeding. When I was breastfeeding my two older children, we didn't have lactation consultants available to help us out and give us information. We couldn't afford the books available at that time to learn about breastfeeding. We certainly didn't have the Internet, Google, Facebook, Twitter, and the like— well the Internet *was* in the "early stages", but we didn't have a computer, and the World Wide Web (WWW) didn't have the vast information it has now.

I had a small chest size when my oldest two were babies and I was breastfeeding. So, when each was going through a "growth spurt", I didn't realize it at the time. I thought that my milk was drying up because the baby was nursing and wasn't getting fully satisfied. It never occurred to me that with the growth spurt they wanted more food, and instinctually they were trying to get more food by making my body produce what they wanted. Needless to say, I didn't breastfeed my first for longer than 6-7 weeks— when I went back to work. My 2nd got about 3 months because I had gotten a handy-dandy little hand pump in my hospital "gift bag" that helped me to pump during breaks at work. I don't know why I stopped breastfeeding then. I guess I didn't want to do it anymore. The point is— with all the education I am providing you (and others are providing through lactation consultants, nurses, books, the Internet, etc.), if I had to do it all again I would have made sure to breastfeed my babies for longer than they got— and would have known that the more frequent feedings were just to help produce more milk for them, *and* that I was not just "drying up". So be sure and stick with it for *a lot* longer than I did. I continue to regret that I did not breastfeed longer.

Documenting Feedings

While you are in the hospital, your nurse will ask you to keep track on a log of when you feed the baby and how long, and when you change the baby's wet and/or poopy diapers. This information will be documented on your baby's chart for the pediatrician to see, so the baby's progress can be tracked. Each time you attempt to feed the baby and he or she was too sleepy at the time to eat, document those as well. The pediatrician knows that the baby will be going through some sleepy periods in the first few days, and will not feed, but they want to see that documented on the chart. This way they know you are at least attempting to feed your baby and not just seeing a big gap between feedings. The doctor wants to be sure you are not just letting your baby sleep for prolonged periods without attempting or offering a feeding.

The hospital should provide you with a log to keep record of everything. Note the time each event occurs and document what occurred. Some mothers will download an app on their smart phone to keep track of these things and that's okay. Either way of documenting is fine, so just update your nurse when she asks. This is essential to monitor your baby's progress during the hospital stay to be sure your baby is well hydrated, and their systems are functioning like they should. If they are not getting enough to eat to produce at least one wet diaper and one poopy diaper the first day, two of each the second day, and so on— then your baby is not getting the necessary nourishment needed and supplementation may be in store.

Supplementation

When your baby does not get enough to eat at the breast, because you have very small quantities of colostrum or no colostrum production, the pediatrician will usually intervene with the order to supplement along with each breastfeeding.

There are some mothers with the mindset of exclusively breastfeeding— and *only* breastfeeding— from the beginning. This is acceptable by the pediatricians, in fact, they encourage it. But if your baby is not getting the quantities to produce enough pees and poops, and they lose too much weight (remember 10% is the threshold), then intervention is needed to prevent other issues the baby might encounter.

Banked breast milk: If you want to exclusively breastfeed and do not want your baby to have *any* formula, the pediatrician may write an order for banked breast milk based off the baby's need for an increased volume of milk due to your current lack of production. Usually in the hospital, banked breast milk is reserved for the preterm or premature babies that have a greater need to receive this milk, but the pediatrician can order this for you if it is available. If formula is suggested, and banked breast milk is not— just ask the pediatrician. Since your baby has a need, this shouldn't be a problem.

But if banked breast milk is not currently available to your baby for the time being, then the supplement will be done with formula.

Formula supplementation: This usually is a short-time need for your baby either way. Once you start producing more colostrum or start producing milk and the volume goes up, the need for the banked breast milk or formula will go down. Your baby will produce more wet and dirty diapers, and slow down or stop weight loss. When your milk completely comes in, the need for supplementation will no longer be necessary, unless you continue to be unable to produce enough for your baby. During this timeframe, your baby will continue to be monitored for however long the pediatrician deems necessary for your baby's well-being.

Supplemental Nursing Systems

Supplementation *can* be done without the use of a bottle. There is supplemental nursing systems (SNS), which can be used at the breast to give your baby more volume at the same time the baby is suckling and stimulating your breast. Your hospital should have SNS available for use during your hospital stay, and your nurse or lactation consultant can help you set this up and demonstrate how to use this system. If the hospital does not have a system available, a 10 or 20 ml syringe and a small neonatal feeding tube can be used to accomplish this. With the push for more lactation education, and the policies and protocols of hospitals changing to follow the World Health Organization (WHO) and UNICEF's "Exclusive Breastfeeding" initiative, your hospital should have this system available for you, and personnel available to assist you.

Nipple Damage from Breastfeeding

One issue with breastfeeding is a chance you may start having problems with *nipple soreness, cracking, blistering, bleeding, or extensive trauma to the nipple.* You might even receive a "*hickey*" around the area of the nipple if baby isn't latching in the correct spot (this can happen if you have flat or inverted nipples or very large breasts which make correct placement visually difficult). This may also come from putting your baby to breast incorrectly, baby not latching deep enough, baby sliding down to the end of the nipple when you relax your hold, or not requesting help from your nurse or lactation consultant when you think you know what you are doing. (There *are* some moms out there— and you know who you are— who are either too embarrassed to ask for help *or* refuse help because they think "I've got it.") Help is there for you to hopefully avoid some or all of these issues— so don't be afraid to use it.

If you do have sore, cracked, blistered, bleeding or damaged nipples, here are some ways to combat any of these problems:

Expressed colostrum or milk: Starting off, for sore nipples the first line of defense: expressed colostrum or milk. If you can express some colostrum or milk after the feeding and rub it into the nipple, this will help. This has natural healing elements already there and available for you, which help to keep the nipple and areola soft and supple. Take the expressed colostrum or breastmilk and rub it onto and around the nipple and areola. Let the breasts dry completely before replacing your bra, and do this each time after you feed your baby.

Lanolin ointments: If the soreness is early on, and your baby has *"sucked you dry"*, then Lansinoh® or Medela® Tender Care lanolin ointments should be available for your use in the hospital. (If not, have someone go out to the drug store or department store and get some for you.) Each of these ointments are easy to use and do not require you to "wipe it off" before putting the baby to breast. The ingredients in these ointments will not harm your baby— but the baby might hesitate a few times when latching because your breast is "tasting a little different now." Eventually, the baby will get used to it and will start latching right on again without hesitation.

Place a small bead of ointment on the pad of your clean finger and rub it all over the area of the nipple and areola where your baby is latching on to. This will help to keep the nipple and areola supple, and help with your soreness.

Hydrogel pads: If you start getting blistering, cracking or bleeding, then hopefully they have the Medela hydrogel pads to place on your breasts after feeding, which are very helpful. These soothing gels are a wound healer, and will help to heal your nipples while you are breastfeeding. They are especially good if you can place them in a refrigerator and use them when they are cold. This can give you additional relief with the added coolness. If you do not have a personal refrigerator in your hospital room, then do this once you have returned home from the hospital. You will be glad you did!!

These hydrogel pads are about 3 x 3 and can be cut in half horizontally or diagonally to be placed on your nipples. Be sure and have your nursing bra on, which will keep them in place between feedings. And— you can continue to use the Lansinoh or Medela ointments along with the pads. These pads are good for about 48 hours of use, or until the gel just starts to disintegrate, before needing to be thrown away.

**Just a reminder: be sure and wash your hands each time you handle your breasts, at *least* after the feeding. Before you handle the colostrum or breast-milk, ointment, or hydrogel pads and place any of these on the breasts, be sure your hands are clean. Remember, you have wounds now on your nipples, and they will be prone to infection from anything you transfer to them.

All-purpose nipple cream: For those of you that have extensive nipple tissue trauma where the nipple is really "torn up", there may be made available to you an all-purpose nipple cream. This is a prescription that only some pharmacists will fill, but the lactation consultant or your obstetrician can order this for you if needed. However, with this nipple cream there is an active steroid in the cream to promote healing, so it is not intended for long term usage— just until the nipple(s) heals. (For about 2-3 weeks, then if it is still a problem you need to follow up with your doctor.)

Nipple shells: Your hospital may have what is called "nipple shells" which are available for your use if you are having very sore nipples and you don't want anything touching them because it's irritating, or it hurts. The cloth from the bra you are wearing may be too abrasive on your nipple, therefore, making you want to take it off. Nipple shells can help remedy this for you.

These nipple shells are made of a hard-plastic case on the outside, with a number of holes around the shell, and made in a cup shape like the breast. There is a pliable silicone covering on the underneath side with a large hole in the center to be placed over your nipple area for your comfort. These will help to let air circulate around your nipple and not allow anything to touch it while it's sore. It will also help keep the bra from rubbing against the sore nipple. There are also two small "1/8 of a moon-shaped" pieces of foam to be placed on the lower segment of the shells— to catch any colostrum or milk leakage from your breasts.

Place one shell over the nipple on each breast and place your bra cup over the shell to keep it in place. This will help to give you some relief from your over-sensitive nipples. But there *is* a catch— you *do not* want to wear these nipple shells when you are sleeping. They are hard and may be very uncomfortable to wear during sleep. Also, the shells may cause some suction when applied to the breast and if you sleep and the shells move out of position, you may cause them to start a "hickey" on your breast elsewhere and you will lose the protection around your nipple.

Breast Augmentation/Reduction

If a mother had surgery for enlarging or reducing breast size and she is worried breastfeeding might not be possible because of this, the nurses or lactation consultants can help put the baby to breast which will help stimulate milk production. Pumping with a hospital-grade breast pump will accomplish this, and provide proof for the mother and nurse or lactation consultant if there are milk ducts which are open and transporting colostrum thru the breast. If drops or milliliters of colostrum are produced, then breastfeeding can be established for these mothers. Continued monitoring during the hospital stay and after discharge would be necessary to establish how much milk is being produced, and if mother is providing enough volume and nourishment for the baby.

If enough milk is being produced for the baby— that's *Fantastic!!* The mother will be able to provide exclusive breastfeeding for her baby and know her baby is getting what is needed. If the milk provided is not sufficient enough for long-term breastfeeding, then what is produced can be given to the baby first and supplementation of donor breast milk or formula given after. Mothers who *cannot* provide sufficient amounts or any breastmilk can qualify for donor milk, instead of using formula to fill the gap. Some insurance companies may provide some or all coverage, if this is the case. Be sure to check into this option if you fall in this category.

Flat or Inverted Nipples

For mothers who have flat or inverted nipples, there are tools that can be used to help with this. Flat or inverted nipples can be stimulated to pull out far enough to allow the baby to latch on successfully. A breast pump used for a few minutes can help draw out the nipple as well as a latch assist. These two options have been successful for many moms out there.

Latch assist: A latch assist is a device which is like a small meat baster or nasal aspirator, but made for the nipple. By depressing the bulb and placing the small "horn" over the nipple, you can use suction to draw the nipple out.

Nipple shields: For those of you who cannot draw out the nipple because of the anatomical make-up of your breast and nipple, or the nipple does not remain out long enough for the baby to latch on correctly— there is still hope! There are nipple shields, made of silicone, which are in the shape of a nipple that can be placed over your nipple area and the baby can latch on to this. This will allow the baby to suckle at the breast and stimulate some milk production. But this does have a downside. The nipple shields cover the nipple and some or all the surrounding area of the areola with a thin, but durable silicone. Your baby can suck and draw the nipple out some, but cannot compress the areola around the nipple which help compress the milk sinuses effectively to promote good stimulation and milk production. Usually this is a temporary tool used by mothers whose nipples may start to evert (stand out) permanently at a later time where baby can latch on effectively.

Breast pump: For those whose nipples will not cooperate and stand out eventually on their own, and must continually use this tool for each breastfeeding, pumping the breast afterwards would be necessary to help effectively stimulate adequate milk production. This may be cumbersome and time-consuming for you, but it can be an effective way to ensure your baby is getting your breast milk.

If these methods are not a good fit for you, an alternative way to ensure your baby is getting your breast milk is to pump and feed this to the baby by bottle. This might be a better alternative for some, which will allow you to provide baby with the best nourishment and allow dad to feed his baby, thus letting him in on both the feeding and the bonding process.

This can also be helpful for those mothers who have no desire to put baby to the breast for personal reasons but want their baby to receive their breast milk, or for mothers who become too anxious or stressed out with the thought of breastfeeding. Some mothers do feel this way, and that is okay. By pumping and bottle feeding, you will still be able to provide your baby with the best nourishment available.

Pacifier Usage During Breastfeeding

It is strongly recommended that you *do not* give the baby a pacifier in the beginning stages of breastfeeding. The reasoning is that the baby may have "nipple confusion" from taking the pacifier when breastfeeding. I like the wording, "nipple preference", a little better the "nipple confusion". It has been called both.

When your baby is at the breast, you are wanting the baby's mouth to open wide to get in a large amount of nipple and areola for a good latch. If the baby uses a pacifier, they are generally not large enough in size to mimic the baby latching onto the breast, so the mouth must clamp down, which would then mimic a smaller latch. Then when your baby goes to latch onto the breast, they may not open the mouth big enough. Here's where the "nipple confusion" comes in. If you begin using a pacifier, it is not recommended until the breastfeeding is well established, at approximately 3-4 weeks. This is the firmly held belief of the World Health Organization (WHO), UNICEF, La Leche League International, and various other organizations.

However, according to SIDS research, the use of pacifiers during sleep time is encouraged because it *decreases* the risk for SIDS. So, what recommendations do you follow? A pediatrician, Dr. Clay Jones, from Newton-Wellesley Hospital in Newton, MA wrote a very good article about this very thing. He is a regular contributing writer for the Science-Based Medicine blog, which discusses "issues and controversies between Science and Medicine." He discusses in the blog the above recommendations, and, also breaks it down to further discuss "Is nipple confusion real?"

His thought that it doesn't seem plausible. [In other words, reasonable, credible, believable, or conceivable.] Babies will suck on anything, and they all aren't shaped like the breast. We talked about suck blisters previously, already on newborns hands or forearms from when they were sucking on them before they were born. He talks about that same thing along with sucking on blankets, hands, feet, gloved fingers (he uses this during his assessment of babies to quiet them, so he can hear their heartbeat and heart sounds), anything they can get into their mouth. And— he stated that they don't seem to alter their suck with the breast, so why would the pacifier be any different??

Another concern for breastfeeding, for the WHO, UNICEF, LLLI, and others, is that a pacifier would take the place of breastfeeding— that mothers might choose to offer "the pacifier instead of the breast, thus causing a delay in milk letdown from the breast and increase the likelihood of breastfeeding cessation." [Breastfeeding ending, terminating.] But then Dr. Jones also states that "a pacifier would not appreciably [noticeably] space out breastfeeding because a hungry baby is rarely soothed by one." I have found this true in my many years of nursing.

I have seen babies take pacifiers between feedings and "spit them out" after being repeatedly placed back in their mouths; when what they really want is to breastfeed. With some, I have even witness them "shot putting" them from their mouths. Then after they do breastfeed as requested, the babies take the pacifier again after the feeding— without a problem. Some babies want to suck, because sucking is comforting and soothing to them. Why deny that if a baby wants to constantly suck, even *after* a long breastfeeding session??

Before the "mandate" in hospitals was passed down about "no pacifiers" except during painful procedures, babies were given pacifiers routinely between feedings to help soothe and comfort those who wanted to just suck. (Our hospital is going to "locking down" pacifiers by putting them in our medicine machine and we must *only* get them out for painful procedures. If a parent wants to use a pacifier for baby just to suck, they must bring their own.)

Dr. Jones also concluded; that if a baby wants to suck and is denied a pacifier, wouldn't the exhausted mother be more likely to offer formula during the times when their baby is crying unconsolably, usually on the 2nd day after birth, than if offered a pacifier between feedings? Wouldn't the formula then be *more* detrimental for breastfeeding than the pacifier? Even in Dr. Jones's research he found that the *Cochrane Database of Systematic Review* had a study of pacifier use in breastfeeding in 2012 and here was their conclusion:

"Pacifier use in healthy term breastfeeding infants, started from birth or after lactation is established, did not significantly affect the prevalence or duration of exclusive and partial breastfeeding up to four months of age. Evidence to assess the short-term breastfeeding difficulties faced by mothers and long-term effect of pacifiers on infants' health is lacking."

They then judged it to be of *"moderate-quality evidence"* and further stated:

"Until further information becomes available on the effects of pacifiers on the infant, mothers who are well-motivated to breastfeed should been encouraged to make a decision on the use of a pacifier based on personal preference."

*Jaafar, S. H. (2016). Effect of restricted pacifier use in breastfeeding term infants for increasing duration of breastfeeding. Cochrane Database of Systematic Reviews (8), doi:10.1002/14651858.CD 007202.pub4

Even the *Pediatrics* journal for the American Academy of Pediatrics, which Dr. Jones also reviewed, concluded that *"it raises serious concerns that restricting pacifier availability in the newborn period may even increase the likelihood that breastfeeding mothers will reach for formula."*

> *Laura R. Kair, Daniel Kenron, Konnette Etheredge, Arthur C. Jaffe, Carrie A. Phillipi. (Mar 2013). Pacifier Restriction and Exclusive Breastfeeding. Pediatrics, peds.2012-2203; DOI: 10.1542/ peds.2012-2203*

So, should you or shouldn't you use a pacifier while exclusively breastfeeding?? If your baby has eaten well and continues to look for something to suck on, the decision is *entirely up to you*— as the baby's parent to decide.

Pumping Your Breasts

You may start pumping your breasts while in the hospital: whether it is due to a baby not wanting to eat for long periods of time, and you need breast stimulation until they do, *or* your baby is receiving specialized care in the nursery and unable to eat or even breastfeed at this time. Your hospital should have a hospital-grade breast pump and the accompanying kit for your own personal use.

Starting to Pump

Your nurse or lactation consultant should help you set up the pump at the bedside and demonstrate to you how to use the pump. Pump each breast for about 15-20 minutes per breast if pumping one at a time, *or* pump both for the same amount of time you would one breast. This will help to stimulate the breast when the baby is not at the breast to do so, therefore, helping you to initiate milk production. Be sure to pump every 2 ½ to 3 hours, or the same time frame you would be putting the baby to breast— *around* the clock. If your baby would be breastfeeding at a certain time, then you should be pumping at the same time to keep up production for the baby until he or she is able to get on the breast at a later time. If you will be sleeping, set your phone alarm to wake you for the pumping session.

**One thing you should do each time you pump your breasts: use some of your lanolin ointment before you begin pumping. Place it on the inside of the horn which you place over your nipple. This will help to lubricate the nipple, and keep your nipple from getting damaged from the friction of the nipple pulling in and out inside the horn. I have seen some nipples get extremely damaged from using the pump without the ointment, so be sure to use it each time.

Cleaning Your Pumping Equipment

After you have finished pumping and have collected what you have pumped into another container for storage, you need to take apart the pump kit pieces and wash them in warm soapy water. Then rinse and set each piece on a towel to dry until you need them for the next pumping session. Your hospital may provide you with a container and dishwashing soap, along with towels so you can wash your equipment and keep it separate from everything else.

Breastfeeding Conclusion

Whether you are an old pro or just starting out breastfeeding, your nurses and lactation consultants are there to help you. Each baby is different, each baby's latch may start off differently. One child might be and easy breast feeder, but the sibling is a big challenge. Your first or second baby may have not "figured it out" about breastfeeding, but you want to try with this one last baby. We want each breastfeeding mom to get it right, each and every time, and make each breastfeeding experience successful.

Q & A on Breastfeeding

Q   *My baby is sleeping a lot and not breastfeeding, and I'm worried he/she isn't eating enough. What can I do?*

A   It's not uncommon on the first day of life that your baby will be very alert the first couple of hours and then slip off to "dreamland". Your baby has been through a lot with the labor and birth, possible pain medications given during labor or your cesarean section, and being passed around like a football to every visitor he or she encounters the first day. Your baby is tired and in need of rest. He or she may also have a full stomach of amniotic fluid, like we discussed in the section on *Q & A on Baby*. If the stomach is full of amniotic fluid, baby won't have the urge to eat very much until the fluid is working its way out. (Just try eating when your stomach is already full…)

It is important, though, to attempt to wake your baby up to feed every 2-3 hours, and every hour if you cannot arouse him or her to eat, even for a 5-minute period. Change the diaper, sit your baby up and burp baby or rub the back, and/or take off all the blankets and clothing down to the diaper. This will help to wake your baby.

Sometimes during the feeding your baby will attempt to fall asleep as well, so there are a few things you can do to help keep baby awake and feeding during this time. Use your finger tips on the back of the head in a "shampoo massaging" way, quickly but *not* slow and rhythmically. Quickly will help keep baby awake; slow and rhythmic will be soothing and cause baby to fall asleep. Do this only when he or she stops sucking for several seconds to encourage baby to suckle again.

Tickling the feet, ribs, or back may also help keep baby awake and feeding. It will cause your baby to wiggle around when tickled and keep a little more interest on the sucking. You can also take your finger and gently push a few times under the chin against the tongue.

By prodding in this location, it may signal your baby to start sucking again. And, again, only do this when the sucking stops for a few seconds.

Last, but not least, try using a cold, wet washcloth against the exposed skin if the other methods do not work. Try anywhere it might be successful in getting your baby suckling again, including around the face and on top of the head. I've been known to perform a few "wet willies" in the ears to see if it will accomplish our goal, so you can try this one as well.

About your concern with getting enough to eat, there are several things we check on frequently, when assessing your baby, that will help to indicate if your baby is getting enough to eat to keep her hydrated. First, we check the number of wet diapers the baby is producing. At the beginning, there are fewer wet diapers for breastfed babies, since he's not getting the volume yet for the 6-8 wet diapers expected after your milk comes in. This is normal and to be expected, but will change once the volume picks up. Second, we check the mouth and lips for moistness. If it is dry, this is a good indication she might not be getting enough to keep her hydrated. She may need a little supplementation if the doctor feels it is necessary at that time. Last, we check the fontanels or "soft spots" on the top of the head to see if they are sunken in. This is also another good indicator of dehydration, and will supplement if doctor indicated.

Q   *Now my baby wants to eat all the time… why the sudden change?*

A   It's normal for them to eat periodically that first day, and on the second day— after their "refreshing sleep" and spitting up the excess amniotic fluid, he or she will cluster feed to make up for what he or she didn't do the day before. This may last for up to 5-8 hours or more, with feeding for extended periods of time, then a short break 30 mins or so, and then will quickly start up again. As your baby gets "caught up" after not eating much the 1st day, he or she will generally slow back down and eat every 1-1/2 to 3 hours like baby should— but, your baby may have different ideas about that!

Q   *Why is my baby getting upset and pushing me away when I'm trying to get him/her to breastfeed? Does my baby not want me? Am I doing something wrong?*

A   Babies will get upset when breastfeeding if anything is bothering them. They may not like the position they are feeding in; be mad because your breast isn't giving them "instant gratification; they're sitting in a dirty diaper and want it fixed first; or, don't like that nipple or that side to feed on. It can be any number of things. But what you can be assured of is that your baby loves you and depends on you— and *wants* you no matter what.

When a baby is upset and frustrated, they will begin to flail their arms and legs around if they can. If they meet resistance, say like your breast, they may "push off" on your breast— but they *are not pushing you away.* When this happens, the baby may push so hard he or she pops themselves off your breast— *then the real frustration and crying will begin!* They are thinking, "what just happened to my breast… I want it back!!" They do not realize those arms are attached to them yet, so they don't realize they just pushed *themselves* off. They are just mad!

If your baby gets so mad that they are crying uncontrollably, get your baby to calm down by placing him or her on your chest, and cuddle, caress, and "*shuuuuush*", which will soothe your baby. Once you calm your baby down, you can re-attach him or her to the breast. If this continues to happen, try and figure out what may be causing their frustration and fix it— then try the feeding again.

Q   *Which breast do I start on? Why do I need to switch? Why can't I start on the same side each time? I get so confused...*

A   The goal with breastfeeding is to get equal stimulation on both sides, so they get equal milk production. When the baby just starts to feed, he or she will get very vigorous with their sucking which creates *more* stimulation. Once they get to the second side, they are beginning to slow down their sucking, which will stimulate that breast *less*. If you start on the same side each time, that particular breast will get more stimulation than the other one, therefore, you will have unequal stimulation on your breasts.

When starting out breastfeeding, you want to start on one side, then switch to the other side for the rest of the feeding. The goal is 10-15 minutes of good sucking on each side— if possible. When you feed the next time, you want to start on the side you finished on *last*. This way the 2nd breast gets more stimulation than it did the last time and the 1st breast gets less. This is how you get equal stimulation. You will continue this practice throughout breastfeeding.

Now, if your baby is sleepy and you need to wake him (like we discussed above), and you are struggling to get the baby latched, the goal would be to get the baby latched on one side and *stay* feeding on that side. You will struggle to keep the baby awake and suckling during this feeding, so it would be best to keep the baby on this side for the whole time. This way you get a good feeding on the one side, and then you can start with the *other* breast the next feeding, thus again keeping the stimulation on both sides equal. When the baby becomes more awake and more demanding to feed, then you can go back to using both sides and switch accordingly.

Trust me, when you milk has come in a few days down the road, you will definitely know which side you need to feed on first. One breast will be fuller, heavier, and more painful than the other, so you will *know* which side you need to start on.

Q   *What is wrong? My baby is eating all the time and I don't think I have enough to give him/her… Should I give some formula?*

A   Remember, when you are breastfeeding your colostrum is in "a lot" smaller quantities than breast milk will be when it comes in, so, *yes,* your baby may want more than what you are giving to them.

If your baby had a substantial amount of amniotic fluid in the stomach after delivery and has thrown up this fluid, the stomach has been stretched out and, again, the baby may want more. Just think of it like giving the baby "dessert" when they want the "full meal deal". You are only filling up a portion of the stomach and not the whole thing. The solution would be to put the baby to breast "on demand" and continue to do so will help stimulate the breasts and your milk may come in a little sooner.

I know you may be getting little to no sleep at this time because the baby is demanding to eat frequently, and circumstances such as "little to no sleep for an extended time" has been a problem— even before the delivery. *But,* to continue with *exclusive breastfeeding,* you need to keep putting the baby to breast to stimulate the milk production. This is the appropriate way to go about it.

Now, if you are adamant that your baby is "starving" and you feel the need to give the baby formula— this is *your* decision.

Parents have insisted to go this route to make the baby more satisfied— if just to get *some* sleep because they are exhausted. If you do decide you want to do this, it would be best to limit the amount of formula to 10-15 milliliters during the feeding time. This way the baby will more likely wake up and nurse again in a 2 to 3-hour timeframe, following the breastfeeding schedule, than if you completely fill up the stomach.

If you do supplement with formula, you may only have to do this a couple times here and there, when your baby wants more than the colostrum. Then again, if your baby likes having the additional food, he or she may demand to get it for every feeding— until your milk comes in. Every baby is different when it comes to supplementing along with the breastfeeding, so be prepared either way.

Q   *If I do decide to supplement, how can I do this with breastfeeding? Do I feed with a bottle?*

A   There is an alternative way to accomplish this and breastfeed at the same time, *without* the use of the bottle. If you introduce a bottle to the baby during the time you are starting to breastfeed, you may just be "shooting yourself in the foot" or "sabotaging the breastfeeding" by doing this. The reason why is when at the breast, the baby must suck to get the colostrum to come out— so, he or she must work for it to make it happen.

If you introduce a bottle, the nipple "drips" and the baby does not have to work as hard to "get something". Then, when you put the baby back to breast the next time, the baby will then expect the colostrum to "drip" just like the bottle— and maybe make your baby frustrated. Then you have the problem of the baby wanting to refuse the breast, because the baby must "work harder" for it— and they now *expect* it to be simple and less work.

One solution to this would be to use a Supplemental Nursing System (SNS), which can be used at the breast while the baby is nursing. A breastfeeding syringe is filled with the formula and feeding tube is attached to the syringe. The end of the tube can then be placed either right next to the nipple before the baby latches on, or if this doesn't work for your baby, it may be inserted into the side of the mouth after the baby has latched onto the breast. Your nurse or lactation consultant can help you with setting this up and show you how it's done. Any unused formula the baby doesn't take during the feeding is to be discarded after the feeding is completed. Don't worry about "wasting" the formula. It comes in 2 oz bottles, so it's not much to waste. And— be sure to wash the equipment thoroughly after the feeding so it's ready for use the next time.

The idea with using this system is that the flow to the baby can be controlled, so they are only getting "a few drops" at a time when they are suckling— and *only* when they are suckling. If the baby gets the tube in the mouth— *just right*, they may be able to "suck" the formula out of the tube quickly. You have control over that and can pull back on the syringe a little to control how much they take as they suck. This is how you control the flow of formula through the tube, and *mimic* breastfeeding as it occurs now, which is different than when your milk comes in.

Another alternative with the tube and syringe can also be done with finger feeding it to the baby. If you want to breastfeed first and then give the supplement, either you *or* dad can do this. Your lactation consultant can demonstrate positioning of you and the baby if you want to try this. You can control the amount of formula given to the baby in drops, or pull back on the plunger if the baby wants to suck it fast, just like we just discussed above.

Another way to supplement the baby would be to spoon feed or cup feed the formula to the baby. These are methods your lactation consultant will be familiar with, and can show you how to do it. If your nurse is familiar with these methods, they can help you as well. (Not all nurses can work with SNS, cup, or spoon feeding as they may rely on the lactation consultants for this— but some nurses in some smaller hospitals may be familiar with these methods and can help you as well.)

If you decide to decline any of these options and insist on giving your baby a bottle, you have one thing you can do that might help keep the amount your baby is sucking down to smaller quantities— *and* getting the baby to slow down. The option you can use is to let the baby suck only a couple times, then remove the bottle from the mouth. Give your baby time to "pause" for 10-15 seconds, then give the bottle back to the baby, and keep repeating this until the baby *only* takes 10-15 milliliters. (If you are exclusively breastfeeding, then I would encourage you *not* to use this method, but if you do insist, remember, it is *your* choice.)

Just remember, once you introduce formula to the breastfeeding equation, your baby may expect this at *"each and every feeding"*, until your milk comes in and the baby is receiving more volume to fill their tummy up. This may last from anywhere to 1-5 days, so be prepared to go the short haul until your milk comes in.

Q   *What is that dried white stuff around the baby's mouth?*

A   Anytime you see this around your baby's mouth, you should be shouting "hallelujah"!! This is what is called a "milk mouth" and comes when the baby is getting a larger quantity of colostrum, or your milk is coming in. You may also notice your baby seems to be swallowing more frequently while sucking, which is another indicator of more volume for your baby. You can just wipe off the dried stuff from around the mouth with a warm wet cloth when you are finished feeding. This is *definitely* a good thing!!!

Q   *The pediatrician told me that I need to supplement my baby with formula, but I want to exclusively breastfeed and not give my baby any supplement… Why am I being "forced" to do this when it's against my wishes?*

A   The supplementation ordered by the pediatrician generally is done for a reason, and not to undermine your desire to exclusively breastfeed. In fact, it's the total opposite. They encourage exclusive breastfeeding, but may find your baby is not receiving a "sufficient amount" of colostrum at this time. The pediatrician obviously has assessed your baby, and for one reason or another has determined that, at the present time, the lack of volume in the colostrum produced by you is not enough to avoid certain issues that can occur with beginning exclusive breastfeeding, and the health of your baby. Dehydration, jaundice, low blood sugars, low temperatures, loss of 10% of birth weight— any one of these factors may be why the pediatrician has ordered formula supplementation. The increased volume of nourishment for your baby will help remedy these issues, at least until your milk comes in.

One option you might have, would be to ask if donor breastmilk could be ordered for you if you must supplement; since you are not producing enough at this time, and your baby must have something to correct whatever issue he or she is having. This way your baby still gets just breastmilk, in addition to the colostrum you provide, and you would be avoiding the formula, which you do not want your baby to have. This would be a win-win situation for both you and your baby!!

Q   *What if I want to pump my breasts and feed this to my baby?*

A   This is a great alternative for mothers who want to give their baby breastmilk, but do not want to breastfeed, or breastfeeding is not working for them. Your lactation consultant or nurse can set you up with a breast pump and demonstrate how to use it to start building up your milk supply for your baby. They can also give you information on storage options for the pumped breastmilk.

If you do pump your breasts to feed your baby, just remember, you need to pump every 2-3 hours, just as often as your baby would go to the breast. Pump for 15 minutes per breast, or whatever your lactation consultant or nurse recommends.

So... You Chose to Formula Feed Your Baby

Feeding your baby formula may have been an easy decision for you and your family. You may have already had a "not-so-great" breastfeeding experience with a previous child and *do not* want to go through that again... *EVER!!* It may be that you are unable to breastfeed due to medications you *must* take, so you *cannot* breastfeed your baby. Maybe you cannot produce enough breastmilk, so why even start it again? Maybe your mother or grandmother strongly suggested you bottle feed because they had bad experiences, so don't even try! That it's not worth the hassle— easier for others to feed baby, too. Breastfeeding "disgusts you" or "gives you the willies." Don't want to think about the baby "nursing" from your breast because it's just "weird to you." Then there those who know they are too anxious and don't feel they can do it or stick with it. There are countless reasons some mothers give for not wanting to breastfeed, and *that's okay*. It's your *personal choice* to do this if you want to, and no one should force you to do anything you don't want to do with your baby— including breastfeeding. This is your baby— are they going home with you to feed your baby for you? Are they going to raise your baby for you? You are the mother, and as your baby's advocate, you must do what is right for you and your baby's situation. This *is* OKAY!!

Formula fed babies are fed a little differently than breastfed babies are. Breastmilk is easier to digest than formula, so with formula, babies need to eat every 3-4 hours versus every 1 ½ to 3 hours like their breastfeeding buddies. They generally receive a larger amount each feeding, so they also tend to be a little more satisfied after finishing. Newborns within the first couple of days usually start off with between 10-30 milliliters of formula, and gradually adding "smaller amounts" of 5-10 milliliters a feeding if baby seems hungrier. But there are some factors which might come into play when bottle feeding your newborn, so we will go over some of these possible scenarios.

First Thing to Do Before Beginning to Feed

This one seems a little silly because most parents already know to do this, but this is just a reminder for some of the newbies out there or even the ones who "just forget" to do it first, and that is— place a burp cloth under the chin and tuck it in around the neck. I know, some of you are thinking that I am being ridiculous suggesting this to you, but you'd be surprised at even some of the "pros" out there *forgetting* this little step. Just because you may be starting back at square one with the new baby, doesn't mean it hurts to have a few reminders on the "little things" you just may have forgotten since the last time.

Baby's Not Wanting to Eat

This is a common occurrence, usually on the first day following delivery. There are several factors which might cause your little one to not want to eat:

Just too tired: Your baby has been through a lot this first day. The delivery was hard enough, but then there was a bunch of people messing with the baby, bathing the baby, giving shots, measuring, wrapping, passing baby around to a room full of visitors. This little kiddo hadn't been "touched" for 9 months, now everyone "has to" get their hands on him or her. All this overstimulation can make your poor kiddo just plum "tuckered out". SO— sleep is the next solution. Eating… naaah, don't care about that right now. And that goes for almost all babies.

Trying to get a tired baby to eat is sometimes tough, but it is essential the baby gets some nourishment, even if it's just 5 milliliters for a feeding. That small amount will help, and any larger amounts would be better— when they come. You still need to wake baby up if not waking on his or her own. You may need to try to "force feed", even just a little, by wiggling the bottle nipple in between the baby's gums, pushing the nipple in the mouth, and closing the mouth around the nipple. This way the baby will be more motivated to begin sucking, thus taking in some formula. Your nurse can help you with this if you are not so comfortable trying to do it. They can show you how to get your baby to eat something.

Don't want to eat because... BARF!!: Okay, your baby has now thrown up a mouthful or two of the nasty, mucous-y amniotic fluid that's been sitting in their stomach since they delivered. Remember the section Q & A on Baby, where we discussed the amniotic fluid, how it just sits on the stomach and doesn't digest— it just turns to mucous and upsets their stomach— and eventually they will throw it up? Well, that belly full of fluid makes it *really* hard to want to eat because the baby *is just not hungry!* How do you like it when someone tries to force you to eat some more when you are already full??

Once the stomach starts to empty the amniotic fluid, mucous, possibly old blood from the delivery, undigested food mixed with the mucous, then the baby will be hollering to eat now that the stomach is all stretched out and the baby wants to get it filled— again. Then you should have no problem with the little munchkin pestering you that he or she is hungry. And you will be happy to help your baby get what he or she is asking for.

Don't seem to like the taste of formula: In the beginning, your baby may give you some "really funny" faces when getting some formula from the first feedings. Just keep in mind that your baby has not needed to take in *any* food before they were born, and they are used to the amniotic fluid they have been sucking and swallowing for months, so they are kind of used to that "flavor". So, now you are introducing a new "flavor" and it takes a few feedings for your baby to get used to the change.

Just keep offering the formula, even if they seem to not like it. Your baby will begin to get used to the new taste of the food and start taking it when offered.

Baby Having Difficulty Feeding from the Nipple

Just as we discussed before in the breastfeeding section, some of these little kiddos didn't come right out of your tummy knowing just how to suck right.

The tongue might be thrusting out on the nipple instead of them using the tongue to draw it in; they may get the tongue way back in the mouth and now bring it forward to latch onto the nipple correctly; they may not want to close their mouth around the nipple since they have a big mouth wide open for breastfeeding instead; they may even suck on the nipple right but not yet figure out to suck and then swallow, so the formula "pools" in the cheeks and then falls out of the mouth; they may have a very, intense *gag reflex* with anything that barely touches the back of the mouth. These are just some of the problems you may encounter while feeding your new baby, so let's discuss some ways to help fix them.

Stroking the nipple down the tongue: For the babies who have difficulty grabbing onto the nipple and drawing into their mouths to suck: take the nipple, insert it into the mouth, and "stroke" the nipple on the tongue from the back to the front. This is one way to "train" the baby to place their tongue down instead of back so they can grasp the nipple. You may have to continue repeating this method a few times before your baby "catches on" to put the tongue down instead of back. Once the tongue is down you can lay the nipple on top of the tongue and hopefully your baby will close his or her mouth, grasp it and suck.

Using chin support: Using chin support is one way to help your baby close the mouth around the nipple so they can suck on it. You can do this by putting the bottle in your feeding hand and hold it with your thumb and your first two fingers. This leaves the last two fingers to "anchor" against the bottom of the chin and pull up— to help close the gap of the mouth. You may have to use firm pressure against the chin, especially if your baby wants to have a big, wide open breastfeeding mouth instead of a smaller bottle mouth.

You can continue holding your last two fingers there under the chin to continue maintaining chin support throughout the feeding, if needed. Once your baby gets more used to sucking on the bottle correctly, this method would no longer be needed.

Using cheek support: This method is used for the little "chipmunk cheeks" who swallows a little formula, but also likes to hoard some formula in the cheek pockets and not swallow it all— then it dribbles out on the sides of the mouth. This one is a little more difficult to accomplish as it takes a little more coordination pull it off, and you may not be able to successfully achieve the correct hand position— but "we'll give it the ol' college try!"

First, you would need to get the nipple of the bottle into your baby's mouth for them to suck. Next, you then "prop" the bottle against the space between your thumb and first finger. This leaves your thumb and finger free to take and grasp the sides of the baby's cheeks and gently squeeze together. This method helps to close off the sides of the mouth and allow for the formula to stay in, instead of dribbling out when they suck and then swallow. As they get better with the "suck and swallow" coordination, this may be discontinued, and then you can start holding the bottle the normal way.

Working around an intense gag reflex: There are few babies out there that seem to have a really challenging time breastfeeding or bottle feeding because any-thing "too big" or "too long" getting in the mouth causes them to gag. (I'm sure my mother had a tough time with this as I have a _very bad_ one myself— and I still have a major problem with it!!) If the nipple is too long, _they gag;_ if too much formula sits in their mouth, _they gag;_ if they are still trying to work up some amniotic fluid left in the stomach, _they gag._ Sometimes, you just cannot seem to win in this situation.

Fear not!! Your baby can manage to get some of the formula down in the beginning, and when given a little time, will become better able to suck and swallow with coordination. Most babies, when sucking on a nipple, will take most or all of the whole nipple in the mouth when feeding. You would think the baby would choke on all that nipple, but most do just fine with it without any problem. But for your "little gagger", you will have to go slowly and take your time with the feeding.

One way to you can help with this is to slowly push the nipple of the bottle in the mouth, but not to push it in all the way. Give your baby just a small enough amount of nipple he or she can grasp with the tongue, but not have enough to gag on. This may make it easier for your baby to suck on the bottle without gagging.

Another idea is you can try taking the nipple out of your baby's mouth after a few sucks. This would allow your baby to take a breath or two and swallow what is in the mouth before getting too much formula, which might cause them to choke and gag. Once your baby has taken a few breaths and swallowed what is in the mouth, then you can re-introduce the nipple and repeat throughout the feeding. As your baby's coordination begins to get better over time, you may stop using this method or only use when your baby "forgets" again what he or she needs to do.

Forgetting to breathe while sucking the bottle

Every so often, I encounter one of those little munchkins who get so intense with sucking the bottle and swallowing that they forget to take a breath. If this seems to be a problem for your baby, just take the bottle out of the mouth after about 10 sucks and *make* your baby pause. During that pause, your baby will then take some breaths and recover. After that, return the nipple to the mouth and resume feeding. Keep repeating this method each time throughout the feeding. This is another one where over time your baby should learn to breathe while sucking and swallowing, then you can stop using this method.

Sucking very hard, thus sucking down the formula

Some little ones get a really strong coordinated suck going when sucking on the bottle— then they "wolf" down the formula way too quickly. This is not a good thing, since they might be overeating during a feeding, and then they *throw up* a large amount of what they just ate afterwards. You can use the same technique discussed above: *you take the nipple out of your baby's mouth between 10-15 sucks and make the baby* pause. In this case, let your baby rest a good minute or two before giving back the bottle, even if your baby starts searching for it or crying. Some little ones don't like to wait when they are hungry, but if they eat too fast they will bring it back up if they eat too much.

In between the pauses, sit your baby up and burp him or her. (See below on how to burp your baby.) With this attempt at "fast food eating", they just might take in a large amount of air. So, getting the air out during those long pauses might keep your baby from spitting up a big amount of formula when they burp.

Our brains are hard wired with our stomachs, in that our stomachs will send a signal to the brain when the stomach is full. If we eat too much too fast, we usually have the feeling of being overly full after our stomach catches up to our brain. If we eat slowly, when are stomach is just full, then it signals to the brain we *are full,* so we stop eating— or at least some of us do. This usually takes about 20 minutes of slow eating for this to occur, so, it makes sense that if the baby is "wolfing" down his or her food really fast— say in 5-10 minutes, the baby still thinks they are hungry— so they continue to eat *more.* Thus, throwing up a lot of formula afterwards when they overeat.

Overfeeding Your Baby Formula

One of the problems with formula fed babies is the potential to overfeed the baby. This is not necessarily the amount of the feeding, but the frequency of feeding. Some babies may root around for something to suck on sooner than they are due to eat. The first thought of the parent is "I guess the baby's hungry again, so I guess I'll feed again." This may be true that your baby is hungry again, but in some instances, it is not. If your baby starts a pattern of "requesting to eat" every 1 ½ to 2 hours, and the baby is getting anywhere from 1 oz to 1-1/2 oz of formula a feeding, then this may not be a hunger cue— unless the baby is a BIG baby and would have more room to eat. Your

baby may have a tummy ache and the only thing the baby would like to do—
is suck!! Since sucking is a comfort measure, and the baby's tummy is hurting,
your baby may just want to suck. Offer a pacifier in between feedings to see
if this is just what the baby wanted.

If the baby spits out the pacifier and is still showing a hunger cue too soon
to eat, it would be necessary to hold the baby off with a pacifier until at least
the 3-hour mark. When a baby gets into a consistent pattern of eating "too
much, too soon", what happens is you begin to see thinner stools, which start
soaking into the diaper. What your baby is beginning to experience is what
we call "water-loss stools".

Water-loss stools are when the baby is getting too much formula to eat and
the body starts not digesting the larger, frequent amounts. The formula begins
to just "run right though the baby" and stops long enough along the way to
take some of the baby's body water with it. If this happens for a long time, the
baby can start getting dehydrated from the loss of body water, and become
sick. To avoid that, if you start seeing water-loss stools in your baby and the
baby is trying to eat too frequently, make the baby wait until it is time to feed
again. That would be *no earlier* than 3 hours. Keep feeding the baby this way
and continue to make the baby wait the full 3 hours minimum before feeding
again, and when enough feedings have occurred, and the baby gets used to
eating at 3 hours, then your baby should be out of the clear. You should also
begin to see the stools start to become soft again and not soaking into the
diaper. If the water-loss stools continue to be a problem, be sure and let your
nurse know so the baby can be evaluated for dehydration.

Burping your Baby

No matter if you are bottle feeding or breastfeeding, you should try to burp
your baby several times during a feeding. Babies take in extra air that gets
trapped in the stomach when they eat, so burping your baby periodically
during the feeding will help to get rid of this air.

With breastfed babies, they don't generally take in very much extra air, but some "little snarfers" really get into what they are doing and make a lot of heavy breathing noises or "popping" noises with the mouth while feeding. When they do this, the baby may take in some air, so burping is a good idea. You may have read in some other places that "you don't need to burp a breast-fed baby". Well— I tend to disagree with this little *tidbit* of misinformation. I have first-hand knowledge with some of the babies that have shown up in our nursery after a feeding, and that if a baby had not been burped previously during or after a feeding, they usually let you know quite loudly that a burp is in order. Their shrilly cry and body stiffening up completely in a straight line is a good indication they need a burp.

When the body stiffens up, it's the baby's way of trying to "get away" from the pain the gas is causing them. The shrilly cry is an indication *they are in* a lot of pain. I've seen sleeping babies come back to the nursery and be sleeping peacefully for about an hour— then— the screaming and crying and stiffen-ing up begins!! So, burp your poor breastfed baby between breasts and after the feeding.

With bottle fed babies, they do take in quite a bit of air with their sucking, so periodically burping them during the feeding is needed as well. And— for the "snarfers" out there who tend to try and eat really fast, there should be several *extra* burps during the feeding session.

I find it very difficult for me to get a baby to burp on my shoulder, like so many of us have seen done throughout the years, but I find that sitting them up when burping seems to work the best. So, this is the technique I use, and also teach my parents to do:

First, sit the baby up on your lap sideways, in a sitting position, facing either the right or left depending on which hand you will use on their backs to burp. (One side may be more comfortable than the other, so try whichever side works best for you.) Then, place your first two fingers around your baby's chin for support and your third finger underneath the armpit and close your second and third finger together. This helps you hold your baby steady, since they like to wobble around. Next, lean your baby forward a little and rest their tummy against the side part of your hand below. This will help to put a little counter-pressure against the tummy which helps "push" up some of the gas.

Once you have your baby positioned this way, take your other hand and pat your baby just enough that their whole body moves a little during each pat. This helps to "dislodge" or move the air bubbles around to the top so the baby can burp it out. If you pat way too soft, you won't be getting the air bubbles to move around enough for the baby to burp the air out. And— you *don't* want to pound on their backs *really* hard, because this isn't necessary, and you can possibly injure your baby doing this.

You know, for instance, when you pour out some soda into a glass and "bubbles" cling to the sides, and if you bump the glass *just right*, the air bubbles will rise to the top, right? Well, this is the same idea when you burp your baby. You need the "right" amount of patting on the back to dislodge the bubbles to bring them to the surface of the stomach so they can come out when your baby burps.

The second technique that goes along with this is to stroke your baby's back in an upward motion several times and alternate with patting the back. When you stroke the baby's back, firmly stroke it in an upward direction— from the waist up to the shoulders. While doing this, gently lift your baby up just a little bit... maybe, and inch or less— and then set them back down. Keep repeating the stroking and lifting about 10 times, then go back to patting the back. Repeat back and forth on both until the baby give you several good burps. This technique also helps to move the air bubbles around, so the bubbles move to the top and the baby can "burp" them out.

Now, some babies are a little harder to burp than others, and that's just normal. Sometimes you may get a *really, big burp*— that would make *any* dad proud!! LOL! Sometimes, you may get only a little burp, so continue to burp the baby for a little while longer to make sure you're not leaving some gas behind— *or* they may let you know in about an hour or so, when the gas pain is uncomfortable!! Thus, the stiffened up, shrilly crying baby—.

For the ones that are harder to burp, you may have to sit there and continue to burp your baby and stroke their back for 5, 10, maybe even 15 minutes before you get them to burp. If you still cannot get a burp out, it's possible there is no gas in the tummy and you can stop for now. If your baby does wake up in a short while and start a shrill cry and stiffen up, you can bet the gas is in there and needs to come out— so start burping your baby again. Usually, once the gas is gone babies will go back to sleep rather quickly— unless it's time to eat again, or the diaper needs changing, or they are awake now and want to stay up— you get my drift.

After the Feeding and Burping is Over...

Once you have completed the task of feeding and burping your baby and it's time for the little one to go to sleep, be sure and place a burp cloth underneath the chin and tuck it in and around the neck. Since most of the new babies spit up amniotic fluid and sometimes whatever they ate, it's a very good idea to place the burp cloth so that if the baby spits up it doesn't get all over everything— their clothes, the blanket they are wrapped in, the blanket over the bed pad. This is just an easier way to eliminate a lot of changing of bedding, wrapping blankets and clothing frequently— especially if they are spitting up a lot. Doing this will save you some time and energy— time that would be better spent resting between those feedings.

Q & A on Bottle Feeding

Q   *How much formula should I feed my baby?*

A   When first starting off, you will want to feed your baby anywhere from ½ oz (15 mls) to 1 oz (30 mls) to start off. The first day your baby may not take much if the tummy is full of amniotic fluid, it may be closer to ½ oz to ¾ oz (15-22.5 mls). Once your baby starts getting rid of all the fluid, he or she will begin eating a little larger amount of formula to fill the void where the fluid was.

If the baby, after feeding and burping, is still rooting around for the bottle and starts to fuss, then give the baby another 5 mls of formula and stop. Burp your baby and then see if he or she is still wanting more. Repeat another 5 mls, stop, and check again. When your baby is finished, record the amount of formula the baby took. If during the time before the next feeding the baby vomits up a large amount of formula, then this is a good indication he or she over-ate during the last feeding, so back off 5 mls from what you gave the last time. If he or she eats that much again, wait and see if your baby holds it down this time. If your baby does, then this would be the new amount of formula to feed your baby for several more feedings— until he or she again asks for more.

Q   *Can I use the same bottle the baby ate from for the next feeding? There's still a lot left in the bottle…*

A   If it is within 1 hour of the baby's last feeding, then the answer is "Yes". If it is longer than 1 hour, then the answer is "No". The reason behind the two answers is due to the length of time the formula has been left out, and the chance of bacteria starting to grow in the formula. That sounds "gross" and here's why… When your baby puts his or her mouth on the bottle, they have now left germs on the bottle's nipple and the formula has now had contact with those germs. The formula now has been contaminated by the baby, therefore, when the bottle has been left out at room temperature for too long, there is a greater chance for the bacteria to grow.

We all know parents hate to waste formula, especially since it seems like a lot to waste, but there is only 2 oz of formula in the bottle. And— the bottle is meant for "one-time use only". So— don't be afraid to throw away the extra that's left. It's a lot safer for your baby if you just discard the leftovers.

Q   *Since I'm bottle feeding, how do I keep my milk from coming in?*

A   There are several things you can do to help keep milk production at bay, but it's not guaranteed that you may not have some milk production or engorgement. Your body will naturally work to make milk when your baby is born. The key to helping suppress milk production would be to provide no stimulation to the breasts, or at least as little as possible. This means do not put baby to breast to suckle, even a few times for the "heck of it".

Some moms will do this just to give the baby some colostrum before solely going to formula feeding. They think, "Oh… I just give a little colostrum, so my baby can get the benefit of the immunities for a couple days, and then I'll just bottle feed after." It is strongly suggested you do not do this if you *will be* solely formula feeding. Any stimulation to the breasts can bring on milk production, so no stimulation of any kind would be more beneficial for you.

If you decide to go ahead and breastfeed, even just a little, and then stop breastfeeding— be prepared for your milk to come in! It might be possible if you do decide to put the baby to breast for just a little of the colostrum, that you do change your mind and decide to breastfeed. This would be great, so be sure and utilize lactation consultants and nurses to help you with your quest for breastfeeding, and answer any questions you may have on changing back over to bottle feeding in the future. If you want to go back to bottle feeding and your breastmilk is in, you may decide to pump the breastmilk and bottle feed it to your baby. This is a great alternative to feeding your baby formula.

Several things to do when you are not breastfeeding are:

- Wear a well-fitting support bra to decrease the chances of stimulation.

- Place ice packs on top of the breasts. This will help with breast swelling and constrict the blood vessels, which will help reduce the swelling and rapid blood supply to the breasts if engorgement is becoming a problem.

- Take a pain reliever, such as acetaminophen or ibuprofen, to relieve breast pain. Be sure to get the okay from your doctor first.

- Use clean cold cabbage leaves placed over the breasts and hold them in place with your bra. There are some enzymes in the cabbage leaves which help with milk suppression. Remove the leaves when wilted and replace with new clean, cold leaves. The coolness of the leaves will help with comfort.

- Avoid warm packs which increases the blood supply to breasts.

- Avoid direct shower spray of warm water to the breasts. This causes stimulation.

Contrary to what your mother or grandmother will tell you about pills to dry up your milk production, this method is no longer used. The medication used in previous years was found to increase the chances of heart attacks and stroke, so a prescription for this is no longer an option from your doctor.

Circumcisions (The "Boys Only" Club)

This is a controversial topic in that there are two sides to the circumcision subject of the newborn male baby. It is thought by some, and this includes some medical professionals, that circumcision is an unnecessary elective surgery which is performed on the penis to remove the additional foreskin. With proper education from the parents on good hygiene, and performance of good hygiene by the male child later on and into adulthood, there is no need to remove the foreskin. Then there are the others who decided that circumcision has definite health benefits, or that due to religious or personal beliefs circumcisions should be or will be performed.

In 2012, the American Academy of Pediatrics (AAP) posted a technical report in the *Pediatrics* journal on the subject of male circumcision. A task force was made up of members of the AAP, the American Academy of Family Physicians (AAFP), the American College of Obstetrics and Gynecology (ACOG), and the Centers for Disease Control and Prevention (CDC). They concluded that factual, current, non-biased information regarding circumcision along with post-circumcision care instructions be provided to parents. This allows for an informed decision by the parent on whether or not to have a circumcision performed on their baby. They also want benefits as well as risks presented to parents, so their decision can be weighed based on the correct information given. There is also information given regarding the need to provide educational material to all clinicians who care for newborn baby boys, which will enhance their knowledge base on education, care, and instructions given to parents. The decision whether or not to have their son circumcised is up to the parents and what they feel is in the baby's best interest— along with personal, cultural, or religious preferences.

According to the task force, the current recommendations are that benefits of newborn circumcision *outweigh* the risks, and here are the findings:

- To prevent Urinary Tract Infections (UTIs);

- To prevent the acquisition (contracting, catching) of HIV or sexual transmitted infections;

- To prevent the transmission (passing on) of HIV and sexually transmitted infections;

- To decrease the risk of penile cancer;

- That circumcision does not adversely affect the sexual function, sensitivity, or sexual satisfaction in the adult circumcised male

Not all parents decide to have their boys circumcised: it may be for personal reasons, such as the father or other males in the household are not circumcised and the baby will not be either; it may be because the parents do not believe the benefits outweigh the risks, therefore, decide against circumcision. There may be many other reasons that help to make up the parent's mind regarding the refusal of the circumcision. This is the parent's *right* to decide against the circumcision of their newborn baby boy.

Currently, most of the infant male circumcisions are performed using what is called a Plastibell, which is a small plastic device made in several different sizes to accommodate the glans (head) size on the infant male's penis. This device helps to protect the glans (head) of the penis until it is healed, and then the ring that is placed around the glans (head) falls off after several days and the penis finishes healing. For those who decide to proceed with the circumcision of their son, here is some information on how the procedure is performed.

(*WARNING*: This detailed information is *graphic*, and is provided for parents who want to learn how the circumcision is performed on their son. Anyone who doesn't want to know the details may skip the next two paragraphs.)

The pediatrician or other clinician trained in performing the circumcision starts off by having the baby placed in a harness or restraint, which keeps both arms and legs down and out of the way during the sterile procedure. The baby may be given a pacifier along with a concentrated sucrose solution of up to 2 milliliters. Sucrose is believed to have a pain relieving affect for infants, like being given some Morphine or other pain reliever, and is used frequently during painful procedures such as heel sticks, lab draws, or in this case, circumcisions. The pediatrician or clinician then uses a local anesthetic to numb the penis, both on the top and bottom close to the baby's scrotum. They then wait for several minutes before proceeding with the procedure to allow the anesthetic to take effect.

Once the anesthesia has taken effect, the pediatrician or clinician will use some small clamps to grasp the skin of the foreskin and clip downward approximately ½ to ¾ centimeters, to allow for the Plastibell to be placed over the glans. Once the Plastibell is in the correct position, then a small piece of sterile string is half-knotted loosely and slipped over the glans. When the string is in the correct position to follow the groove in place to accommodate the string, the string is then tightened very tightly and tied in a knot to cut off the blood flow to the upper foreskin tissue. The remaining foreskin tissue is then clipped off around the upper portion of the Plastibell ring all the way around the glans. Once this is complete, the plastic positioning piece used by the pediatrician or clinician is snapped off and the head of the penis is checked for any bleeding after the procedure is complete.

After completion and bleeding is minimal or non-existent, the baby is removed from the harness or restraint, diapered, and returned to the parents for continued comfort care. Instructions are then given to the parents for care of the circumcision until it is healed. If you notice a black ring around the Plastibell ring area, this is normal and not to be concerning. This is the remaining tissue in and around the outer ring where the string has cut off the blood supply. What you are seeing is a little of the necrotic (dead) tissue that will fall off when the ring falls off.

Eventually over the 5-8 days the necrotic (dead) tissue along with the Plastibell falls off, leaving a completed circumcised penis. Any remaining edges of the circumcision site may still need to heal for another day or two. During the healing period over the next 5-8 days, parents or caregivers should be looking for bleeding, redness, swelling, foul odor indicating infection, or tightening of the ring around the top of glans. If you notice any of these during your hospital stay, notify your nurse so it can be assessed and treated if needed. And, if you have returned home, notify the pediatrician, or primary care physician who will be taking over the baby's care, so that prompt medical attention can be obtained.

There are two other types of devices used still for the removal of the foreskin: the Gomco clamp and Mogen clamp. With these devices, the clamp is placed around the glans of the penis snuggly and the foreskin is then clipped off. With this method, there is generally a potential for more bleeding, but usually pressure applied with gauze and the clinician's fingers applying pressure to the site will stop the bleeding. There may be a need for silver nitrate or Gelfoam® gauze tape to stop the bleeding from the circumcision site, if pressure to the site is unsuccessful. These procedures also leave the head of the penis exposed and raw around the site of foreskin removal, and have more detailed care instructions than with the Plastibell device. These devices are being used less and less by clinicians, who are now in favor with the use of the Plastibell device instead.

Care of the Circumcision Site

Depending on the type of device used for the circumcision, certain care instructions would be given to the parents upon completion of the procedure.

Mogen or Gomco Clamps: The head of the glans penis is raw and exposed, and, during the healing time, is likely to stick to any surface coming in contact with the glans; specifically, the diaper. To prevent the glans from sticking to the diaper from some of the healing drainage and possibly "small amounts" of oozing blood, the glans of the penis needs to be well lubricated with a water-soluble lubricant, such as Vaseline®, and be covered with a small amount of gauze.

During the diaper change, once the bottom and around the penis is cleaned— *taking care to lightly rub the exposed glans with a soft wash cloth and warm water, and remove any remaining urine or stool during cleaning*— take a 4 x 4 square of gauze with a pea to grape sized amount on Vaseline®, rub it lightly together so the Vaseline® is covering a larger area on the gauze, and then place it gently over the glans of the penis. Carefully, pull up the diaper in between the legs and fasten around the waist snugly. But— be sure the diaper area around the circumcision site is "baggy", so there is very little pressure of the diaper against the penis. When making the next diaper change, remove the soiled 4 x 4 of gauze, clean the bottom area, and apply a new 4 x 4 with Vaseline® on the glans. Repeat this process for the next 24 hours, then only apply the Vaseline® on the glans before replacing with a clean diaper until the site is healing, for the next couple of days. There may be some spotting of blood, and anything less than quarter-sized is okay.

Plastibell: This is an easier type of circumcision to clean, as there is no need to use a lubricant with this device. When changing the diaper, you need to take care with cleaning around the Plastibell with a diaper wipe or soft washcloth with warm water. The best way to clean around the Plastibell without coming in contact with the tip of the glans is to take your index finger and place it on the side of the shaft, essentially shielding it with your finger. Then wipe all along the diaper area on that side and clean thoroughly. Repeat the process on the other side to protect the glans again. Once you have cleaned the entire diaper area, place a new diaper on the baby loosely so the diaper doesn't come in much contact with the exposed tip of the glans. (Tape the diaper snugly around the waist, but make sure the diaper is "baggy" around the site of the circumcision.)

If there is stool in and around the Plastibell ring, take a washcloth full of warm water and squeeze it out *over* the top of the Plastibell. This will help rinse out the ring and remove the stool without wiping on the sensitive glans. Be sure and leave the dirty diaper under the bottom during this so the diaper can catch any water that flows off your baby. Repeat with another washcloth full of water if necessary to remove all the stool. Then once the ring is clear, clean around the remainder of the diaper area like discussed above, remove the old diaper, and replace with a new one.

Drainage or Oozing from the Site

With either procedure, there may be a small amount of oozing or bleeding from the site. As long as it is less than quarter sized, it is normal. You may also notice a yellow drainage, especially on the tip of the glans. Unless this has a foul odor, this is *not* infection. This is a normal healing drainage which will dry to a scab on the site and will go away when the site is close to healing completely. You may even notice a pinkish, salmon color on the glans as well. This is uric crystals from the concentrated urine and is also normal. (Refer to section *Diapering Your Baby* under *Some "Oddities" Found in the Diaper* regarding the pinkish color found on the diaper.)

Your son may have the procedure done in the hospital a few days before discharge, but some may have it done the morning before discharge. Either way, be sure and watch for any heavier bleeding than normal. If you are in the hospital, be sure and let your nurse know if you are finding blood spots which seem to be soaking in the diaper and larger than a quarter-sized. The pediatrician may order some silver nitrate to be placed on the bleeding site, or may need to come back in to correct the issue. If you have gone home and notice the site bleeding more than it should, contact the pediatrician for further instructions— either to come into the office or an urgent care facility.

Watching for the 1st Post-Circumcision Void

After the circumcision is completed, your son may be a little fussy and need some comforting from you. Over the next several hours, you need to keep a close eye on your baby's diapers and to report when you have the 1st urine since the baby's circumcision. This is very important information for the pediatrician in that they want to be sure your son is able to urinate after the circumcision, so be sure to report it to your nurse so she can document this on his chart.

Don't be surprised if your son does not urinate for a long time— in fact, it may be closer to 12-15 hours before your baby has the 1st one. There are a couple reasons why there may be a delay in your son beginning to urinate again: You are breastfeeding, and the smaller amount of colostrum may delay having much output— and he doesn't want to pee— BECAUSE IT HURTS!!!

Now that your poor son had his "weenie wacked", any time he starts to urinate, he will start to pull the pee back. This is because the tip of the glans is raw, and the concentrated urine is hitting the area— and IT STINGS!! So— you may find a couple little tiny spots of pee, but not a whole lot. This would not count as a wet diaper— yet. Over the next several hours your son will continue to pee and pull back again, until at last— he cannot hold it any longer! He will have a very large wet diaper that might have very dark urine in it. Now— you can report this void to your nurse.

The penis is still functioning like it should, because we now have proof your son is able to urinate after the circumcision. He may still hold back on urinating again for the next few diapers until the stinging and soreness lessens and lessens. Once it subsides, he will urinate again without it bothering him.

Crying or Sleeping... Which One is it Going to Be??

After a baby boy has been circumcised, I have found that usually the baby reacts in one of two ways: they either *sleep* through their pain *or eat* through their pain.

The ones who *sleep* through their pain become difficult *again* to wake up and get to feed when it's time to eat. During that time, use the same techniques described under *Q and A on Breastfeeding* your sleepy baby wake up your baby to feed.

For the ones who want to *eat* through their pain, this is almost like the cluster feeding phase on the 2nd day. They seem to want to be permanently attached to the breast, or suck on anything to help soothe them. Sucking, remember, is a comfort measure for babies and when they are in pain, such as with a circumcision, they sometimes want to suck— *A LOT!*

We talked about pacifiers earlier under *Q and A on Breastfeeding,* so the use of one now for your baby's comfort is still *your* choice. If you decide to allow the baby a pacifier, the one used during the circumcision may still be in your son's crib and available there for your use. If it was discarded after the circumcision and your hospital does not give any extra out, have someone purchase some for you and bring them in, if you want one for him. This way he'll get some of the comfort he needs, and you won't feel like your nipples will fall off!!

And— if you are bottle feeding, don't be tempted to put a bottle in the baby's mouth every time he is crying. This can lead to overfeeding. If your baby is overfeeding, this can lead to water loss stools like we discussed in the section, *So You Want to Bottle Feed Your Baby*

Other Topics of Discussion

In this section, we will go over several topics on issues which are concerns for parents or healthcare workers. We will go over things such as SIDS, co-sleeping, rooming-in, and just some general topics which would be beneficial for me to address with regards to you and your baby. This information is not only for you during your hospital stay, but is also beneficial information for you after you have returned home.

Sudden Infant Death Syndrome (SIDS)

This is the most concerning issue parents worry about when a new baby arrives. SIDS can strike at any time within the first year of life, but is most prevalent in the first few months of age. The death of an infant with SIDS is unexplainable, meaning they cannot come up with a cause of death. The cause is unknown, but is thought to be a defect in the brain which controls breathing and awaking from sleep.

Other beliefs of factors for SIDS are that babies are subjected to asphyxiation or strangulation in their sleep environments, whether bedsharing or in their own cribs, yet there is no definitive proof of what was the actual cause of death upon the coroner's autopsy. Most coroner's death certificates were filed as *unknown* or *unspecified* unless there was proof of strangulation or asphyxiation.

"Although SIDS rates have declined by more than 50% since the early 1990s, SIDS remains the third-leading cause of infant mortality and the leading cause of post neonatal mortality (28 days to 1 year of age)."

> *SIDS and Other Sleep-Related Infant Deaths: Expansion of Recommendations for a Safe Infant Sleeping Environment* Pediatrics Nov 2011, 128 (5) e1341-e1367; DOI: 10.1542/peds.2011-2285

Several risk factors have been identified which may contribute to SIDS and have identified measures you can take to lessen the chances for SIDS to affect your baby. Place baby on the back to sleep, which is the most important measure for parents to follow.

A combination of physical and sleep environment factors can make your baby more vulnerable to SIDS, but each child is different, so any combination of these can contribute to SIDS.

Physical Factors

- *Brain defects:* Some babies have problems which make them more vulnerable because the breathing and sleep-arousal centers of the brain are not fully mature or are not functioning properly.

- *Low birth weight:* Premature or Low Birth Weight babies have a higher risk for SIDS because the brain is more likely very immature in development, which baby has little or no control of automatic responses to breathing or heart rate.

- *Respiratory infections:* Babies that have recently had a respiratory infection are at greater risk for SIDS, which contribute to breathing problems.

Environmental Factors

- *Sleeping on sides or stomach:* Babies may have more difficulty breathing when in these positions than when on the back.

- *Sleeping on a soft surface:* Fluffy pillows, comforters, or blankets can block the airway, especially if baby manages to turn over to their stomach to lie face down.

- *Bed sharing:* Even though co-sleeping is recommended to reduce the incidences of SIDS, bed sharing is not. Bed Sharing increases the risk of SIDS— therefore, it is not recommended for baby to sleep in any bed with parents, siblings, or family pets.

- *Overheating:* This is another environmental factor which may contribute to SIDS. These babies cannot move away from a person's body or unwrap themselves from a blanket if they get overheated.

Infant Risk Factors

- *Sex of baby:* Male babies are at a slightly higher risk for SIDS than their female counterparts.

- *Age of baby:* Most vulnerable between the 2-4 months of age

- *Race:* It is unknown why, but non-white babies are more vulnerable to develop SIDS.

- *Family history:* Siblings or cousins of the baby who have died of SIDS, make them vulnerable to SIDS.

- *Second-hand smoke:* Babies who live with smokers are at a higher risk for SIDS.

- *Prematurity:* Also puts your baby at risk for SIDS.

Maternal Risk Factors

Risk factors which puts her baby at risk for SIDS are:

- Under the age of 20

- Smokes cigarettes

- Drinks alcohol or uses drugs during the pregnancy and after

- Has inadequate or no prenatal care.

Prevention

Back to sleep: Always place the baby on the back to sleep, and not the side or stomach, for the first year of life. If the baby is starting to roll on his or her own, don't be concerned with trying to keep your baby on the back.

Don't always assume any other caregiver will place the baby in this position to sleep. Let your wishes be known to them to place the baby on the back for sleeping.

Don't overheat your baby: Either outfit your baby to stay warm with the clothing they have on or place a blanket over their body around the waist and tuck it in on the sides of the mattress to keep it from coming loose.

If baby is beginning to move around in bed more often and the blanket becomes dislodged, then forego placing a blanket around them and just dress them warmly.

Have your baby sleep in the same room: Ideally, it is best for baby to sleep in the same room with you, but in their own crib or on their own sleep surface. Do not place them in bed with you, as this is not safe sleeping for your baby, as this puts them at risk for suffocation.

Breastfeed your baby, if possible: Breastfeeding for at least six months lowers the risk of SIDS related deaths.

Bare baby crib: To protect your baby, it is recommended that when outfitting your baby's crib, you do not place anything in the crib with the baby. Stuffed toys, bumper pads, loose blankets, baby hats, and pillows are not to be placed in the crib. As baby gets a little more active when sleeping, they can move around in bed and get caught up in the blankets or snugged up to the bumper pads, stuffed toys or pillows, and re-breathe carbon dioxide they are exhaling, which is also a contributing factor for SIDS.

Don't use baby monitors: Some baby monitor companies will advertise the safety of using monitors to reduce the risk of SIDS. The American Academy of Pediatricians discourage use of monitors or other devises as ineffective at preventing SIDS.

Pacifier usage: Offer the use of a pacifier to your baby. If not interested, don't force it. And, if the pacifier falls out of the mouth while sleeping, don't replace it.

Immunize baby: There is evidence to support decreased risk for SIDS by immunizing your baby, but no evidence that immunizing puts them at risk.

Co-Sleeping

This is different from bed sharing, in that the baby sleeps in the same room with you, but not in the same bed. According to the American Academy of Pediatricians, co-sleeping in the same room, but on separate sleep surfaces, reduce the risk for SIDS by as much as 50%, and is safer than bed-sharing. Should you, or shouldn't you? Is it helpful or harmful? There are definitely two sides to this coin, so we will weigh the pros and cons found about the subject of co-sleeping.

Benefits of Co-Sleeping:

- Learn your baby's feeding cues and can attend to baby quicker; more convenient
- Synchronizing sleep cycles together between mom and baby
- Babies fall asleep easier and go back to sleep easier after waking up
- Helps lead babies to more nighttime sleep overall
- Gives parents a sense of more intimacy with their baby, especially if apart during the daytime (or nighttime, if you work nights)

Cons to Co-Sleeping:

- Less sleep for mom – babies make all kinds of noises during sleep, and moms wake up to every little noise

- Less sleep for baby - moms tend to pick up baby during first noises (super-attentive), which may make things more difficult with you and baby getting more sleep

- Less intimacy with your partner – noisy baby may make getting "in the mood" or concentrating on your partner's needs very difficult

Bed Sharing

This is a big ol' hot topic of discussion and debate among parents, advocates, and the healthcare community. There are many advocates and studies done about the positive aspects of bed sharing, but there are several out there with regards to the dangerousness of it. Which ones are right? Did they do a measurable study or were the results not conclusive? According to the American Academy of Pediatrics, the infants at greater risk for SIDS are from the ages of 0-3 months in a bed-sharing situation. Here's a list of recommendations of what not to do when bed sharing, if you do decide bed sharing is the way you want to go:

- No smoking around your baby. This increases exposure to second-hand smoke and risks for SIDS;

- Avoid alcohol, drugs or over-the-counter medications which might cause you to fall asleep and not awaken easily;

- Do not bed share on a sofa, recliner or chair. Risk for baby to accidentally suffocate/smother or becoming entrapped between cushions, parents, armrests, back of sofa, etc.;

- Do not place baby on top of a pillow, head on a pillow, or around one. Increases risk for suffocation/SIDS;

- Make sure there's no bedding bunched up around the baby's face;

- Do not swaddle baby while bed sharing. Increases baby's risk for overheating from blankets and parents radiating heat and increases risk for SIDS;

- Moms and dads, bundle up your very long hair. Increases risk for wrapping around baby's neck.

- Do not bed share if parent(s) are obese. Increases risk for mom and/or dad not to be able to feel how close the baby is to the body, therefore, increasing the risk for suffocation;

- Do not breastfeed your baby lying in bed, on a reclining chair, or on a sofa if you are tired and in danger of falling asleep

Rooming-In

There seems to be a differing of opinions with regards to rooming-in during your hospital stay. It is shown that rooming-in is beneficial for breastfeeding. Babies are put to the breast quicker for feedings, and it increases the number of breastfeedings, allowing for feeding on demand. Bonding is also established and continued with rooming-in, which are proven to be beneficial for the mother-baby couplet. It is also proven that babies are at less risk to develop newborn complications and less risk for SIDS.

Although rooming-in has become or is becoming the norm in the hospital setting, there should still be some lee-way in the hospital policies which allow for exceptions. Alison Steube, MD and assistant professor of Obstetrics and Gynecology at the University of North Carolina School of Medicine, puts rooming-in in the correct perspective. *"Rooming in should be the norm, but flexibility is needed to individualize care when circumstances require it,"* she said. What is being said here is that, "Yes" rooming-in is a good thing and should be done routinely in the hospital setting, however, certain situations need to be *"taken into account"* or addressed which might be beneficial for some separation time between mother and baby.

When babies remain in the room continuously for several days, there are some issues which happen more frequently with rooming-in than not:

- Baby knows you are near "at all times". He or she can hear you talking and can smell you in the room, so they know you are near. If the baby wants to be held "at all times" or put to the breast continuously, this might interfere with mother's sleep. If she is already sleep deprived before entering the hospital, then after baby is born it gets even worse with continued rooming-in. Mom then goes home sleep deprived and "anything goes" if it will allow for some sleep.

- Sometimes sending the baby out to the nursery for a few hours can allow for mom to get some "much needed" sleep she otherwise would not get with her baby continually fussing.

- Baby develops a "bed allergy" to sleeping in the crib, even if it is next to mom in the room. Baby falls asleep while being held or finished with feeding, and when placed back into the crib begins to fuss and cry until held again. This is what we lovingly call a "bed allergy". Baby "wants those nice warm arms versus that cold hard bed", therefore, will fuss every time you put him or her back into the crib. They may fuss and root around for food, then when it's offered again, the baby falls back to sleep, put back in the crib, and the process starts all over again. This can be very exhausting— at least until your breastmilk comes in.

- Baby wants only mom to hold him or her, and will cry until her or she gets what they want. Doesn't matter who attempts to quiet or soothe the baby, the baby fusses, cries or gets downright angry until mom holds him or her again. Sorry, dad, but baby has been with mom continuously for nine months, so naturally, mom is the #1 person the baby wants right now. Unfortunately, this could lead to unsafe co-sleeping on mom's part because of the exhaustion she's experiencing due to all the baby's demands.

- From sheer exhaustion, mom might be tempted to place baby in bed with her, essentially co-sleeping, which puts the baby at risk for SIDS.

- Mom may become sick after delivery, and caring for the baby may not be possible at this time. She may need additional medical support and rest to recuperate, and caring for the baby might put her at additional personal risk.

Anxiety Around the Baby

When a baby is crying, and you don't know what to do or what the baby is crying for, sometimes parents get anxious around the baby. This happens quite frequently with new parents, because they are learning constantly or have questions or concerns about lots of things. This is normal behavior for first-timers, but it can be an issue when you are anxious around the baby.

Babies sense when the one holding them or even just near them are anxious or tense. If they sense this, then they may get tense and distressed just because *you* are. Then they start fussing or crying even more, which gets you even more anxious or tense, then baby gets even more— and so on and so forth!

It may seem hard to do when you start feeling this way, but try to remain calm and soothing during this stressful time for your baby. This will help him or her to start relaxing and winding down. Talking to the baby soothingly, no matter what words are coming out of your mouth, can not only help calm the baby down, but can also help in calming you down as well.

If you cannot calm down around the baby, then it's okay to step out of the room or even out of the house, if you have returned home, to help you calm down. It's not good to continually be around a baby who is distressing to you, until you can calm yourself down. You'll just keep "feeding" off each other and making the situation escalate, which could put you in the perfect position to cause harm to your baby. (Which I know you don't want to do— but situations like this can be a precursor to child abuse.)

If the anxiety around the baby does not subside, then it might be beneficial for you to talk to your doctor about helping to manage your anxiety. You may need some medication to help you get "over the hump" until things begin to smooth out for you. Enlisting the help from family, friends, or other caregivers to take over for a little while so you can get away for some *me time*, will also go a long way in helping to reel in the anxiety.

Passing Around Baby "Like a Football"

There is one thing which might stress your baby out the first few days, and that would be being passed around like a football. Everybody and their brother wants to get a hold of that baby as soon as he or she is born, so passing the baby around to everybody who comes in to visit may not be the best thing to do— at least for your baby.

Your baby has not been touched for a whole 9 months while in your tummy, so naturally your baby may get a little distressed by being held by so many people in a relatively brief period of time. I have always taught my parents this— imagine every one of those people that came in and held your baby, gave you a hard hug for 10 minutes— each! How would you then feel? Overstimulated? Sore? Stressed out? Now think of this in relation to your baby. I think this is a pretty good analogy to use to describe what your baby might be feeling.

If this does happen to your baby, don't be surprised he or she gets either very fussy and inconsolable, or tries to sleep for a very long time. To avoid this, you might want to limit the number of visitors holding your baby for the first time.

Sick Visitors

With regards to your visitors— don't allow them to visit you while they are sick!! This is considered a well floor at the hospital, so you don't want them coming in and exposing you and your newborn to cold, flu, chicken pox, etc. (And we certainly do not want to be exposed either.)

During the official flu season, visitors that have any signs or symptoms of having the flu will not be allowed in to visit. It is recommended that only essential persons to the mother's well-being visit. This is in accordance to the CDC guidelines during the flu season, which runs from October thru the end of March, to prevent transmission to the mother or baby. Also, children who are approximately 13 years of age or younger will not be allowed in at all, unless they are siblings with no signs of illness. Since they come in constant contact with other children and can contract or pass on the flu easily, they will not be allowed to visit. Generally, this ban does not take full effect unless there is a documented local outbreak of the influenza virus.

But this does not just mean the flu, this covers anything that could be passed on to the mother or baby, from a simple cold to any highly contagious virus. We want our patients to be protected, so be vigilant at screening your visitors before they come to visit. Make sure you ask them if they are sick to not visit you or the baby until they are well, and to certainly not bring any children with them who are showing signs of illness.

Coughing, sneezing, congestion, nausea and vomiting, diarrhea, fever, spots on the skin, rashes, and sore throat are all signs and symptoms of illness. If someone does come to visit you and are showing any of these signs, ask them to leave. If you do not wish for your sick visitor to leave, then they need to wear a hospital facemask and wash their hands. It would be best if the sick individual stays at the perimeter of the room and not close to you, baby or your significant other so as not to pass anything on to any of you.

For the health of you and your new family, it's important to be aware of any sick individuals coming in to the hospital.

Generational Pictures

When your baby is born, and you have your parents, grandparents, great-grandparents, or even great-great grandparents, it's wise to get a photograph of all the generations you can get together with you and your new baby. Life is short, and with elderly family members we don't know when their time will come, and they will no longer be with us. The sooner you can get the family together for a generational picture, the better— and you will be glad you did!! This will be a valuable piece of family history which can be passed down through the family, so you don't want to miss the opportunity to capture this special moment.

I have been researching my family history for several years now, and I treasure all the pictures I have captured or pictures that have been shared with me. Family is very special, and photographs can keep those memories alive for a long time.

Your Discharge from the Hospital

There are several things that need to be finished before you are, or will be discharged from the hospital. Once these tasks are completed, you will be able to take your newly expanded family home.

Birth Certificate/Affidavit

Your hospital will give you a form to fill out for the birth certificate, which will be filed with the state after your discharge. This will need to be completed before you go home. You may have a form which will be the original sent off to the state, or you may have a worksheet to fill out and the hospital secretary will type it up for you. Our hospital provides a worksheet for our parents to fill out and we produce a state issued typed copy for our parents to review prior to filing. We give the typed copy back to the parents to make sure everything on the birth certificate is correct, and they have to initial the copy before it is submitted to the state. This ensures there are no errors on the birth certificate, which can be very difficult to get corrected once the state has processed it. (Lots of red tape…)

If the parents are not married, then an affidavit is also produced to accompany the birth certificate when it is filed. This is signed by both parents in the company of two hospital witnesses, as this is a legal document.

Car Seat Check

Before your baby can go home, the car seat you will place your baby in must be checked to be sure it is safe to transport your baby home. This is a necessary safety feature most, if not all, hospitals today complete before dismissal.

Your car seat is checked with the national registry, National Highway Traffic Safety Administration (NHTSA), to make sure your car seat is up-to-date and there are no pending recalls with your car seat. If there are recalls on your make and model of car seat, you will be notified by your nurse to either purchase a new car seat before discharge, or if the recall is not significant enough where you can still use the carrier safely, you will have a choice whether to use the car seat or purchase a new one. (i.e. Some recalls have been with the carrier and the base not latching well and can come apart during an impact. The carrier could still be used, but not with the base until latch the mechanism is replaced by the manufacturer.)

Car seats are good for 6 years, and anything older can compromise the safety of your baby. Car seats are often times left in the car on a continuous basis, therefore, subjected to heat and cold for several years. The plastic frame of the car seat begins to become brittle after 6 years and can break easily, thus not providing a safe and secure seat for your baby in the event of a car accident.

We also check to make sure the car seat is registered with your current residence so that if, at a later date, there is a recall on the seat, you can be notified of this recall. Most times you can register directly with the manufacturer on the company website, and if not, you can send the registration card in by mail. Be sure and contact the manufacturer if you move during any time you are still using the car seat. (Some parents may move in between children and still be using the original car seat from the first child, but forget to make the change with the manufacturer.)

It is important *not* to purchase an unknown car seat from a garage sale, consignment shop, or thrift store. Even though parents want to save money when purchasing baby needs, the car seat is one you *do not* want to compromise on. You will have no idea whether that car seat has ever been in a car accident. If it had been in one, you are now compromising on the safety of your baby, as car seats are only good for one accident before they must be replaced. Save your money on other things, such as baby clothes, blankets, etc. that can be safely reused.

Car seats are also checked to see if there are anything "added on" to the carrier. Baby toys, cushioned back and head rests, anything that did not come with the car seat is considered an "add on" and not recommended to be placed on the car seat when in use in the vehicle. These "add on(s)" have not been crash tested with the car seat, therefore, can compromise the *safety* of the car seat itself. Most infant car seat carriers come with a padded back and head rest and these are okay. They have been tested by the manufacturer for safety with the car seat. Added cushioned back and head rests which did not come with the car seat are *not* recommended. These have not been crash tested with the car seat and can compromise the safety of your baby.

Toys attached to the car seat handle for the baby to play with can become projectiles within the car in the event of an accident, which can harm your baby or any other passenger in the vehicle. If you are carrying your baby in the carrier, say to the pediatrician's office or the store, you may attach the toys during this time. But, be sure to remove them when placing your baby in the car before you drive away.

Screenings for Baby

There are several screenings which take place before your baby is discharged from the hospital. Bilirubin levels, hearing screening, PKU testing, and CCHD testing are performed right before discharge. We will go over each one to give you a better understanding of why these are performed on your baby.

Bilirubin Levels: As discussed earlier in the section *Skin Color and Conditions* under *Jaundice*, labs are drawn on all babies just before discharge, or within 48 hours of birth. By testing all babies before discharge, we are making sure there are no babies missed that may have become jaundiced enough and now require phototherapy. Some babies do not become visibly jaundiced enough to alert their caregiver that the bilirubin levels may be too high and need to be treated. By testing every baby before discharge, this helps to eliminate the chance for a jaundiced baby to be dismissed before phototherapy is initiated when needed. Remember, if bilirubin levels become too high and are not treated, this can be deadly to your baby. (Refer to *Jaundice* under treatment)

Critical congenital heart disease (CCHD) testing: This is a very simple screening completed within a 5-10 min period which can help detect whether your baby might have a congenital heart defect. An otherwise healthy-looking baby may have a cardiac issue which can worsen over time if not treated in a timely manner.

A pulse oximeter, which detects the oxygenation in the blood (like the one placed on you during your hospitalization), is place on the right hand and the right or left foot. After a few minutes we will get a reading of the blood oxygenation levels of your baby. If they are 95% or higher, and the hand and foot are within 3% difference, your baby is showing a negative result for a cardiac issue. If they are saturating less than 95% or there is a significant difference of 4% or more, then your baby may have a cardiac issue and further testing would be needed.

When the testing is done, and a baby shows a positive result, usually the nurse or practitioner will retest after an hour to make sure this is not a false positive result before jumping right in to testing. False positives can result from baby's cold hands or feet, or improper attachment of the pulse oximeter. The baby would be re-screened in one hour, and a 3rd time if the 2nd screening is also positive. If there are 3 positive screenings and your baby is not immediately symptomatic of a cardiac issue, your baby will then be referred to a neonatologist or pediatric cardiologist for further testing. If the screening result is less than 90% or greater than 3% difference and the baby is symptomatic, then immediate care and testing will be initiated in your hospital. If your hospital cannot provide the needed care for your baby, they will be transferred to a tertiary pediatric care center where immediate testing and treatment can be performed.

This is a quick, easy screening for several major cardiac issues, but is *only a screening.* This does not guarantee there is not a cardiac issue which may not be detected early on. This only test for seven major cardiac issues which require immediate testing and treatment, but some other cardiac issues might be detected as well.

Hearing screening: This is a screening used to detect if your baby may have a hearing problem, which can start the process early for follow-up with a pediatric audiologist. Early detection of a hearing problem is beneficial for your baby's language and communication development. By further testing and pinpointing the hearing loss of your baby, treatment can begin earlier rather than later. Instead of having a frustrated 2-year old who cannot communicate with those around him or her, the problem can be detected well before that age and treatment can be started *before* communication can become a problem.

There are two methods of testing used by hospitals for hearing screenings: OAE (otoacoustic emissions) and ABR (auditory brainstem response). OAE are tested with a small probe placed in the ear, sounds are transmitted into the probe, and a response of the hair cells of the cochlea are measured. These hair cells in the inner ear send signals to the brain through nerve pathways when hearing is detected. With ABR testing, electrodes are held in place with sticky tabs, and sound is transmitted into the ear, and the baby's brain waves response to the sound is measured. Both screenings are very easy to complete and do not harm the baby when performed.

Again, this is a *screening*— so one failed hearing screening does not necessarily indicate your baby's having a hearing problem. Sometimes testing is done too early or the baby may have some fluid or vernix still in the ear canal. Either one can cause a false failed test. Re-testing is usually done to determine if the first test is accurate before a referral to an audiologist is made.

PKU (phenylketonuria) testing: This is a blood test which is performed to detect whether or not your baby's body can break down the amino acid (phenylalanine) found in protein feedings. If the phenylalanine cannot be broken down and it continues to build up in the body, over time it can cause several developmental and mental issues. This is an inherited disorder passed on from *both* parents (both are carriers of the gene) to a child. If only one parent passes on the gene, the baby then becomes a carrier but does not have PKU.

A few drops of your baby's blood (from a heal stick) are place on a special paper for testing. This paper is then sent to the state agency lab for testing to be completed. If the results show a positive result for PKU, your pediatrician or PCP will provide further diagnostic testing to determine if the initial testing results are accurate.

If your baby has PKU, you will be notified by the state agency completing the testing, or directly from your health care provider (pediatrician or primary healthcare physician) when they receive the results. Additional testing will be performed for PKU severity, and then dietary changes will need to be made specific for your baby. Along with dietary changes, routine frequent blood testing will be performed to test the levels of phenylalanine. These will continue throughout your child's lifetime.

It's the "Little Things..."

Everything we do as nurses or practitioners are to make sure you and your new baby have a great start to your new life ahead. We want you to be educated, informed, and comfortable with both your care and your baby's care. Unfortunately, your time in the hospital is *very short*— and there's a lot of information and teaching to pack into those short two or three days. Remember what I stated at the beginning of the book that you are *lucky* if you remember even 25% of what information we give to you during that time??? Well— that's very true!! That time will go by so fast you won't know "which end is up," and then you are left to go home with this new baby.

During you and your baby's hospital stay, if you have questions about anything that is concerning you— *don't* hesitate to ask your nurse or doctor about it. Never be embarrassed to ask questions about anything, even if you feel it might be a "stupid question." There are *"no stupid questions"*!! Anything you aren't sure of just ask— and don't let anyone you ask a question "make" you feel bad *for* asking. You have a question, and you want "clarification" so you can understand, just ask! That's it— end of story!!! Also, don't hesitate to ask a question as 2nd· 3rd· or 4th time if you forget the original answer. Remember— 25% may be the only amount of retention for you during your stay.

Here's another piece of advice directly from me to you all— whatever hospital you may be in and wherever you live, you may have some issues with your nursing care or certain ways things are done. You have a right to be treated with respect and you also have a voice in how you and your baby's care will go. If you don't want to breastfeed— *don't*. What are they gonna do— let your baby *starve*?? They can't bully you into breastfeeding if you do not want to. That is your choice— not theirs. If you want to use a pacifier for your baby, go right ahead. If you don't want to take narcotic pain meds— that's for you to decide. If you want to get some sleep and want your baby to go to the nursery for a little while, just ask. This book is filled with recommendations and suggestions, but there's a lot of it that you may or may not agree on. Just remember, these are recommendations and suggestions— not "hard and fast" rules, only advice. We do want what is best for you and your baby, but you are the ultimate deciding factor of how and when you may use this advice— and *if* you use this advice.

Don't be scared— you'll do just fine. Just listen to your "gut instincts…" If something is not right, or you are concerned with something which you don't think can wait on, call your obstetrician or pediatrician— whichever the case may be. If it is after office hours, call if you feel you cannot wait until the next business day. The doctors are on call 24/7 to help determine if you can wait until the next business day to be seen, or need to go to urgent care or the emergency room.

Last... But Not Least

Here's the last bit of cautionary advice— *beware of the Internet!!* With the vast amount of healthcare information— and misinformation— on the Internet, you may not find the appropriate or accurate answers to your questions— and some information is also *outdated*, too. Stay away from blogs written by just anybody, mostly these are just opinions or someone's personal accounts. Don't Google something and take just anyone's opinion as gospel. Make sure you are looking for reputable and reliable sources when researching any healthcare questions you may have. Government health websites, scholarly journals written by healthcare professionals, government organizations such as Centers for Disease Control (CDC), university studies, etc. I have patients ask healthcare questions all the time about certain things that are either not accurate or outdated information, and I ask where the information came from. Usually, it's from an outdated or inaccurate source. So be diligent in your searches online— look for the *best* sources.

Conclusion

....

I hope you found this book informative— if not a little bit entertaining, too. This has been a labor of love and caring on my part to see that every mother is completely informed on her hospital care and every parent is completely informed on their baby's care. There is so much information and education to be provided, but only so much time during your stay to give you this information that I felt the need to provide this book. As stated at the beginning of the book, there are books galore out there about pregnancy, breastfeeding, baby care, infant loss, etc., etc., etc., but there just wasn't anything out there just on the hospital stay itself. So— here you have a book to read *before* your hospital stay, and book to go back to during your stay. If you can't remember what you read about a "particular situation" that has come up, you now have a reference book to help you get through.

**Just remember… this book is about routine care. There may be some issues or diagnosis that you may come across with your care or your baby's care, which may not be addressed in this book. This is where the obstetrician or pediatrician comes into play to discuss and educate you on any "out of the ordinary" situations and how the care will be administered.

References

Periodicals

AAP Media. (2014, July 14). Bed sharing remains greatest risk factor for sleep related infant deaths. *AAP Pressroom Media Center.* Retrieved from https://www.aap.org/en-us/about-the-aap/aap-press-room/Pages/Bed-Sharing-Remains-Greatest-Risk-Factor-for-Sleep-Related-Infant-Deaths.aspx

Abboud, T. L., Moore, M., Zhu, J., & Kimball, S. (1987). Epidural butorphanol or morphine for the relief of post-cesarean section pain. *Anesthesia & Analgesia, 66*(9), 887-893. https://doi.org/10.1213/00000539-198709000-00015

American Academy of Pediatrics. (2012). Breastfeeding and the use of human milk. *Pediatrics, 129*(3). Retrieved from http://pediatrics.aappublications.org/content/129/3/e827#ref-24

Bartick, M., & Reinhold, A. (2010). The burden of suboptimal breastfeeding in the united states: A pediatric cost analysis. *Pediatrics, 125*(5). Retrieved from http://pediatrics.aappublications.org/content/125/5/e1048

Baxley, E. G., & Gobbo, R. W. (2004). Shoulder dystocia. *American Family Physician, 69*(7), 1707-1714. Retrieved from http://www.aafp.org/afp/2004/0401/p1707.html

Blank, S., Brady, M., Buerk, E., Carlo, W., Diekema, D., Freedman, A., . . . Wegner, S. (2012). Male circumcision [PDF]. *Pediatrics.* Retrieved from http://pediatrics.aappublications.org/content/pediatrics/early/2012/08/22/peds.2012-1990.full.pdf

Checa, A., Holm, T., Sjodin, M. O. D., Reinke, S. N., Alm, J., Scheynius, A., & Wheelock, C. E. (2015). Lipid mediator profile in vernix caseosa reflects skin barrier development. *Scientific Reports.* https://doi.org/10.1038/srep15740

Coco, A. S., & Silverman, S. D. (1998). External cephalic version. *American Family Physician*, *58*(3), 731-738. Retrieved from http://www.aafp.org/afp/1998/0901/p731.html

Colvin, J. D., Collie-Akers, V., Schunn, C., & Moon, R. Y. (2014). Sleep environment risks for younger and older infants. *Pediatrics*, *134*(2). Retrieved from http://pediatrics.aappublications.org/content/134/2/e406

Dancel, R., & Price, D. (2012). Evaluation of newborns with preauricular skin lesions. *American Family Physician*, *85*(10), 993-998. Retrieved from http://www.aafp.org/afp/2012/0515/p993.html

Eidelman, A. I., & Schanler, R. J. (2012). Breastfeeding and the use of human milk. *Pediatrics*, *129*(3). Retrieved from http://pediatrics.aappublications.org/content/129/3/e827

Feldman-Winter, L., & Goldsmith, J. P. (2016). Safe sleep and skin-to-skin care in the neonatal period for healthy term newborns. *Pediatrics*, *138*(3). Retrieved from http://pediatrics.aappublications.org/content/early/2016/08/18/peds.2016-1889

Fuloria, M., & Krieter, S. (2002). The newborn examination: Part I. emergencies and common abnormalities involving the skin, head, neck, chest, and respiratory and cardiovascular systems. *American Family Physician*, *65*(1), 61-69. Retrieved from http://www.aafp.org/afp/2002/0101/p61.html#sec-1

Gozen, D., Caglar, S., Bayraktar, S., & Atici, F. (2014). Diaper dermatitis care of newborns human breast milk or barrier cream. *Journal of Clinical Nursing*, *23*(3-4), 515-523. https://doi.org/10.1111/jocn.12047

Grosse, S. D., Riehle-Colarusso, T., Gaffney, M., Mason, C. A., Shapira, S. K., Sontag, M. K., . . . Iskander, J. (2017). CDC grand rounds: Newborn screening for hearing loss and critical congenital heart disease. *MMWR: Morbidity and Mortality Weekly Report*, *66*(30),

888-890. Retrieved from https://www.cdc.gov/mmwr/volumes/66/wr/
mm6633a4.htm?s_cid=mm6633a4_w#suggestedcitation

Hoath, S. B., Pickens, W. L., & Visscher, M. O. (2006). The biology of
vernix caseosa. *International Journal of Cosmetic Science*, *28*(5). https://
doi.org/10.1111/j.1467-2494.2006.00338.x

Hoeger, P. H., Schreiner, V., Klaassen, I. A., Enzmann, C. C., Friedrichs, K.,
& Bleck, O. (2002). Epidermal barrier lipids in human vernix caseosa:
Corresponding ceramide pattern in vernix and fetal skin. *The British
Journal of Dermatology*, *146*(2), 194-201. Retrieved from https://www.
ncbi.nlm.nih.gov/pubmed/11903227

Horsley, T., Cliffored, T., & Barrowman, N. (2007). Benefits and harms
associated with the practice of bed sharing: A systematic review. *Archives
of Pediatrics and Adolescent Medicine*, *161*(3), 237-245. https://doi.
org/10.1001/archpedi.161.3.237

Hunter, W. (2016, June 6). Scary baby symptoms (That are perfectly
normal). *Parents*. Retrieved from http://www.parents.com/baby/health/
scary-but-normal-baby-symptoms/

Kair, L. R., Kenron, D., Etheredge, K., Jaffe, A. C., & Phillipi, C. A.
(2013). Pacifier restriction and exclusive breastfeeding. *Pediatrics*,
131(4). Retrieved from http://pediatrics.aappublications.org/content/
early/2013/03/12/peds.2012-2203

Kelly, J. C. (2011). AAP sets guidelines for neonatal hypoglycemia.
Pediatrics, (127), 575-579. Retrieved from https://www.medscape.com/
viewarticle/738204#vp_2

Kibler, V. A., Hayes, R. M., Johnson, D. E., Anderson, L. W., Just, S.
L., & Wells, N. L. (2012). Early postoperative ambulation: Back to
basics [PDF]. *American Journal of Nursing*, *112*(4). Retrieved from
http://unmhospitalist.pbworks.com/w/file/fetch/66026896/Early%20
Postoperative%20Ambulation%20Back%20to%20Basics%20A%20
quality%20improvement%20project.pdf

Kwek, K., & Yeo, G. S. (2006). Shoulder dystocia and injuries: Prevention and management. *Current Opinion in Obstetrics & Gynecology, 18*(2), 123-128. https://doi.org/10.1097/0000192976.38858.90

Leighton, B. L., & Crock, L. W. (2017). Case series of successful postoperative pain management in buprenorphine maintenance therapy patients. *Anesthesia & Analgesia, 125*(5), 1779-1783. https://doi.org/10.1213/ANE.0000000000002498

McLaughlin, M. R., O'Connor, N. R., & Ham, P. (2008). Newborn skin: Part II. birthmarks. *American Family Physician, 77*(1), 56-60. Retrieved from http://www.aafp.org/afp/2008/0101/p56.html

Montag, S., & Palmer, L. S. (2011). Abnormalities in the penile curvature: Chordee and penile tortion. *The Scientific World Journal*, (11), 1470-1478. Retrieved from https://www.researchgate.net/publication/51536266_Abnormalities_of_Penile_Curvature_Chordee_and_Penile_Torsion

Moon, R. Y. (2011). SIDS and other sleep-related infant deaths: Expansion of recommendations for a safe infant sleeping environment. *Pediatrics, 128*(5), 1341-1367. Retrieved from http://pediatrics.aappublications.org/content/128/5/e1341.full

Moore, D. B., & Catlin, A. (2003). Lactation suppression: Forgotten aspect of care for the mother of a dying child. *Pediatric Nursing, 29*(5). Retrieved from https://www.medscape.com/viewarticle/464568

Neville, K. (2014, September/October). Besting breastfeeding bullies: A case for supporting, not shaming. *Food & Nutrition.* Retrieved from http://foodandnutrition.org/september-october-2014/besting-breastfeeding-bullies-case-supporting-not-shaming/

O'Connor, N. R., McLaughlin, M. R., & Ham, P. (2008). Newborn skin: Part I. common rashes. *American Family Physicians, 77*(7), 47-52. Retrieved from http://www.aafp.org/afp/2008/0101/p47.html

Oral dextrose gel for treatment of newborn infants with low blood glucose levels [Review *Oral dextrose gel for treatment of newborn infants with low blood glucose levels*, by P. J. Weston, D. L. Harris, M. Battin, J. Brown, J. E. Hegarty, & J. E. Harding]. (2016). *Cochrane Database of Systematic Reviews*. https://doi.org/10.1002/14651858.CD011027.pub2.

Quinlan, J. D., & Murphy, N. J. (2015). Cesarean delivery: Counseling issues and complication management. *American Family Physician*, *91*(3), 178-184. Retrieved from http://www.aafp.org/afp/2015/0201/p178.html

Sachs, H. C. (2013). The transfer of drugs and therapeutics into human breast milk: An update on selected topics. *Pediatrics*, *132*(3). https://doi.org/10.1542peds.2013-1985

Sauberan, J. B., Anderson, P. O., Lane, J. R., Rafie, S., Nguyen, N., Rossi, S. S., & Stellwagen, S. L. (2011). Breast milk hydrocodone and hydromorphone levels in mothers using hydrocodone for postpartum pain. *Obstetrics & Gynecology Journal*, *117*(3), 611-617. Abstract retrieved from https://www.medscape.com/medline/abstract/21343764

Sinkey, R. G., Eschenbacher, M. A., Walsh, P. M., Doerger, R. G., Lambers, D. S., Sibai, B. M., & Habli, M. A. (2015). The GoMo study: a randomized clinical trial assessing neonatal pain with Gomco vs Mogen clamp circumcision [Abstract]. *American Journal of Obstetrics and Gynecology*, *212*(5). https://doi.org/10.1016/j.ajog.2015.03.029

Spain, J. E., Frey, H. A., Tuuli, M. G., Colvin, R., Macones, G. A., & Cahill, A. G. (2015). Neonatal morbidity associated with shoulder dystocia maneuvers. *American Journal of Obstetrics & Gynecology*, *212*(3), 353-358. Abstract retrieved from https://www.ncbi.nlm.nih.gov/pubmed/25291256

Stokowski, L. J. (2004). Hypospadias in the neonate. *Advances in Neonatal Care*, *4*(4). Retrieved from https://www.medscape.com/viewarticle/489956_11

Nonperiodicals

ACOG Committee on Obstetric Practice. (2017, March). *ACOG Committee Opinion: Delivery of a newborn with meconium-stained amniotic fluid* (Research Report No. 689). Retrieved from https://www.acog.org/Resources-And-Publications/ Committee-Opinions/Committee-on-Obstetric-Practice/ Delivery-of-a-Newborn-With-Meconium-Stained-Amniotic-Fluid

ACOG Committee on Obstetric Practice. (2017, August). *ACOG Committee Opinion: Opioid use and opioid use disorder in pregnancy* (Report No. 711). Retrieved from https://www.acog.org/Resources-And-Publications/ Committee-Opinions/Committee-on-Obstetric-Practice/ Opioid-Use-and-Opioid-Use-Disorder-in-Pregnancy

Ball, H., & Blair, P. S. (2017). Health professionals' guide to: "Caring for your baby at night". In *UNICEF* [PDF]. Retrieved from https://www. unicef.org.uk/babyfriendly/wp-content/uploads/sites/2/2011/11/ Caring-for-your-Baby-at-Night-A-Health-Professionals-Guide.pdf

Baskin, L. S. (n.d.). Neonatal circumcision: Risks and benefits. In C. J. Lockwood, J. G. Bartlett, D. Wilcox, & K. Eckler (Eds.), *UpToDate*. Retrieved from https://www.uptodate.com/contents/ neonatal-circumcision-risks-and-benefits?source=search_ result&search=circumcision&selectedTitle=2~90

Baskin, L. S. (n.d.). Patient education: Circumcision in baby boys (beyond the basics). In C. J. Lockwood, D. Wilcox, & K. Eckler (Eds.), *UpToDate*. Retrieved March 9, 2017, from https://www.uptodate.com/ contents/circumcision-in-baby-boys-beyond-the-basics?view=print

Berens, P. (n.d.). Overview of postpartum care. In C. J. Lockwood & V. A. Barss (Eds.), *UpToDate*. Retrieved September 14, 2017, from https://www.uptodate.com/contents/overview-of- postpartum-care?source=search_result&search=shivering%20 postpartum&selectedTitle=1~3

Berghella, V. (n.d.). Cesarean delivery: Postpartum issues. In
    C. J. Lockwood & V. A. Barss (Eds.), *UpToDate*. Retrieved
    October 3, 2017, from https://www.uptodate.com/contents/
    cesarean-delivery-postoperative-issues

Caput succedaneum. (2015). In K. G. Lee, D. Zieve, & A.D.A.M. Editorial
    Team (Eds.), *Medical encyclopedia: MedlinePlus*. Retrieved from https://
    medlineplus.gov/ency/article/001587.htm

Chordee. (n.d.). In J. Robinson (Ed.), *WebMD*. Retrieved from https://
    www.webmd.com/men/guide/chordee-repair-treatment#2

Dahlke, J. D., & Magann, E. F. (2015). Immune and non-immune hydrops
    fetalis. In R. J. Martin, A. A. Fanaroff, & M. C. Walsh (Eds.), *Fanaroff
    and Martin's neonatal-perinatal medicine* (10th ed.). Retrieved from
    http://www.umm.edu/health/medical/ency/articles/hydrops-fetalis

Eichenwald, E. C. (n.d.). Overview of cyanosis in the newborn.
    In L. E. Wilseman & M. S. Kim (Eds.), *UpToDate*. Retrieved
    May 26, 2016, from https://www.uptodate.com/contents/
    overview-of-cyanosis-in-the-newborn

Garcia-Prats, J. A. (n.d.). Neonatal polycythemia. In D. H. Mahoney, L. E.
    Wiseman, & C. Armsby (Eds.), *UpToDate*. Retrieved September 19,
    2016, from https://www.uptodate.com/contents/neonatal-polycythemia

Grant, G. J. (n.d.). Adverse effects of neuraxial analgesia and anesthesia for
    obstetrics. In D. L. Hepner & M. Crowley (Eds.), *UpToDate*. Retrieved
    June 28, 2017, from https://www.uptodate.com/contents/adverse-
    effects-of-neuraxial-analgesia-and-anesthesia-for-obstetrics?source=see_
    link&sectionName=Shivering&anchor=H18#H12560398

Healthwise, Inc. (n.d.). Childbirth: Epidurals - topic overview. In J.
    Robinson (Ed.), *WebMD*. Retrieved from https://www.webmd.com/
    baby/tc/childbirth-epidurals-topic-overview#2

Horli, K. A. (n.d.). Diaper dermatitis. In M. J. Levy, J. E. Drutz, & R. Corona (Eds.), *UpToDate*. Retrieved September, 2017, from http://www.uptodate.com/contents/diaper-dermatitis

Kaneshiro, N. K. (n.d.). Fontanelles - bulging. In D. Zieve, B. Conaway, & A.D.A.M. Editorial Team (Eds.), *Medical encyclopedia: MedlinePlus*. Retrieved from https://medlineplus.gov/ency/article/003310.htm

Kaneshiro, N. K. (n.d.). Skin findings in newborns. In D. Zieve, I. Oglevie, & A.D.A.M. Editorial Team (Eds.), *Medical encyclopedia: MedlinePlus*. Retrieved November 19, 2015, from https://medlineplus.gov/ency/article/002301.htm

Kaneshiro, N. K. (2017). Hormonal effects in newborns. In D. Zieve & B. Conaway (Eds.), *Medical encyclopedia: MedlinePlus*. Retrieved from https://medlineplus.gov/ency/article/001911.htm

Lee, K. (2015). Apnea of prematurity. In D. Zieve, I. Oglevie, & A.D.A.M. Editorial Team (Eds.), *Medical encyclopedia: MedlinePlus*. Retrieved from https://medlineplus.gov/ency/article/007227.htm

Lee, K. G. (n.d.). Bilirubin encephalopathy. In VeriMed Healthcare Network, D. Zieve, I. Oglivie, & A.D.A.M. Editorial Team (Eds.), *Medical encyclopedia: MedlinePlus*. Retrieved April 27, 2015, from https://medlineplus.gov/ency/article/007309.htm

Lessaris, K. J. (2016, January 2). Polycythemia of the newborn. In T. Rosenkrantz (Ed.), *Medscape*. Retrieved from https://emedicine.medscape.com/article/976319-overview

Ma, C. B. (2017). Tailbone trauma - aftercare. In D. Zieve, B. Conaway, & A.D.A.M. Editorial Team (Eds.), *Medical encyclopedia: MedlinePlus*. Retrieved from https://medlineplus.gov/ency/patientinstructions/000573.htm

Mastitis. (2008). In *Gale encyclopedia of medicine*. Retrieved from https://medical-dictionary.thefreedictionary.com/mastitis

McKee-Garrett, T. M. (n.d.). Assessment of the newborn infant. In L. E. Wiseman & M. S. Kim (Eds.), *UpToDate*. Retrieved July 21, 2017, from https://www.uptodate.com/contents/assessment-of-the-newborn-infant?source=search_result&search=eye%20color&selectedTitle=1-150

McKee-Garrett, T. M. (n.d.). Assessment of the newborn infant. In L. E. Wiseman & T. K. Duryea (Eds.), *UpToDate*. Retrieved July 21, 2017, from https://www.uptodate.com/contents/assessment-of-the-newborn-infant?source=search_result&search=umbilical%20hernia&selectedTitle=3-43

McKee-Garrett, T. M. (n.d.). Neonatal birth injuries. In L. E. Wiseman, W. Phillips, M. C. Patterson, & M. S. Kim (Eds.), *UpToDate*. Retrieved May 19, 2017, from https://www.uptodate.com/contents/neonatal-birth-injuries?source=search_result&search=petechiae%20neonate&selectedTitle=1-150

Milk fever. (2009). In *Mosby's medical dictionary* (8th ed.). Retrieved from The Free Dictionary database.

Milk fever. (2012). In *Medical dictionary for the health professions and nursing*. Retrieved from The Free Dictionary database.

Miller-Keane encyclopedia and dictionary of medicine, nursing, and allied health (7th ed.). (2003). Retrieved from https://medical-dictionary.thefreedictionary.com/mastitis

Newborn appearance. (n.d.). In *Stanford children's health*. Retrieved from http://www.stanfordchildrens.org/en/topic/default?id=newborn-appearance-90-P02691

Newborn appearance: What does a newborn look like? (n.d.). In L. C. Adler & D. Freeborn (Eds.), *Health encyclopedia: University of Rochester Medical Center*. Retrieved from https://www.urmc.rochester.edu/encyclopedia/content.aspx?ContentTypeID=90&ContentID=P02691

Nixon, H., & Leffert, L. (n.d.). Anesthesia for cesarean delivery. In D. L. Hepner & M. Crowley (Eds.), *UpToDate*. Retrieved July 26, 2017, from https://www.uptodate.com/contents/anesthesia-for-cesarean-delivery?source=see_link

Penile torsion. (n.d.). In J. Donohoe (Ed.), *Cleveland clinic health library*. Retrieved from https://my.clevelandclinic.org/health/articles/penile-torsion

Pielop, J. A. (n.d.). Benign skin and scalp lesions in the newborn and infant. In M. L. Levy, L. E. Wiseman, & R. Corona (Eds.), *UpToDate*. Retrieved July 31, 2017, from https://www.uptodate.com/contents/benign-skin-and-scalp-lesions-in-the-newborn-and-infant

Pielop, J. L. (n.d.). Benign skin and scalp lesions in the newborn and infant. In M. L. Levy & L. E. Wiseman (Eds.) & R. Corona (Author), *UpToDate*. Retrieved July 31, 2017, from https://www.uptodate.com/contents/benign-skin-and-scalp-lesions-in-the-newborn-and-infant

Pielop, J. L. (n.d.). Vascular lesions in the newborn. In M. L. Levy, L. E. Wiseman, & R. Corona (Eds.), *UpToDate*. Retrieved May 10, 2016, from https://www.uptodate.com/contents/vascular-lesions-in-the-newborn?source=see_link

Premature infant. (n.d.). In E. Gibson & U. Nawab (Eds.), *Merck manual: Professional version*. Retrieved January, 2015, from http://www.merckmanuals.com/professional/pediatrics/perinatal-problems/premature-infant

Save your life: Get care for these post-birth warning signs (Association of Women's Health, Obstetrics and Neonatal Nurses, Comp.) [Leaflet]. (2016). Retrieved from http://c.ymcdn.com/sites/www.awhonn.org/resource/resmgr/files/Post-Birth_Warning_signs_160.pdf

Sobol, J. (2015). Undescended testicle. In D. Zieve, I. Ogilvie, & A.D.A.M. Editorial Team (Eds.), *Medical encyclopedia*. Retrieved from https://medlineplus.gov/ency/article/000973.htm

Stack, A. M. (n.d.). Etiology and evaluation of cyanosis in children. In S. J. Teach & J. F. Wiley (Eds.), *UpToDate*. Retrieved December 16, 2016, from https://www.uptodate.com/contents/etiology-and-evaluation-of-cyanosis-in-children

STDs during pregnancy - CDC fact sheet [Leaflet]. (2016). Retrieved from https://www.cdc.gov/std/pregnancy/stdfact-pregnancy.htm

What are the benefits of breastfeeding? (n.d.). In *Eunice Kennedy Shriver: National institute of child health and human development*. Retrieved from https://www.nichd.nih.gov/health/topics/breastfeeding/conditioninfo/Pages/benefits.aspx

When is a cesarean delivery necessary & what are the risks? (n.d.). In *Eunice Kennedy Shriver: National institute of child health and human development*. Retrieved from https://www.nichd.nih.gov/health/topics/obstetrics/conditioninfo/pages/risks.aspx

Wong, R. J., & Bhutani, V. K. (n.d.). Patient education: Jaundice in newborn infants (Beyond the basics). In S. A. Abrams & M. S. Kim (Eds.), *UpToDate*. Retrieved April 28, 2017, from https://www.uptodate.com/contents/jaundice-in-newborn-infants-beyond-the-basics?source=see_link

World Health Organization, & UNICEF. (2009). Baby-Friendly hospital initiative: Revised, updated and expanded for integrated care. In *World Health Organization*. Retrieved from http://www.who.int/nutrition/publications/infantfeeding/bfhi_trainingcourse/en/

Web sites, e-sources

Agrawal, R., & Elston, D. M. (2017, June 30). Diaper dermatitis. Retrieved from https://emedicine.medscape.com/article/911985-overview

Antipuesto, D. J. (2011, February 9). Difference between caput succedaneum and cephalohematoma [Blog post]. Retrieved from Nursing Crib website: http://nursingcrib.

com/nursing-notes-reviewer/maternal-child-health/
difference-between-caput-succedaneum-and-cephalhematoma/

Assessments for newborn babies. (n.d.). Retrieved
from http://www.stanfordchildrens.org/en/topic/
default?id=assessments-for-newborn-babies-90-P02336

BabyCenter Medical Advisory Board (Ed.). (n.d.). Baby sensory
development: Sight. Retrieved September, 2016, from Baby Center
website: https://www.babycenter.com/0_baby-sensory-development-
sight_6508.bc

Bed-sharing. (n.d.). Retrieved from https://www.marchofdimes.org/baby/
co-sleeping.aspx

Boyd, K. (2017, May 22). Baby's vision development: What to expect
the first year (S. N. Lipski, Ed.). Retrieved from American Academy
of Ophthalmology website: https://www.aao.org/eye-health/
tips-prevention/baby-vision-development-first-year

Brown, T. (2015, October 6). Breastfeeding support on upswing in
many US hospitals. Retrieved from https://www.medscape.com/
viewarticle/852227?src=trendmd_pilot#vp_2

Caput succedaneum vs cephalohematoma. (2015, March 4). Retrieved from
Health Research and Funding website: https://healthresearchfunding.
org/caput-succedaneum-vs-cephalohematoma/

Care for an uncircumcised penis. (n.d.). Retrieved June 19, 2017, from
Healthy Children: The American Academy of Pediatrics website:
https://www.healthychildren.org/English/ages-stages/baby/bathing-skin-
care/pages/Care-for-an-Uncircumcised-Penis.aspx

Co-sleeping and bed-sharing. (n.d.). Retrieved May 21, 2017, from https://
kellymom.com/parenting/nighttime/cosleeping/

Dekker, R. (2014, March 18). Evidence on: The vitamin K shot in newborns. Retrieved from https://evidencebasedbirth.com/evidence-for-the-vitamin-k-shot-in-newborns/

Demerol. (n.d.). Retrieved from Drugs.com website: https://www.drugs.com/demerol.html

Demerol injection. (n.d.). Retrieved December 27, 2017, from Drugs.com website: https://www.drugs.com/pro/demerol-injection.html

Dilaudid. (n.d.). Retrieved December 27, 2017, from Drugs.com website: https://www.drugs.com/dilaudid.html

Facts about critical congenital heart defects. (n.d.). Retrieved June 27, 2017, from Centers for Disease Control and Prevention website: https://www.cdc.gov/ncbddd/heartdefects/cchd-facts.html

Facts about hypospadias. (n.d.). Retrieved from Centers for Disease Control and Prevention website: https://www.cdc.gov/ncbddd/birthdefects/hypospadias.html

Facts about jaundice and kernicterus. (n.d.). Retrieved November 7, 2016, from Centers for Disease Control and Prevention website: https://www.cdc.gov/ncbddd/jaundice/facts.html

Fentanyl injection. (n.d.). Retrieved December 27, 2017, from Drugs.com website: https://www.drugs.com/pro/fentanyl-injection.html

For babies receiving donor milk. (n.d.). Retrieved from Three Rivers Mother's Milk Bank website: http://www.threeriversmilkbank.org/recipients/

Geller, D. (n.d.). Is it normal for my baby's genitals to be so swollen? Retrieved from https://www.babycenter.com/404_is-it-normal-for-my-babys-genitals-to-be-so-swollen_9940.bc

Gibson, E. (n.d.). Premature infant (E. Gibson & U. Nawab, Ed.). Retrieved January, 2015, from http://www.merckmanuals.com/professional/pediatrics/perinatal-problems/premature-infant

Granberg, C. (n.d.). Hypospadias. Retrieved October 25, 2017, from Mayo Clinic website: https://www.mayoclinic.org/diseases-conditions/hypospadias/symptoms-causes/syc-20355148

Grosse SD, Riehle-Colarusso T, Gaffney M, Mason CA, Shapira SK, Sontag MK. CDC grand rounds: newborn screening for hearing loss and critical congenital heart disease. *MMWR: Morbidity and Mortality Weekly Report* 2017; 66:888–890. DOI: http://dx.doi.org/10.15585/mmwr.mm6633a4

Guidance for the prevention and control of influenza in the peri- and postpartum settings. (n.d.). Retrieved from Centers for Disease Control and Prevention website: https://www.cdc.gov/flu/professionals/infectioncontrol/peri-post-settings.htm

Heart murmur. (n.d.). Retrieved November 21, 2015, from Health Children: The American Academy of Pediatrics website: https://www.healthychildren.org/English/health-issues/conditions/heart/Pages/Heart-Murmur.aspx

Hepatitis B vaccination. (n.d.). Retrieved from Centers of Disease Control and Prevention website: https://www.cdc.gov/vaccines/vpd/hepb/index.html

Hill, D. L. (2012, May 11). Erythromycin ointment. Retrieved from Healthy Children: The American Academy of Pediatrics website: https://www.healthychildren.org/English/ages-stages/prenatal/delivery-beyond/Pages/Erythromycin-Ointment.aspx

HIV transmission. (n.d.). Retrieved June 6, 2017, from Centers for Disease Control and Prevention website: https://www.cdc.gov/hiv/basics/transmission.html

Hunter, W. (n.d.). It's not a seizure: Great baby fake-outs. Retrieved from Baby Science website: http://babyscience.info/its-not-a-seizure-great-baby-fake-outs/

Infant vision: Birth to 24 months of age. (n.d.). Retrieved October 30, 2017, from American Optometric Association website: https://www.aoa.org/patients-and-public/good-vision-throughout-life/childrens-vision/infant-vision-birth-to-24-months-of-age?sso=y

Jaafar, S. H., Ho, J. J., Jahanfar, S., & Angolkar, M. (2016, August 30). Effect of restricted pacifier use in breastfeeding term infants for increasing duration of breastfeeding. Retrieved from Cochrane Database System Review. (Accession No. CD007202)

James, A. (2009, October 18). What your newborn baby looks like. Retrieved from About Kids Health website: http://www.aboutkidshealth.ca/En/ResourceCentres/PregnancyBabies/NewbornBabies/YourNewbornBabysBody/Pages/What-Your-Newborn-Baby-Looks-Like.aspx

Johnson, S., & Calfasso, J. (n.d.). Umbilical hernia (S. Kim, Ed.). Retrieved September 29, 2015, from https://www.healthline.com/health/umbilical-hernia#overview1

Jones, C. (2013, September 23). Separating fact from fiction in the not-so-normal newborn nursery: Pacifiers and nipple confusion. Retrieved from https://sciencebasedmedicine.org/separating-fact-from-fiction-in-the-not-so-normal-newborn-nursery-pacifiers-and-nipple-confusion/

Karp, H. (2015, November 5). The 5 S's for soothing babies [Blog post]. Retrieved from Happiest Baby website: https://www.happiestbaby.com/blogs/blog/the-5-s-s-for-soothing-babies

Kuehn, B. M. (2017, August 24). Newborn screening guidelines not followed by all hospitals. Retrieved from https://www.medscape.com/viewarticle/884692

[LACTMED: Acetaminophen: Summary of use during lactation]. (n.d.). Retrieved from National Library of Medicine: National Institutes of Health: TOXNET website: https://toxnet.nlm.nih.gov/cgi-bin/sis/search2/f?./temp/~Jw1wrB:1

[LACTMED: Diphenhydramine: Summary of use during lactation]. (n.d.). Retrieved from National Library of Medicine: National Institutes of Health: TOXNET website: https://toxnet.nlm.nih.gov/cgi-bin/sis/search2/f?./temp/~dOqAeS:1

[LACTMED: Fentanyl: Summary of use during lactation]. (n.d.). Retrieved from National Library of Medicine: National Institutes of Health: TOXNET website: https://toxnet.nlm.nih.gov/cgi-bin/sis/search2/f?./temp/~YqDwyz:1

[LACTMED: Hydrocodone: Summary of use during lactation]. (n.d.). Retrieved from National Library of Medicine: National Institutes of Health: TOXNET website: https://toxnet.nlm.nih.gov/cgi-bin/sis/search2/f?./temp/~w4lOkh:1

[LACTMED: Ibuprofen: Summary of use during lactation]. (n.d.). Retrieved from National Library of Medicine: National Institutes of Health: TOXNET website: https://toxnet.nlm.nih.gov/cgi-bin/sis/search2/f?./temp/~ugQnNL:1

[LACTMED: Morphine: Summary of use during lactation]. (n.d.). Retrieved from National Library of Medicine: National Institutes of Health: TOXNET website: https://toxnet.nlm.nih.gov/cgi-bin/sis/search2/f?./temp/~kxPahY:4

[LACTMED: Oxycodone: Summary of use during lactation]. (n.d.). Retrieved from National Library of Medicine: National Institutes of Health: TOXNET website: https://toxnet.nlm.nih.gov/cgi-bin/sis/search2/f?./temp/~Yh5Orp:1

Lockhart, T. (2017, May 8). Circumoral cyanosis: Causes, symptoms, and how to treat it. Retrieved from Doctors Health Press website:

https://www.doctorshealthpress.com/general-health-articles/
circumoral-cyanosis-causes-treatment/

Making the decision to breastfeed. (n.d.). Retrieved May 3, 2017,
from Women's Health: U.S. Department of Health & Human
Services website: https://www.womenshealth.gov/breastfeeding/
making-decision-breastfeed

Maternity care practices. (n.d.). Retrieved from Centers for Disease Control
and Prevention website: https://www.cdc.gov/breastfeeding/pdf/bf_
guide_1.pdf

Mayo Clinic Staff. (n.d.). Phenylketonuria (PKU). Retrieved October
17, 2017, from https://www.mayoclinic.org/diseases-conditions/
phenylketonuria/basics/definition/CON-20026275

Mayo Clinic Staff. (2014, April 3). Diseases and conditions: Infant jaundice.
Retrieved from https://www.mayoclinic.org/diseases-conditions/
infant-jaundice/basics/causes/CON-20019637

Mayo Clinic Staff. (2014, November 27). Diseases & conditions: Premature
birth. Retrieved from https://www.mayoclinic.org/diseases-conditions/
premature-birth/basics/definition/CON-20020050

Mayo Clinic Staff. (2015, August). Cesarean birth after care. Retrieved from
American Pregnancy Association website: http://americanpregnancy.
org/labor-and-birth/cesarean-aftercare/

Mayo Clinic Staff. (2015, October 15). Diseases and conditions:
Sacral dimple. Retrieved from https://www.mayoclinic.org/
diseases-conditions/sacral-dimple/basics/definition/CON-20025266

Mayo Clinic Staff. (2015, November 6). Thermometer basics: Taking
your child's temperature. Retrieved from https://www.mayoclinic.org/
healthy-lifestyle/infant-and-toddler-health/in-depth/thermometer/
art-20047410?pg=2

Mayo Clinic Staff. (2015, November 25). Lactation suppression: Can medication help? Retrieved from Riverside website: https://riversideonline.com/health_reference/Healthy-Baby/FAQ-20058016.cfm

Mayo Clinic Staff. (2017, July 12). Sudden infant death syndrome (SIDS). Retrieved from https://www.mayoclinic.org/diseases-conditions/sudden-infant-death-syndrome/symptoms-causes/syc-20352800

Mayo Clinic Staff. (2017, August 22). Undescended testicle. Retrieved from https://www.mayoclinic.org/diseases-conditions/undescended-testicle/symptoms-causes/syc-20351995

Medical Advisory Committee. (n.d.). Sexually transmitted diseases (STDs) and pregnancy. Retrieved May 1, 2017, from American Pregnancy Association website: http://americanpregnancy.org/pregnancy-complications/stds-and-pregnancy/

Medical Advisory Committee. (n.d.). Your child's first test: The APGAR. Retrieved from American Pregnancy Association website: http://americanpregnancy.org/labor-and-birth/apgar-test/

Medical reasons for a c-section. (n.d.). Retrieved June, 2013, from https://www.marchofdimes.org/pregnancy/c-section-medical-reasons.aspx

Morphine. (n.d.). Retrieved December 27, 2017, from Drugs.com website: https://www.drugs.com/morphine.html

Morphine injection. (n.d.). Retrieved December 27, 2017, from Drugs.com website: https://www.drugs.com/cons/morphine-injection.html

Ondansetron. (n.d.). Retrieved December 27, 2017, from Drugs.com website: https://www.drugs.com/ondansetron.html

Ostrower, S. T., & Bent, J. P., III. (2017, February 7). Preauricular cysts, pits, and fissures (A. D. Meyers, Ed.). Retrieved from Medscape website: https://emedicine.medscape.com/article/845288-overview

Patient controlled analgesia. (n.d.). Retrieved December 27, 2017, from Drugs.com website: https://www.drugs.com/cg/patient-controlled-analgesia.html

Phenergan. (n.d.). Retrieved from Drugs.com website: https://www.drugs.com/phenergan.html

Phenergan. (n.d.). Retrieved December 27, 2017, from Drugs.com website: https://www.drugs.com/phenergan.html

Phenylketonuria. (n.d.). Retrieved October 24, 2017, from National Institutes of Health: Genetics Home Reference website: https://ghr.nlm.nih.gov/condition/phenylketonuria

PKU (Phenylketonuria) in your baby. (n.d.). Retrieved February, 2013, from https://www.marchofdimes.org/baby/phenylketonuria-in-your-baby.aspx

Pros & cons of co-sleeping. (n.d.). Retrieved from https://www.whattoexpect.com/first-year/cosleeping.aspx

R, A. (2011, May 13). Mottled skin in infants and babies: Causes and treatment. Retrieved from Simple Remedies website: http://www.simple-remedies.com/childrens-health/mottled-skin-in-infants.html

Reece, T. (2014). When do babies' eyes change color? Retrieved from http://www.parents.com/baby/development/physical/when-do-babies-eyes-change-color/

Sacral dimple (pilonidal dimple). (n.d.). Retrieved from Internal Medicine and Pediatric Clinic website: http://www.impcna.com/intranet/Nelson%20Pediatric/Newborn/SacralDimple%5B1%5D.pdf

Shu, J. (Ed.). (n.d.). Movement: Birth to 3 months. Retrieved August 1, 2009, from Healthy Children: American Academy of Pediatrics website: https://www.healthychildren.org/English/ages-stages/baby/Pages/Movement-Birth-to-Three-Months.aspx

Smith, L. J. (n.d.). Guidelines for rapid reduction of milk supply. Retrieved from Bright Future Lactation Resource Centre website: http://bflrc. com/ljs/breastfeeding/dryupfst.htm

Stadol. (n.d.). Retrieved December 27, 2017, from Drugs.com website: https://www.drugs.com/pro/stadol.html

Stevens, S. (2012, August 14). Evidence to support that 'rooming in' for mother and baby after birth could be beneficial. Retrieved from https:// medicalxpress.com/news/2012-09-evidence-rooming-mother-baby-birth.html

Thompson, E. G., & London, W. T. (n.d.). Function of the liver. Retrieved from https://www.webmd.com/hepatitis/function-of-the-liver

Turner, B. (n.d.). How to deal with swelling after pregnancy. Retrieved from https://health.howstuffworks.com/pregnancy-and-parenting/pregnancy/ postpartum-care/deal-with-swelling-after-pregnancy2.htm

Turner, B. (n.d.). What causes swelling after pregnancy. Retrieved from https://health.howstuffworks.com/pregnancy-and-parenting/pregnancy/ postpartum-care/deal-with-swelling-after-pregnancy1.htm

Tuteur, A. (2014, September 5). Is the baby friendly hospital initiative really the baby deadly hospital initiative? [Blog post]. Retrieved from The Skeptical OB website: http://www.skepticalob.com/2014/09/ is-the-baby-friendly-hospital-initiativ-really-the-baby-deadly-hospital-initiative.html

What are undescended testicles (cryptorchidism)? (n.d.). Retrieved from Urology Care Foundation website: http://www.urologyhealth.org/ urologic-conditions/cryptorchidism

What is hypospadias? (n.d.). Retrieved from Urology Care Foundation website: http://www.urologyhealth.org/urologic-conditions/hypospadias

Whitlock, J. (n.d.). What to do if you can't urinate after surgery (R. N. Fogoros, Ed.). Retrieved July 7, 2017, from https://www.verywell.com/what-to-do-if-you-cant-urinate-after-surgery-3157318

Your baby's eyes. (n.d.). Retrieved from Bausch and Lomb website: http://www.bausch.com/vision-and-age/infant-eyes/eye-development

Zofran. (n.d.). Retrieved December 27, 2017, from Drugs.com website: https://www.drugs.com/zofran.html

Unpublished & other sources

del Castillo-Hegyi, C. (2015, April 18). *Letter to doctors and parents about the dangers of insufficient exclusive breastfeeding.* Retrieved from https://fedisbest.org/2015/04/letter-to-doctors-and-parents-about-the-dangers-of-insufficient-exclusive-breastfeeding/

MacDonald, L. (2016, May). *Becoming baby friendly: Rooming-in for patient centered care in the maternal setting.* Unpublished working paper, Honors college thesis. University of Massachusetts, Boston, MA.

About the Author

· · · · · · · · · · · ·

Karen Brewer is a certified mother-baby nurse who has been working over the past 20 years for a health system in the Greater Kansas City area. She is passionate about her career as a register nurse specializing in mother/baby care postpartum, and wants the utmost care for her patients, as well as for other patients out there.

While not finishing college the first time around (a business major that didn't go so well), she went on to work a state government job and raise a family. Soon she realized that this was not the path she wanted to continue on, so she went another route and returned to school when the older two were very young. Changing directions and completing her nursing degree became the turning point of her new career and her family's future.

She is married to her college sweetheart, Bobby, has two adult children with another one ready to fly the coop, and a beloved "puppy" Gordy and calico cat, Lilo. She lives in Kansas City, Missouri.